Minority Rights in South Asia

Rainer Hofmann / Ugo Caruso (eds.)

Minority Rights in South Asia

PETER LANG
Frankfurt am Main · Berlin · Bern · Bruxelles · New York · Oxford · Wien

Bibliographic Information published by the Deutsche Nationalbibliothek
The Deutsche Nationalbibliothek lists this publication in the Deutsche Nationalbibliografie; detailed bibliographic data is available in the internet at http://dnb.d-nb.de.

Cover Design:
Olaf Glöckler, Atelier Platen, Friedberg

The research leading to these results has received funding from the European Community's Seventh Framework Programme [FP7/2007-2013] under grant agreement n° 216072)

ISBN 978-3-631-60916-3

www.peterlang.de

Dedicated to the memory of Cristina Boglia and Kaiyan Homi Kaikobad
invaluable colleagues and beloved friends

TABLE OF CONTENTS

Foreword

Financial aid, trade and economic relations with Europe are very important for South Asia but policy makers do not take in consideration Europe as a major strategic player in Asia. EU needs to pay more attention to the still under-developed political relationship with countries in South Asia. In South Asia, EU has not yet shown so much sign of acting as a political power or as credible political and collective entity in foreign policy. Politicians remain therefore much more focused on US and Asia rather than on Europe. Even on major security concerns like terrorism, human rights abuses, post conflict reconstruction or environmental questions South Asian opinion leaders observe that EU lays more stress on financial aid and less on geo-politics or transfer of knowledge of so called European values. Despite this understanding, South Asian countries, especially India, have growing economic and political ties with the major European national States like UK, France and Germany. Researches included in the present publication have been conducted in the frame of the EU-funded EURASIA-Net project, whose aim is precisely to change this image towards a greater mutual understanding of instruments for the promotion of human rights, minority issues and supranational policies. Most activities of the project are fostering reciprocal knowledge exchange between EU and South Asia. The unique nature of European institutions and mechanisms on human rights and minority issues which create usually an information sharing and consultation forum involving different local, regional, national and EU political powers, civil society, academia and other interest groups or power sharing through federal systems and autonomy regimes have been analyzed and studied in detail in the frame of the project. The present publication is elaborating human and minority rights case studies in South Asia by a country by country approach with a special focus on SAARC (South Asian Association on Regional Cooperation) and different forms of National Human Rights Commissions. *The book "Minority Rights in South Asia"* supports knowledge and dialogue between representatives from the scientific community, policy-makers and civil society in Europe and should contribute to create background awareness and understanding among a wide range of actors from different countries and institutions in Europe.

Günther Rautz
European Academy of Bolzano
Institute for Minority Rights

Introduction

Taking fully into account the current considerable increase of the relevance of regionalism and regional instruments for the protection of human and minority rights, the present publication on minority rights in South Asia is in line with today's international concern for the development of common grounds for mutual analysis and knowledge, beyond the pure economic nature of present world interactions. In such circumstances, the history of European human and minority rights protection mechanisms is marked by the increasing consciousness of the comprehensiveness of the approach to be followed by the international community in setting significant standards of protection. Nowadays, as Europe and specifically the EU endeavour to obtain an even more prominent role in the world arena, the above mentioned historical background is used as the reference frame in a time which is characterized by a growing interest for comparative analysis with other regional instruments and minorities. The quite considerable increase of the relevance of South Asian states as well as South Asia as a region has encouraged European efforts in trying to gain a deeper understanding of the human and minority rights situation in the region. In this context, we are fully convinced that a book on minority rights in South Asia, as part of a broader international effort undertaken in the frame of the EU-funded project EURASIA-Net, complements academic results already produced by the EURASIA-Net project by targeting specifically the European audience. The publication is designed to function as a guide for academics and practitioners wishing to familiarize themselves with South Asian human and minority rights issues. Fully aware of the importance of mutual learning practices in the present human rights law-making process, we hope to provide a useful contribution to the process of enhancing the mutual awareness and understanding between South Asia and Europe, in particular among human rights activists and scholars from both regions.

The publication is developed along a country by country presentation and begins with a set of reports on the status of human and minority rights at the national level, which is followed by a broader focus on National Human Rights Institutions and the South Asian Association for Regional Cooperation (SAARC). Finally, in order to take account of the increasing linkages between the two regions, the publication ends with a specific chapter on the immigration to the UK from Commonwealth countries and the issue of "new minorities". This chapter constitutes, in our opinion, additional evidence of the crucial importance, for both Europe and South Asia, to create even more significant opportunities for further mutual understanding.

Rainer Hofmann & Ugo Caruso

CHAPTER 1

Human and Minority Rights in Afghanistan

Dr Gulshan Sachdeva*

I. INTRODUCTION

For the last few decades, Afghanistan has been in transition. It has witnessed diverse projects of nation building and socio-political transformation. Every new project has created a new set of social, political and economic problems. The Soviet project of building communism in Afghanistan resulted in over a million dead and five million Afghan refugees, mainly in the neighbouring countries. Similarly, when Pakistan pushed backward theocracy in Afghanistan, the world faced disastrous consequences, including the 9/11 attacks. The current international project of building democracy and a market economy is mandated by the United Nations and is being implemented mainly by the western alliance led by the United States. So far, this endeavour has produced mixed results. Apart from installing a democratic government, the country has made significant achievements in infrastructure, education and economy in the last eight years. After reaching records levels in 2007, opium cultivation and production have been somewhat moderated in the last two years. Despite significant success in many areas, however, the Taliban insurgency is gaining strength in some parts of the country and the security situation has deteriorated. There is also an alarming rise in suicide bombings.

Most analysts believe that there is a need to rethink the present strategy.[1] The new "Af-Pak" policy in Afghanistan has failed to show any significant improvement. Instead of weakening, anti-government forces have been able to increase their strength, even in northern Afghanistan.[2] Within six months of announcing a 'comprehensive new strategy for Afghanistan and Pakistan' in which the new US president Barack Obama aimed "to disrupt, dismantle and defeat al Qaeda in Pakistan and Afghanistan, and to prevent their return to either country in the future,"[3] he was again considering shifting his strategy.[4] The new *Afghanistan-Pakistan Regional*

---

* Associate Professor, School of International Studies, Jawaharlal Nehru University, New Delhi. The Author can be contacted at: gulshanjnu@gmail.com

1 See Grey Bruno, "*Rethinking Afghanistan*", Daily Analysis, 1 September 2009, Council on Foreign Relations, available at http://www.cfr.org/publication/20114/rethinking_afghanistan.html (accessed on 1 October 2009).

2 See B Raman, *Obama's Af-Pak Troika Fails to Deliver,* South Asia Analysis Group, Paper No. 3433, 27 September 2009, available at http://www.southasiaanalysis.org/papers35/paper3433.html (accessed on 1 October 2009).

3 Remarks by the President (of the United States) on a New Strategy for Afghanistan and Pakistan, March 27, 2009, available at:
http://www.whitehouse.gov/the_press_office/Remarks-by-the-President-on-a-New-Strategy-for-Afghanistan-and-Pakistan/ (accessed on 1 April 2009).

4 See "Obama Considers Strategic Shift in Afghanistan" *The New York Times,* 23 September 2009, available at http://www.nytimes.com/2009/09/23/world/asia/23policy.html (accessed on 5 October 2009).

Stabilization Strategy outlined by the US State department in January 2010 focuses on reintegration, expanded civilian presence and regional diplomacy. At the recent London Conference participants "re-affirmed the goals of greater Afghan leadership, increased regional cooperation and more effective international partnership". To end the stalemate, consensus is also emerging on reconciliation with the Taliban.
The historical background and current situation has created unique circumstances for human rights issues in Afghanistan. On the one hand, the human rights situation has improved tremendously, particularly in the areas of education, empowerment of women etc. On the other hand, the situation has deteriorated due to insecurity, corruption and weak government institutions. This paper will take a close look at human rights issues in Afghanistan within this broader context.

II. Background

Decades of war, followed by the Taliban regime, destroyed the core institution of the Afghan state. The heavily war-torn economy faced high levels of absolute poverty, ill health, large scale illiteracy and complete marginalization of the female population. In addition, millions of Afghans left the country and became refugees mainly in the neighbouring countries. After the fall of Taliban, all Afghan factions who were opposed to Taliban met in Bonn in December 2001. The meeting was sponsored by the United Nations. The Bonn agreement charted the roadmap for the political transformation of the county into a democratic state.[5] The UN Security Council endorsed the agreement through its resolution 1383.[6] Under the leadership of Mr Hamid Karzai, a Transitional Administration was established to guide the process of transformation. The interim administration derived its authority through the *Loya Jirgha* (Grand Council) convened by former Afghan King Zahir Shah. In early 2002, international donors pledged about $4.5 billion in Tokyo for the reconstruction efforts in Afghanistan. In March 2002, the UN also established the UN Assistance Mission in Afghanistan (UNAMA). The constitutional *Loya Jirgha* adopted a new constitution in January 2004, with the presidential form of government. In April 2004 in Berlin, 23 donor nations pledged a total of $8.2 billion aid to Afghanistan over three years.[7] Under the new constitution, presidential elections were held in October 2004 and parliamentary elections in September 2005. More than 75 percent of voters participated in the presidential election and a significant number of women were elected to the National Assembly. The constitution also established legal protection for the private property and it was presumed that economic development in the country would be based mainly on the market economy. These were remarkable achievements for a country destroyed by decades of war. Once these landmarks were

---

5 For text of Bonn Agreement see *Agreement on Provisional Arrangements in Afghanistan Pending the Re-establishment of Permanent Government Institutions*, available at: http://unama.unmissions.org/Portals/UNAMA/Documents/Bonn-agreement.pdf (accessed on 1 July 2009)
6 See UN Security Council resolution number 1383, 6 December 2001, available at: http://daccess-ods.un.org/TMP/5722597.html (accessed on 6 October 2009).
7 See *Berlin Declaration,* available at: http://reliefweb.int/rw/rwb.nsf/db900SID/SNAO-634SXS?OpenDocument (accessed on 12 October 2009).

achieved, international community and the Afghanistan government agreed on the *Afghanistan Compact* at the London Conference in 2005.[8] The compact set ambitious targets for security, governance, development, regional cooperation and counter narcotics measures. While reviewing the *Afghanistan Compact,* at another international conference on Afghanistan in Paris in June 2008, the international community made further commitments for the next five years.[9] Despite serious difficulties, the process of second presidential elections has been completed in 2009.

III. ACHIEVEMENTS

According to the *Afghanistan National Development Strategy*[10] (ANDS) more than 5 million Afghan refugees have returned home since 2002. In 2006 alone 342,925 Afghan refugees returned from Pakistan and Iran and another thousand from other countries. The number of school-going children has grown from under one million in 2001 to about 6 million in 2007 (one third of them are girls). In 2007, there were more than 9,000 schools (including 1337 all girls and 4,325 co-educational). The number of teachers has increased seven-fold to 142,500, which included 40,000 female teachers. In the health and nutrition sector, more than US$1 billion has been invested in the last five years. As a result, the percentage of people living in areas where basic health care facilities are made available has increased from 9 percent in 2002 to 85 percent in 2008. The infant mortality rate has been reduced by 26 percent in five years.[11] 76 percent of children under the age of five have been immunized against childhood diseases. Between 2002 and 2008, there has been 38 percent reduction in child mortality and 40 percent in maternal mortality. As a result, the lives of approximately 500,000 children have been saved since 2003.[12]

It is remarkable that despite a difficult legacy, macroeconomic stability in Afghanistan has been maintained in the last few years (see table 1). This has been the result of disciplined fiscal and monetary policies. A new currency was successfully introduced. Until 2007, inflation remained reasonably low and the exchange rate has been stable. More than a dozen private commercial banks, two private airlines and 13 microfinance institutions are operating successfully. About 150 cities across Afghanistan now have access to mobile phone networks and internet provider services. Many multinationals, including Coca Cola, Siemens, Nestle and Etisalat, are already operating or are showing an interest in Afghanistan. In 2001, only 15,000 people had access to telecom facilities. Today the number of telephone users (mainly

---

8 See *Afghanistan Compact*, available at:
http://unama.unmissions.org/Portals/UNAMA/Documents/AfghanistanCompact-English.pdf

9 See *Paris Declaration*, 12 June 2008, available at:
http://unama.unmissions.org/Portals/UNAMA/Documents/Paris-con-Declaration-English.pdf (accessed on 20 September 2009).

10 See Government of the Islamic Republic of Afghanistan, *"Afghanistan National Development Strategy: A Strategy for Security, Governance, Economic Growth, & Poverty Reduction,"* (Kabul: Government of the Islamic Republic of Afghanistan, 2008).

11 See United Nations Assistance Mission in Afghanistan (UNAMA), "*Afghan Update*", UNAMA, No.20, Summer 2009 Special Health Issue, p.7.

12 See Government of the Islamic Republic of Afghanistan *"Afghanistan: 38% Reduction in Child Mortality, 40% Reduction in Maternal Mortality Achieved During 2002-2008"*, News Report available at: http://www.reliefweb.int/rw/rwb.nsf/db900SID/MYAI-7Z555Z (accessed on 26 December 2009).

mobile) has exceeded 4 million, which is more than 15 percent of the population. Afghan Telecom has installed 86,000 fixed digital lines and 233,000 wireless lines in all 34 provinces. By mid-2009 the process of constructing a 3,200-kilometre optical-fibre network connecting major provincial capitals with one another and with neighbouring countries will be complete. A broadly free and privately owned media sector has developed. Presently Afghanistan has seven national TV stations (six of which are private), numerous radio networks, plus a diverse and increasingly professional print media. According to government sources about 12,000 kilometres of roads have been rehabilitated, improved, or built. This includes the 2,200 kilometre ring road which connects all major towns in Afghanistan. More than US$ 2 billion has been spent on roads. All these projects are implemented in difficult security situations, which are normally not mentioned while discussing broader security and strategic matters concerning Afghanistan.

Table 1: Some Macroeconomic Indicators in Afghanistan, 2004-10[13]

Year	*GDP Growth*	*Inflation*	*Exchange Rate to US$ (annual average)*
2004	8.0	N.A	47.8
2005	16.1	12.3	49.7
2006	8.2	5.3	49.9
2007	12.1	12.9	49.8
2008	3.4	28.3	50.2
2009*	9.0	6.0	N.A
2010*	7.5	6.8	N.A

**projected*

IV. Security Situation and Narcotics

After initial successes up until 2004-05, the situation in Afghanistan has become more difficult, complex and challenging. One of the main reasons has been the deteriorating security situation, particularly in the south and east of the country. A major change, which has happened in the last three years, is the rise of suicide bombings, which reached almost 150 in 2007 and increased further in 2008. As the following table shows the figures of coalition casualties in Afghanistan are growing with every passing year making 2009 the bloodiest year since 2001.

Table 2 : Coalition Military Fatalities in Afghanistan, 2001-2009 (by year and month)[14]

Year	*Jan*	*Feb*	*Mar*	*Apr*	*May*	*Jun*	*Jul*	*Aug*	*Sep*	*Oct*	*Nov*	*Dec*	*Total*
2001	0	0	0	0	0	0	0	0	0	3	5	4	12
2002	10	12	14	10	1	3	0	3	1	6	1	8	69
2003	4	7	12	2	2	7	2	4	2	6	8	1	57
2004	11	2	3	3	9	5	2	4	4	8	7	1	59
2005	2	3	6	19	4	29	2	33	12	10	7	4	131
2006	1	17	13	5	17	22	19	29	38	17	9	4	191

13 From *Asian Development Outlook 2009* (ADB: 2009), pp. 296, 303, 314.
14 From http://icasualties.org/oef/ (accessed on 15 January 2010).

2007	2	18	10	20	25	24	29	34	24	15	22	9	232
2008	14	7	19	14	23	46	30	46	37	19	12	27	294
2009	25	24	28	14	27	38	76	77	70	74	32	35	520

In addition, opium production continues to be a serious problem in Afghanistan, although 2008 and 2009 opium surveys by the United Nations Office of Drugs and Crime (UNODC) have shown that there has been some moderate decline. In 2008 it was shown that 98 percent of the total cultivation was confined to seven provinces with serious security problems. Five out of these provinces were in the south and two in the west of Afghanistan. The seven provinces that contributed to 98 percent of Afghan opium cultivation and production in 2008 were Hilmand, Kandahar, Uruzgan, Daykundi, Zabul, Farah and Nimroz, clearly indicating strong linkages between opium production and security situation. Opium cultivation in Afghanistan has decreased by 22 percent, from 157,000 hectares in 2008 to 123,000 in 2009. In 2008, Hilmand remained the single largest opium-cultivating province where 66 percent of total Afghan cultivation was done. In 2009, cultivation declined by a third, to less than 70,000 hectares in Hilmand. The 2009 survey also shows that compared to 13 in 2007 and 18 in 2008, 20 provinces (out of 34) were poppy-free. All the seven provinces in the Northern region should then be poppy free in almost a decade. The survey rightly asserts that "controlling drugs in Afghanistan will not solve all of the country's problems, but the country's problems can not be solved without controlling drugs".[15]
Various official and unofficial reports and studies have broadly pointed out that Afghanistan today is at a crossroads. The *Afghanistan Study Group* report which was released in early 2008 sums up the mood by asserting that "the progress achieved after six years of international engagement is under serious threat from resurgent violence, weakening international resolve, mounting regional challenges and a growing lack of confidence on the part of the Afghan people about the future direction of their country".[16] Similarly, the *Centre for Strategic and International Studies* (CSIS) in its 2007 report sums up its findings as: (1) Afghans are losing trust in their government because of an escalation in violence; (2) Public expectations are neither being met nor managed; and (3) Conditions in Afghanistan have deteriorated in all key areas targeted for development, except for the economy and women's rights.[17] In September 2008, the UN Secretary General observed in its report that, "the overall situation in Afghanistan has become more challenging".[18] Despite enhanced capacities, he notes that the "security situation has deteriorated markedly." Furthermore, "the influence of the insurgency has expanded beyond traditionally volatile areas" and "incidents stemming from cross-border activities from Pakistan have increased significantly in

15 For details see "*Afghanistan Opium Survey 2008*" (UN Office of Drugs & Crime, 2008); and "*Afghanistan Opium Survey 2009 Summary Findings*" (UN Office of Drugs & Crime, 2009).

16 See Centre for the Study of the Presidency, "*The Afghanistan Study Group: Revitalising Our efforts, Rethinking our Strategies*", Centre for the Study of the Presidency (Washington DC: Centre for the Study of the Presidency, 2008), 5.

17 See Centre for Strategic and International Studies (CSIS), "*Breaking Point: Measuring Progress in Afghanistan*", (CSIS, Washington DC, March 2007).

18 See "The Situation in Afghanistan and its Implications for International Peace & Security", report of the UN Secretary General to the General Assembly Security Council, 23 September 2008.

terms of numbers and sophistication."[19] In addition, he mentions that the humanitarian situation has also deteriorated. The report also draws particular attention to the increase in the number of civilian casualties, "which are caused mainly by anti-government activities but are also the unintended consequence of operations by pro-government forces."[20]

In August 2009, General Staley A McChrystal, the then commander of International Security Assistance Force (ISAF) and US forces in Afghanistan, warned that situation is serious and "neither success nor failure can be taken for granted" and "many indicators suggest that the situation is deteriorating." He further wrote that "we face not only a resilient and growing insurgency, there is also a crisis of confidence among Afghans - in both their government and in the international community - that undermines our credibility and emboldens the insurgents".[21] During the conformation hearings, the new US commander in Afghanistan General David Petraeus accepted that "there is no question that levels of violence in Afghanistan have increased significantly over the last several years". To turn the tide he emphasized an integrated civil-military effort in Afghanistan.[22]

V. Reconstruction

Overall, more than 70 nations have committed over US$ 57 billion for reconstruction in Afghanistan. As of February 2009, the United States had pledged US$ 38.6 billion, out of which $22 billion had already been disbursed. As the following table shows, more than 50 percent of this aid has gone into building Afghan National Army and Afghan National Police. Other commitments are in the areas of economic and social development, governance, counter narcotics and support to many civil society activities. Apart from this, the number of US troops serving in Afghanistan could touch 100,000 in 2010.[23]

The next major commitment to Afghanistan is from Europe. Individual EU member states and the European Commission are making a significant contribution to security and justice reforms, development and reconstruction, counter narcotics and regional cooperation activities in Afghanistan. The EU has also deployed a police mission. Together they have committed around €8 billion (around $11.5 bn) for reconstruction activities. Furthermore, 25 EU nations are participating in the NATO-led International Security Assistance Force (ISAF) with around 30,000 troops. Their military involvement in Afghanistan has been controversial at times because of limits to their deployment and "national caveats" on many of their troops. Many EU nations

---

19 *Ibid.*

20 *Ibid.*

21 See *"Commander's Initial Assessment"*; unclassified Report prepared by Stanley A McChrystal, US Commander in Afghanistan, 30 August 2009, p. 1-1, available at: http://media.washingtonpost.com/wp-srv/politics/documents/Assessment_Redacted_092109.pdf

22 See Opening Statement during the Confirmation Hearing at the Senate Armed Services Committee by General David H. Petraeus, Commander ISAF/US Forces in Afghanistan, 29 June 2010, available at http://graphics8.nytimes.com/packages/pdf/world/2010/petraeus-opening-statement.pdf (accessed on 5 July 2010).

23 See BBC *"Obama to Send 30,000 More Troops"* available at: http://news.bbc.co.uk/2/hi/8388939.stm (accessed on 10 December 2009).

committed themselves thinking that it would mainly be a peacekeeping and reconstruction effort rather than a "War on Terror project" in which they have to engage with the resurgent Taliban. There have also been problems in coordinating with other international partners as well as within the EU nations themselves. Despite significant success in many areas (economy, education, infrastructure, health, women rights) defeatism is spreading in many European capitals. Exit strategies are being worked out including through "negotiated settlements" with the Taliban. On reconstruction, the UK has spent over £740 million (around $1,175 million) in the last eight years and have committed to more than 510 million ($810 million) over the next four years.[24] Germany also increased its funding in 2008-09 and by 2010, it is likely to have made available resources worth some €1.2 billion ($1.72 billion).[25] From Asia, Japan has pledged around $1.8 billion to Afghanistan including reconstruction ($919 million), security involvement ($212 million) and governance ($247 million). Together with the UN, Japan is the lead nation in Disarmament, Demobilisation and Reintegration (DDR) and also involved in the construction of the Kabul-Kandahar highway and Kabul international airport terminal. With a broad understanding that a peaceful and stable Afghanistan is crucial for regional stability, India has also been playing an active role in reconstruction since 2002. So far it has pledged assistance for about $1.3 billion, with projects covering the whole country mainly in the areas of road construction, power transmission lines, hydroelectricity, agriculture, telecommunication, education, health and capacity building.

VI. Human and Minority Rights

At the policy level, the ANDS, approved in April 2008, envisages a series of priorities and programmes for the period 2008-2013. Within the ANDS, human rights are largely treated as a question of civil and political rights. The ANDS also addresses country's international commitments to Universal Declaration of Human Rights and the six international human rights conventions (discussed below) that the country has ratified. Under the issue of governance, rule of law and human rights, many benchmarks concerning support and monitoring and development of human rights, consolidation of democratic institutions and rule of law, providing public services, accountability, gender equality etc have been outlined. Under the 2005 Action Plan on Peace, Justice and Reconciliation, the government tried to tackle the issue of past human rights violations.

Without resorting to revenge, and in the spirit of inclusion and tolerance the Independent Afghanistan Independent Human Rights Commission (AIHRC) was put in charge of conducting a public consultation by 2008, aimed at drafting a strategy for transitional justice. To implement transitional justice, the AIHRC has taken many measures; these include, for instance, declaring the December 10 as the day of Victims of Human Rights Abuses and documenting human rights abuses etc. Due to

---

24 See *The UK in Afghanistan*, 14 October 2009, available at:
http://www.number10.gov.uk/Page20961
(accessed on 28 December 2009).

25 See the Federal Foreign Office of Germany, *"Bilateral Relation: Afghanistan"*, available at: http://www.auswaertigesamt.de/diplo/en/Laenderinformationen/01-Laender/Afghanistan.html
(accessed on 26 December 2009).

prevailing difficult conditions as well as many misunderstandings, the process of transitional justice has not been followed thoroughly. Through the implementation of various national strategies, the government is trying to achieve better human rights conditions in the country. These strategies include the so-called Justice for All Strategy (2005), the National Justice Sector Strategy (2007), and the National Justice Sector Action Plan (2007). The adoption of different National Strategies concerning Education (2007) Public Health and Nutrition (2008) and Children at Risk (2004) has created the framework for the social and economic human rights in the country. Under the National Strategy for a Higher Education for the years 2008 to 2013, one hundred thousand students, 30 percent of them girls, will be enrolled in the universities.

Constitutionally, all Afghans have been granted the Right to Work under Article 48. They are free to choose occupation and profession as provided by law. Similarly, under Article 53, the state is legally bound to adopt measures for active participation of citizens in the society. Citizens also have been provided Right to Food, Right to Shelter, Right to Education and Right to Health. Under Article 47 of the Constitution, the state is responsible for effective plans for promotion of science, culture, and art. Under civil and political rights, Right to Life has been considered the most important right of any individual. Article 23 of the Constitution says that "life is a gift of God and humans have a natural right to it. Nobody shall be deprived of this right, unless the law rules otherwise." In the prevailing security situation, however, ensuring and protecting the Right to Life has been the biggest challenge faced by the state, particularly when coalition forces' operations are not under its control and a significant territory is under the influence of anti-government forces. According to article 33 of the Constitution "Afghan citizens have the right to elect or to be elected." This article ensures Right to Political Participation for all eligible citizens. Under this provision, 2004 and 2009 presidential elections as well as 2005 parliamentary elections have been conducted. In the 2004 presidential elections, 70 percent of the total 10,567,834 eligible voters participated in the election, out of which 41 percent were women. The 2009 presidential election was marred with allegations of corruption and bogus voting. Moreover, the government has not been able to conduct local elections.

Freedom of expression and media are provided by Afghan laws. According to the government statistics, there are three national television broadcasters and 21 local television stations in the country, both state-run and private. In addition, there are 57 state-run and private radio stations. Similarly, hundreds of publications, including newspapers, weekly, monthly, quarterly and annual publications are published. In the last few years, however, there have been many instances of intimidation of journalists by government authorities.

Under the Law of Formation and Registration of Social Organizations (2002) and the Political Party Formation Law (2003) some 102 political parties and 1,348 social organisations have been registered. Article 36 of the Constitution also states that all citizens have the right to stage peaceful protests. This provision has been used quite frequently by Afghan citizens.

Article 22 of the Constitution says that "discrimination and favouritism of any kind is prohibited. Afghan citizens – men and women alike – have equal rights and responsibilities." Still, discrimination against women and social minorities is a daily fact of life. The 2004 Afghan constitution mentions Pashtun, Tajik, Hazara, Uzbek,

Turkmen, Baluch, Pahsai, Nuristani, Aimaq, Arab, Kyrghiz, Qizilbash, Gujur, Brahui and others as ethnic groups. All these groups have the right to Afghan citizenship. The languages of these ethnic groups are also recognised in the constitution. The constitution of Afghanistan does not use the world minority and there are no special provision listed for minorities. In fact, an earlier report by the Minority Rights Group International called the country *A Nation of Minorities*.[26] However, in everyday life certain ethnic and religious groups (Hazaras, and Non Muslim Hindus and Sikhs) are considered minorities.

Dari and Pashto are the official languages of the state.[27] Recently, the Ministry of Education has also developed a 1-6 grade curriculum in Uzbeki, Turkmeni, Baluchi, Pashaie and Nooristani languages. Out of 249 seats of *Wolesi Jirga* (House of Representatives), 65 seats are reserved for women. In addition, 10 seats are reserved for Kuchis (including at least 3 women). The Kuchis, pashtun nomads, are another social minority that has also faced enduring discrimination. The Independent Directorate for the Affairs of the Kuchis has estimated their population close to 5 million. Ongoing conflict and droughts have disrupted the nomadic lifestyle of Kuchis. Unclear land tenure policies and pasture rights have brought them into conflict with settled communities. There has been long standing dispute between the nomadic Sunni Kuchis and settled Shi'a Hazara populations over access to pasture lands in parts of the Central Region and Central Highlands. The last few years have seen violent clashes between these two communities which have led to significant loss of life and property.

The adoption of the Shi'a Personal Status Law has also been a regressive step for human and women rights. The new law regulates marriage, divorce, inheritance, rights of movement and bankruptcy for Shi'a population. The original version of the bill subjected Shi'a women to restricted movement, mandatory marital sex, limited ability to seek work, pursue an education or visit the doctor without their husbands' permission and special regulation on matters like inheritance. After international pressure and protests by Afghan women the law was amended. The revised version, however, still allows a man to deny his wife food if she does not submit to his sexual requests. It also grants guardianship of children exclusively to their fathers and grandfathers. The law also requires women to get permission from their husbands to work.[28]

Torture is used very extensively in Afghanistan, despite the fact that, to prevent slavery and human trafficking, a new Law on Combating the Abduction and Human Trafficking was enacted in 2008. The law also authorises the formation of the Commission for Combating Abduction and Human Smuggling. Due to old traditions, about 40 percent of marriages in Afghanistan are at an early age and in many cases, forced upon young girls. The age in which marriage is permitted under Afghan law is 18 years of age for boys and 16 for girls. As Article 14 of the law considers family as

26 See Nasim Jawad, "*Afghanistan: A Nation of Minorities*" (London: Minority Rights Group International, 1992).

27 See Article 16 of the Constitution of Afghanistan.

28 See Human Rights Watch, "*Afghanistan: Law Curbing Women's Rights Takes Effect*" of 13 August 2009, available at: http://www.hrw.org/en/news/2009/08/13/afghanistan-law-curbing-women-s-rights-takes-effect.

a cornerstone of the society, many efforts are made to protect young girls from forced marriage.

A. Human Rights (Protecting) Institutions

Within the state structure, the main institutions which deal with human rights issues are the Supreme Court, the National Assembly, the Ministry of Justice (MoJ), the Office of the Attorney General (OAG), the Ministry of Interior (MoI) and the National Directorate of Security (NDS). Under new constitution, the Supreme Court is one of the state's tools of power and under its jurisdiction about 1,370 judges are working in 365 courts all over Afghanistan. Apart from limited capacity, these judges are working under difficult security situations prevailing in the country. So far 12 judges have been assassinated and six have been kidnapped. Under international support, many programmes of capacity building and observation of principles of fair trial and human rights of individuals in the courts have been implemented in the last few years. The National Assembly also monitors and approves the development of social, cultural, and economic national programmes.

According to the 2009 Report prepared by the Ministry of Foreign Affairs, "MoJ administers the affairs of prisons, juvenile correction centres (JCC), solicit public rights and properties, settling of public and individual disputes, raises public legal awareness, provides legal aid to the indigent before the courts, establishment of a bar association, facilitating the establishment of human rights section, registers and grants operation licenses to political parties and social organisations".[29] Despite its clear responsibilities, MoJ faces many challenges due to non-separation of children in JCC centres and lack of human rights standards in prisons. The OAG, an independent body, has the responsibility to observe and enforce law to protect individuals and society at various stages of monitoring, investigation and judicial prosecution. The OAG has been very active in the last few years through some high profile cases. However, it is pointed out that it "faces problems such as insufficient legal awareness of suspects and accused, limited access to defence lawyers especially in the provinces, insecurity of prosecutors, shortage of technical equipment during detection and investigation of crimes, manipulation and pressure by influential individuals, low salaries of prosecutors and lack of proper facilities for investigation".[30] The MoI is responsible for ensuring security (including combating terrorism) and public order, protecting borders, counter narcotics efforts and the prevention of violations of the law. Despite its efforts to train national police in observing human rights issues, the police have been criticized for violations of human rights on many occasions. The NDS is in charge of combating organised crimes and terrorist activities, countering economic crimes and sabotage and combating misuse of public properties. Despite efforts to observe human rights standards in its activities, it has been criticised on many occasions for mistreatment and torture of prisoners and intimidation to journalists and human rights activists.

---

29 See Ministry of Foreign Affairs, "*National Report Submitted in Accordance with Paragraph 15(A) of the Annex to Human Rights Council Resolution 5/1*", (Ministry of Foreign Affairs, Kabul Afghanistan, 2009).
30 *Ibid.*

To monitor and review human rights issues in prisons, the government has established a High Council for Prisons (HCP). Similarly, Special Advisory Board evaluates human rights records of individuals while recommending appointments to high ranking official positions. Since corruption is all-pervasive in Afghanistan, the government has set up the High Office for Monitoring of the Strategy against Official Corruption, the Special Prosecutor Office, judicial departments dealing with administrative corruption, the Civil Service Commission and the Commission for Combating Official Corruption.

Article 58 of the Constitution provides the establishment of an Afghanistan Independent Human Rights Commission (AIHRC). Its main job is to protect and promote human rights and strengthen capacities in the area of human rights throughout the country. According to MoFA report its mandate is to "monitor the implementation of the provisions of the Constitution, statutes and human rights commitments, activities of administrative, legal and judicial systems, relevant performance of governmental and non-governmental agencies and detention centres on a regular basis. AIHRC is also promoting rights of children, women, and disabled people, observing cases of human rights violations, transitional justice and raising human rights awareness."[31] The same report asserts that the AIHRC has been able to train 207,419 individuals by holding 6,569 workshops and special programmes on human rights. It has received around 13,400 cases of human rights complaints and has addressed around 12,500 cases. Under its guidance, fifty private prisons have been closed and more than 3,600 individuals, who were illegally detained have been released. Although AIHRC has not been able to visit Coalition Forces Detention Centres, it has been able to monitor detainees.

Apart from the AIHRC, there are many other special commissions for the monitoring of the human rights situation, such as the Commission Addressing Observance of Human Rights in Investigation, Interrogation and Detention Stages (established in 2007), the Commission Addressing Problems of Children and Juveniles (established in 2008), the Commission on Addressing Capital Punishment and Retaliation Files (established in 2006), the Board for Addressing Complaints of Prisoners Transferred from Bagram and Guantanamo (established in 2007, identified 300 prisoners as innocents), the Board for Addressing Situation of Prisoners in Kabul Prisons and Detention Centres (established in 2007, resolved around 3,600 cases), and the Commission for the Elimination of Violence against Women (established in 2005).

B. Commitment to International Treaties

Afghanistan has signed and ratified many international treaties concerning human and minority rights (see appendix). For instance, it ratified International Covenant on Economic, Social and Cultural Rights in 1983; after submitting its first report in 1991, the second report was submitted to the United Nations only in 2007. The Convention on the Rights of the Child was ratified in 1994 and the Convention on the Elimination of All Forms of Violence against Women was ratified in 2003. The International Convention on the Elimination of All Forms of Racial Discrimination was ratified in 1983 but no reporting has been done so far. Afghanistan ratified Convention against

---

31 *Ibid.*

Torture in 1987 and submitted its initial report in 1992. The International Covenant on Civil and Political Rights was ratified in 1983. Similarly, Afghanistan has also ratified the Optional Protocol on Children in Armed Conflict in 2003 and the Optional Protocol on the Sale of Children, Child Prostitution, and Child Pornography in 2002.

C. Achievements in Women & Children Rights

Since the conditions of women during the Taliban regime were so bad, the international community and the Afghan government have focused specifically on the rights of the women. After forming a separate Women Affairs Ministry, in 2003 Afghanistan acceded to the UN Convention on the Elimination of all Forms of Discrimination against Women (CEDAW) and provided more or less equal rights of men and women in the constitution. Many women have also started participating actively in the social and political life. The Constitution ensures the presence of at least 2 female deputies from each province to the Parliament. In addition, at least 25 percent of parliament members must be women. According to government statistics currently women make up 28 percent of the National Assembly and out of 1,652 judges working in military and civil courts, a total of 189 are women. Similarly, out of 1,095 prosecutors employed by the Office of Attorney General, 103 of them are women. Excluding the Ministry of Interior and Defence, out of total 221,684 state employees, 47,790 are women.

The second group which has been affected by decades of conflict is children, whose rights have been grossly violated. During Taliban regime, girls were denied schooling. Now about 6 million children have started attending schools, a third of who are girls. Still there are numerous examples where girls' schools have been burned down and children, specially girls, have been physically attacked for attending schools. Hundreds of children die because of malnutrition and water-borne diseases. In healthcare many successful vaccination drives have been concluded. Although infant mortality rate is still high, it has come down significantly.

D. Status of Refugees, Disabled and Civilian Killings

As a result of decades of war, there are about 1000,000 disabled people. To tackle the problem of these people, the Afghan government has also initiated measures for the rehabilitation of disabled people so that they can actively participate in public life and society. To ensure their participation, the Law of Disables Rights has also been adopted. With regards refugees, more than 3 million Afghan refugees are still living in neighbouring countries. The Ministry of Repatriates along with the UNHCR is working for the rights of the returnees and the internally displaced people. This is one major issue which the Afghan government is going to tackle in the coming years, particularly arranging humanitarian assistance, finding jobs and housing for these people.

One another major issue in Afghanistan is the rights of civilians during military operations. In the last few years, rights of civilians have been violated both by the pro and anti government forces. In the absence of a required number of security forces, the coalition forces have relied more on airpower in counter-insurgency operations. According to the 2008 Human Rights Watch report, 116 civilians were killed in 2006 in 13 bombings. Similarly, 321 civilians were killed in 2007 in 22 bombings while hundreds more injured. In the first seven months of 2008 at least 119 civilians were killed in 12 air strikes.[32] According to latest UNAMA report in 2009, 2,412 civilians died in Afghanistan due to conflict. Out of this, 67 percent (1,630 deaths) were caused by Anti Government Elements (AGE) and 596 deaths (25 percent) by Pro Government Forces.[33] As the number of civilian killings has increased, the Afghan government has openly criticised many times various operations of the coalition forces. In recent months, security forces are trying to be more careful in their operations.

VII. Conclusion

Along with human rights issues in a poor, under-developed and highly conservative country, decades of war had destroyed all the basic institutions of the state in Afghanistan. The major task in the last eight years has been to build up the basic institutions of governance. In addition, the conflict is still continuing in many parts of the country. Terrorist attacks by insurgents and counter-insurgency operations conducted by the coalition forces have further aggravated human rights conditions in the country. Despite all these problems, Afghanistan has made significant gains in political participation, infrastructure, education, health, economic development and the empowerment of women, which needs to be consolidated. At the same time, the security situation in the last few years has deteriorated. Poppy cultivation and corruption still remain serious problems. Currently, some of the major issues affecting the human rights situation in Afghanistan include insecurity in many parts of the country, the overlapping of authority between different branches of the state, weakness of democratic and civil society institutions, rampant corruption, weak capacity of law enforcement agencies, violence against women and children, deportation of refugees from neighbouring countries, existence of powerful warlords and impunity of their past records, existence of international detention centres, poverty, unemployment and lack of social protection. Many of these issues can be tackled once the security situation improves. Some others issues which are affected by weak government capacities, lack of development, and social customs will take much longer.

---

32 See Human Rights Watch, "*Troops in Contact: Air strikes and Civilian Deaths in Afghanistan*" (Human Rights Watch, September 2008).
33 See United Nations Assistance Mission in Afghanistan (UNAMA), *"Afghanistan: Annual Report on Protection of Civilians in Armed Conflict 2009"*, (UNAMA, Kabul 2009).

APPENDIX[34]

Table A: Main International Human Rights Conventions and Protocols Ratified by Afghanistan

Name of the Convention	*Date of Adoption by the General Assembly and Monitoring Body*	*Date of Signature by Afghanistan*	*Date of Ratification by Afghanistan*	*Reservations given by Afghanistan*
International Convention on the Elimination of All forms of Racial Discrimination (ICERD)	21/12/1965	14/08/1980	05/03/2003	Reservation on art.22 Declaration on arts 17,18 Acceptance of amendment to Art 8
International Convention on Civil and Political Rights (ICCPR). This convention is supplemented by two optional protocols (OPs)which have not been signed or ratified yet by Afghanistan	16/12/1996	Accession	24/01/1983	Decl. on Art 43
International Covenant on Economic , Social and Cultural Rights (ICESCR)	16/12/1966	Accession	24/01/1983	Decl. on Art 26
Convention on the Elimination of All Forms of Discrimination Against Women (CEDAW)	18/12/1979	14/08/1980	05/03/2003	Declaration on Acceptance of amendment to Art 20
Convention against Torture and Other Cruel , inhuman or Degrading Treatment or Punishment (CAT)	10/12/1984	04/02/1985	01/04/1987	Reservations on Art 20 & 30
Convention on the Rights of the Child (CRC)	20/11/1989	27/09/1990	28/03/1994	Acceptance of amendment to Art 43
OP to the Convention on the Rights of the Child on the Involvement of Children in Armed Conflict.	25/05/2000		Accession on 24/09/2003	None
OP to the Convention on the Rights of the Child on the Sale of Children, Child Prostitution and Child pornography.	//	//	Accession on 19/09/2002	Declaration

34 Source: Ministry of Foreign Affairs, Afghanistan.

Table B :Other United Nations Human Rights and Related Conventions Ratified by Afghanistan

Name of the Convention	*Date of Adoption by the General Assembly and Monitoring Body*	*Date of Signature by Afghanistan*	*Date of Ratification by Afghanistan*	*Reservations given by Afghanistan*
Convention on the Prevention and Punishment of the Crime of Genocide	New York, 9/12/1948		22/03/1956	
Slavery Convention , 1926 as amended 1955	Geneva , 25/09/1926	16/08/1954		
Convention for the Suppression of the Traffic of Persons and the Exploitation of the Prostitution	Lake Success, New York, 21/03/1950	Accession on 21/05/1985		Reservation on Art 22
Rome statute of the International Criminal Court	17/07/1998		10/02/2003	
United Nations Conventions against Transnational Organized Crime, 2000, and its protocols against the smuggling of migrants by land, sea and air, and to prevent, suppress and punish trafficking in persons, especially women and children.	15/11/2000	14/12/2000	24/09/2003	

Table C: Conventions of the International Labour Organization (ILO)

Name of the Convention	*Year of Adoption by the General Assembly and Monitoring Body*	*Date of Ratification by Afghanistan*
Night Work Convention	1919	12/06/1939
White Lead Convention	1921	12/06/1939
Weekly Rest (industry) Convention	1921	12/06/1939
Night Work Convention Revised	1934	12/06/1939
Underground Work Convention	1935	14/05/1937
ionProtection of Wages Convent	1949	14/05/1957
Equal Remuneration Convention	1951	22/08/1969
Abolition of Forced Labour Convention	1957	16/05/1963
Weekly Rest (Commerce Office) Convention	1957	16/05/1963
Discrimination (Employment and Occupation) Convention	1958	01/10/1969
Work Convention Dock	1973	16/05/1979

Occupational Cancer Convention	1974	16/05/1979
Paid Educational Leave Convention	1974	16/05/1979
Rural Workers Organizations Convention	1979	16/05/1979
Human Resources Development Convention	1975	16/05/1979

Table D. Geneva Convention and other Treaties on International Humanitarian Law

Name of the Convention	*Date of Adoption by the General Assembly and Monitoring Body*	*Date of Signature by Afghanistan*	*Date of Ratification by Afghanistan*
Geneva Convention (1) for the Amelioration of the condition of the wounded and Sick in Armed Forces in the Field	12/08/1949	8/12/1949	26/09/1959
Geneva Convention (2) for the Amelioration of the Condition of Wounded , Sick and Shipwrecked Members of Armed Forces at Sea	12/08/1949	8/12/1949	26/09/1956
Geneva Convention (3) relative to the Treatment of Prisoners of War	12/08/1949	8/12/1949	26/09/1956
Ottawa Convention on the Prohibition of Use Stockpiling, Production and transfer of Anti- Personnel Mines and Their Destruction	18/09/1997		11/09/2002

CHAPTER 2

Bhutanese Refugees: The struggle in Exile

Jagatmani Acharya*

I. BACKGROUND

Bhutan is a landlocked, Least Developed Country situated in the eastern Himalayas. It is bordered on the east, south and west by India and on the north by China. In 1907, Bhutan became a monarchy with the election of Ugyen Wangchuck as the first hereditary King of Bhutan. Bhutan is now a Democratic Constitutional Monarchy with a total land area of 38,394 sq. km of which 72.5 percent of the total area is under forest cover. The total estimated population of Bhutan is 683.407.[1] The figure, however, does not include the population living in exile and those who have been denied citizenship in the 2005 census. Like other South Asian states, Bhutan is a multi-ethnic country. Yet in the last two decades the Bhutanese state has pursued a policy of marginalizing ethnic, linguistic and cultural minorities such as the Lhotshampas[2] and Sharchhops.[3]

In this context, the Royal Government of Bhutan (RGOB) imposed laws and policies aimed at eliminating the Lhotshampas from southern Bhutan. In addition, the government of Bhutan enforced some laws and policies such as the 1985 Citizenship Act of Bhutan; the Marriage Act of 1988; the 1988 Census policy and the "One-Nation, One-People policy" under which Lhotshampas were forced to practice and follow the culture and tradition of the ruling class. Furthermore, the No-Objection Certificates (NOC), without which one cannot have access to health, education, employment and loans; and the Voluntary Migration Forms (VMFs) which are forms printed in the national language stating that refugees are leaving the country on their own behest. By the early 1990s, 60 percent of the refugees in the camps had signed the VMFs and were forced to leave the country. These only constituted some of the measures adopted by the government of Bhutan in its pursuit to evict thousands of Bhutanese nationals. As a result of these mechanisms adopted by RGOB, more than 100.000 Bhutanese have been forcibly evicted from Bhutan since 1989.

---

* Jagatmani Acharya is a Bhutanese Refugee living in exile since 1991. He is presently involved with the Nepal Institute of Peace (NIP) as a coordinator. He has experience in the fields of peace and human rights, refugee rights, minority rights and displaced populations in South Asia. He is known for organizing and coordinating the South Asian Human Rights and Peace Studies Course and Refugee program of South Asia Forum for Human Rights (SAFHR). He has written numerous reports and articles on refugees, minorities and displaced populations. The author can be contacted at jagatjee@gmail.com

1 See the National Statistics Bureau of the Royal Government of Bhutan, *"Bhutan At A Glance 2009"*, available at: http://www.nsb.gov.bt/pub/baag/BAAG%202009.pdf

2 Lhotshampas are Nepali Speaking Bhutanese, Lho is south and tshampas are people living in the south of Bhutan.

3 Sharchhops are Tshangla speakers that mainly reside in eastern Bhutan.

In the mid-1980s the King of Bhutan initiated plans to homogenize Bhutan's cultural practices on the basis of Ngalong traditions while simultaneously implementing legislation that would reduce the numbers of Lhotshampas. In the early 1990s, due to the introduction of laws revoking citizenship rights by the government, a mass exodus of Lhotshampas began.

The RGOB methodically implemented an expulsion process of the Lhotshampas communities, resulting in the statelessness of over one hundred thousand individuals. Many Sharchops from eastern Bhutan also fled from in 1997 as Bhutan continued its harsh response to any form of political opposition. Ultimately, discriminatory legislation and police efforts compelled thousands of Lhotshampas and Sharchops to flee their homeland in search of refuge. The vast majority of the refugees eventually reached Nepal, where they received assistance from the state and the international community. In these circumstances, in 1991 his Majesty's Government (HMG) of Nepal formally invited the United Nations High Commissioner for Refugees (UNHCR) to coordinate emergency relief assistance for Bhutanese refugees. UNHCR-sponsored camps provided refugees with basic needs such as health care, education and shelter. Likewise, many organizations like the Lutheran World Federation (LWF), CARITAS Nepal, the Association of Medical Doctors of Asia (AMDA), the Nepal Red Cross Society (NRCS) and the World Food Program (WFP) provided food and non-food items to the refugees.

In an attempt to alleviate people's suffering in the refugee camps, the international community offered to resettle refugees to third countries, without denying them the right to return to their homeland. However, even after two decades of exile there is no prospect of return to Bhutan for refugees. The human rights situation inside Bhutan has not changed and the government maintains that the refugees are illegal migrants who left Bhutan voluntarily after signing the VMFs.

II. Constitution of Bhutan, Government Policies, Laws and the Refugee Crisis

Since 2008 the undemocratic laws and policies of the RGOB are gradually changing. The first elected parliament is making efforts to introduce new laws and hopes are high that all new provisions will be promulgated by intensive dialogue involving people from all sectors of society and complying with all relevant international standards. It is regrettable that the Constitution of Bhutan does not reflect the rights of minorities, not a single mention of "Hinduism/Hindu, Lhotshampas, minorities or refugees" is found in the Constitution. Therefore, the fear is that the rights of the Lhotshampas and Sharchops minorities will be violated thus making even more difficult for anyone to promote and protect their rights in Bhutan. The Constitution in its Article 2 (15), gives the monarchy absolute power by placing the King above the Constitution.

Since 1988 the government has implemented the aforementioned laws and policies and, as a result, large numbers of people have continued to live in exile in the last nineteen years. One of the first instances of discrimination is the 1988 "Driglam Namza", an ancient code of social etiquette of western Bhutanese origin made

obligatory for all ethnic communities.[4] The Dzongkha language, the mother tongue of the Ngalong community was made the sole official language. Nepali, the language of the southern Bhutanese was dropped from the school curriculum, thus depriving children from southern Bhutan to an education in their own language. Furthermore, the government of Bhutan introduced the so called "One-Nation, One-People policy" in 1989 through a uniform Ngalongs culture, the culture of the western Bhutanese ruling elite, was imposed on a multicultural, multi-ethnic Bhutanese society. Though Bhutan is a country with 14 different ethnic groups, the government implemented the "One Nation One People Policy", denying other ethnic groups in Bhutan their own culture, their ethnic garb and their own language. Along the same lines, the Marriage Act, enacted in 1980 and then forcefully implemented in 1988 further imposed restrictions and punishments on marriages between Bhutanese and non-Bhutanese. Under its provisions, a Bhutanese citizen who marries a foreigner is for instance denied admission to the Bhutanese Foreign Service and Armed Forces, promotion in the civil service, scholarship and fellowship for trainings abroad, agricultural loans and subsidies. In addition, with the enactment of the Citizenship Act of 1985, children born from such mixed marriages have been denied the right to Bhutanese nationality.[5]
Following the unrest in southern Bhutan in the early 1990s, the government introduced a new rule requiring persons to possess 'No Objection Certificates' (NOC). NOCs are issued by the police and the local administration to confirm that the holder has no involvement in "anti-national activity". The NOCs are considered a pre-requisite for access to healthcare facilities, education, civil service jobs and for the sale of cash crops. Even for children, admission to school is governed by the possession of a NOC.

In 1990-1991, eviction was legitimized with the introduction by the Government of the so called Voluntary Migration Forms (VMF). The 70th National Assembly session in 1991 resolved to evict from Bhutan anyone involved in peaceful demonstrations or being a suspected supporter of the human rights movement. As reported by the Appeal Movement Coordinating Council (AMCC) by "putting the plan into action, the government of Bhutan began to round up prominent citizens from the villages, who were taken to the local schools – turned detention – cum – torture – centres and were put under extreme inhuman torture until they succumbed to signing the VMF".[6]
An estimated 60 percent of the refugees residing in the refugee camps were forced to sign the VMFs, hence "voluntarily" renouncing to their Bhutanese citizenship. In addition, these forms were printed in Dzongkha language: as the Lhotshampas could not read these forms they did not understand the content and most of them did not even know that they were voluntarily renouncing their Bhutanese citizenship. Those who signed the VMF form never understood the content of the forms, nor did they receive appropriate information from the government authorities. According to the

---

4 Driglam Namza further dictated how to eat, how to sit, how to talk, how to dress or how to bow before the authority, and what hair style to adopt. As stated, it was made mandatory to all the Bhutanese despite their cultural diversity.

5 See Article 2 of the Bhutan Citizenship Act, 1985: *"A person whose parents are both citizens of Bhutan shall be deemed to be a citizen of Bhutan by birth."*

6 See Appeal Movement Coordinating Council (AMCC), *"Bhutan: A Report on How Bhutanese Citizens Were Made to Sign Voluntary Migration Forms and Forced Into Exile"*, (AMCC, Jhapa, November 1996).

LWF, "many refugees were coerced (under threat of arrest and torture) to sign papers renouncing their land and citizenship, stating they were leaving voluntarily. The concept of voluntary emigrant is in no way compatible with the reports of violence, summery arrest, vandalism of property and general intimidation."[7]

The RGOB has used religion as tool to harass and evict nationals from the country, specifically targeting adherents of the Christian and Hindu faith. Specific cases were reported by the Association of Human Rights Activists of Bhutan, for instance: "in the year 1992 Mr. Dal Jit Rai and his neighbours were celebrating Christmas. They were arrested, imprisoned and evicted from the country for practising Christianity."[8] Likewise, the harassment of Hindus continues: they cannot practice their religion and have no right to their religion in Bhutan. The religious persecution was also inflicted upon the followers of the Buddhist Nyingmapa sect in eastern Bhutan. During the peace protest in eastern Bhutan in October 1997, 13 Shedras (monasteries) were forcibly closed and more than 600 monks and students were sent to their respective villages by civil administrators, police, army and security forces. Around 200 people, including monks and ordinary people, were arrested and one monk was killed for allegedly being anti-national.

In July 2008, the Constitution of Bhutan was finally adopted. The form of Government under the present Constitution is a Democratic Constitutional Monarchy (Article 1). The credit for such a change goes to pressure from international and regional communities and to the continuous hard work of the Bhutanese refugees in exile. However, while democracy requires inclusiveness, the Bhutanese democracy is premised on the doctrine of exclusion. Its Constitution is an exclusionary document that has omitted the voices and concerns of more than 100.000 Bhutanese refugees in exile.

A. Institution of Monarchy

Upon examination of Article 2 of the Constitution on "The Institution of Monarchy" we can see that King is the most powerful figure in the country: he holds absolute power of the State and is not accountable in any court of law. The Constitution bestows so much power to the King that he holds an executive position instead of a ceremonial role that a King is supposed to have in a parliamentary democracy. To name but a few examples of his authority: he has the power to award titles; decorations; grant citizenship; land kidu and other kidus[9]; grant amnesty; pardon and reduce sentences; command bills and other measures to be introduced in parliament and exercise powers relating to matters which are not provided for under the constitution or other laws. He also holds power to appoint the Chief Justice, Chief Election Commissioner and Election Commissioners, the Auditor General, the Chairperson and members of the Royal Civil Service Commission, the Chairperson and members of the Anti-Corruption Commission, the heads of the Defence Forces and the Attorney General. He also has the power to nominate the Governor of the

---

7 See Lutheran World Federation (LWF), *"Refugees of the Peaceful Dragon"*, (LWF December 1995).

8 See Association of Human Rights Activists (AHURA), *"A Shangrila without Human Rights"*, (AHURA Bhutan, (First edition) June 1993).

9 The land given by the King to a person as a gift is called land kidu in Bhutan.

Central Bank of Bhutan, the Chairperson of the Pay Commission, the Cabinet Secretary, Ambassadors and Consuls, the Secretaries to the Government, Dzongdags (district head) on the recommendation of the Prime Minister.

B. *Buddhism as the spiritual heritage of Bhutan*

According to Article 3 of the Constitution, Buddhism is the spiritual heritage of Bhutan and the King is the protector of all religions in Bhutan. The same Article talks about Buddhist institutions and monks, but does not talk about other religious institutions and their protection and promotion. Going back to the 1990s we can see that people were evicted on the grounds of practising religions other than Buddhism. The King himself decided to stop teaching Nepali language in South Bhutan. The King said "...we recently decided to stop teaching Nepali in our schools. The National Assembly had suggested years ago, but I turned down the proposal then. Now, the situation has changed. More so, because Assam Government has also stopped the teaching of Nepali. I admit this is a very unpopular decision and I fully sympathise with the Nepalese...".[10] Though the Constitution guarantees the freedom of religion, Bhutan is yet to put the tolerance of other religions into practice. Many Hindu temples demolished during the 1990 suppression and Drukpanization process are yet to be restored while Christians are not entitled to form community groups or erect a church. The U.S. Department of State, in its 2008 Human Rights Report on Bhutan reported that: "The government favoured the Drukpa Kagyupa and Ningmapa Buddhist groups through subsidization of monasteries and shrines, as well as aid for monks....NGOs reported that the government required permission to build religious temples but rarely granted it for non-Buddhist buildings. Followers of religions other than Buddhism and Hinduism were free to worship in private homes but could not erect religious buildings or congregate in public."[11]

C. *Fundamental Rights*

The Constitution talks about the fundamental rights of its citizen. For instance, Article 7 of the Constitution deals with the right to freedom of speech, opinion and expression, right to information, freedom of press, right to vote, right to freedom of movement, right to equal access and opportunity to join the Public Service, right to own property, right to freedom of peaceful assembly and freedom of association. Although the Constitution, in its Article 7 (15) states that: "All persons are equal before the law and are entitled to equal and effective protection of the law and shall not be discriminated against on the grounds of race, sex, language, religion, politics or other status," today one-sixth of the population is in exile waiting to return to Bhutan for last two decades. They continue to be in exile for speaking against Tsa-Wa-Sum, the three elements of King, Country and People: speaking out against them is deemed a treasonable offence.

---

10 *Ibid.*, 13.
11 U.S. Department of State, *"2008 Human Rights Report: Bhutan"*, in Section 2 Respect for Civil Liberties, 25 February 2009, available at: http://www.state.gov/g/drl/rls/hrrpt/2008/sca/119133.htm#

Furthermore, the media in Bhutan is not free from government censorship.[12] The media cannot publish sensitive issues or controversial reports, especially on the subject of Southern Bhutan, or that are contradictory to the government positions.
Article 9 (2) of the Constitution emphasises the importance of Gross National Happiness (GNH) over Gross Domestic Product (GDP). It states: "the State shall strive to promote those conditions that will enable the pursuit of Gross National Happiness." Furthermore, according to Article 20 (1) of the Constitution, "The Government shall protect and strengthen the sovereignty of the Kingdom, provide good governance, and ensure peace, security, well-being and happiness of the people." How about the happiness of the people in exile? -as asked by Adhikari & Mishra "With no systematic approach to operationalize the concept of GNH and a significant portion of population still under poverty or in a state of unhappiness in refugee camps in Nepal, it's clear who it (GNH) really makes happy: the regime".[13] Moreover, the Bhutanese Refugee Support Group (BRSG) indicates that "thousands of Bhutanese people live in fear and insecurity, despite the fact that the government of Bhutan has propounded Gross National Happiness as the unifying concept for Bhutan's long-term development".[14]
As to the situation of children in Bhutan, according to the BRSG "Southern Bhutanese children, both refugees and some of those still living in Bhutan, are denied their right to a nationality. Southern Bhutanese children in Bhutan continue to be discriminated against on a daily basis. Yet Bhutan has ratified the Convention on the Rights of the Child without reservation".[15] The government of Bhutan should respect the commitments made by ratifying the Convention. In this context, it is worth recalling that the same government stated that "Happiness of the people was made the guiding goal of development. The exact phrase Gross National Happiness (GNH) is more important than Gross Domestic Product was coined by the Fourth King of Bhutan, who is the author of GNH."[16] Therefore, when we look at the linkages between GNH and the 2008 parliamentary democracy with the declaration of the Constitution of the Kingdom of Bhutan, one could realise that minority communities have been totally excluded from progress made by Bhutan.
The Constitution talks about the protection and promotion of the rights of its citizens, but there is no organization to monitor such issues, nor is there a place to appeal in case of violations. The democratic parliament conferred the responsibilities of safeguarding human rights to the police, who in fact are the perpetrator of frequent human rights violations.

---

12 For instance: Kuensel, is now a daily national newspaper since May 2009, two private independent newspapers started publication in mid-2006 and another in 2008. Besides, there is a TV Channel and a radio station and three FM radio. The internet and satellite TV have also been available since 1999.
13 See I. P. Adhikari & Vidhyapati Mishra, "Bhutan's future in democracy", in *ApfaNews.Com* of 27 October 2009, available at:
http://www.apfanews.com/opinion/bhutan%E2%80%99s-future-in-democracy/
14 See Bhutanese Refugee Support Group (BRSG), *"Some reference points for a sustainable solution"*, available at: http://homepage.eircom.net/~paulbeara/reference.html
15 *Ibid.*
16 See Karma Ura, *"Explanation of GNH Index"*, Centre of Bhutan Studies: Gross National Happiness, available at: http://www.grossnationalhappiness.com/gnhIndex/intruductionGNH.aspx

As to the voting rights, the Druk National Congress (DNC) in 2009 indicated that "monks and religious personalities were deprived of voting rights. The Bhutanese falling in categories other than F1 and F4 and about 80,000 relatives of the refugees still living in Bhutan were also deprived of their right to vote."[17] It is not surprising that the Bhutanese refugees in exile were also left out of this process.

The European Parliament Resolutions of March 1996 and May 2001 expressed awareness that Bhutan's policy of 'national integration' that began in 1990, led to a campaign that suppressed Nepali cultural expression, revoked citizenship and led to intimidation, arrest and torture that resulted in a large-scale exodus of these people to Nepal.[18] It also notes that most of the refugees would, under international law, appear to qualify as genuine citizens of Bhutan's Citizenship Act of 1985.[19]

D. Political parties and the judiciary

According to Article 15 (7), the two political parties obtaining the first and second highest number of votes in the primary election shall be declared the two political parties for the election to the National Assembly.[20] The party which wins the majority of seats in the National Assembly in the general election shall be declared the ruling party and the other the opposition party.[21] The incumbent Prime Minister of Bhutan is a close relative of the King, so it is hard to imagine that the people in exile would trust the present government of Bhutan. Moreover, as stated by Article 15 (3) of the Constitution "Candidates and political parties shall not resort to regionalism, ethnicity and religion to incite voters for electoral gain."[22] This is a direct threat to the candidates who would like to speak out on refugee issues, the Bhutanization policy or the ethnic cleansing policy of the government.

As to the 2008 National Assembly election, in March 2008 79.4 percent of voters exercised their first ever right to vote. However, the election commission rejected the registration of third parties because of the dubious pretext of not fulfilling the election criteria. Only two political parties were allowed: the Peoples' Democratic Party (PDP) led by the brother-in-law of King Jigme Singye Wanghchuk and the Druk Pheunsum

---

17 See Druk National Congress (DNC), Prevailing situation in Bhutan, report to Human Rights Council Working Group, December 2009. During the 1988 census the Government categorized the citizens into seven groups: F1-Genuine Bhutanese; F2-Returned Migrants; F3-Those who had left Bhutan but returned); F3-Drop-outs (those who were not available during the time of census); F4-A non-national woman married to a Bhutanese man; F5-A non-national man married to a Bhutanese woman; F6-Adoption Cases (Children legally adopted); F7-Non-nationals (Migrants and illegal settlers).

18 See European Parliament Resolution on the Plight of Nepali-speaking refugees from Bhutan, Official Journal C 096, 1 April 1996, p. 0296, letter B. See also European Parliament Resolution on Bhutanese refugees in Nepal, Official Journal C 135 E, 7 May 2001, p. 0281-0283.

19 *Ibid.*, § 6.

20 See Article 15 (7) of the Constitution of Bhutan. Furthermore, Article 15 (5) of the Constitution of Bhutan states that: *"Election to the National Assembly shall be by two political parties established through a primary round of election in which all registered political parties may participate."*

21 See Article 15 (8) of the Constitution of Bhutan.

22 See Article 15 (3) of the Constitution of Bhutan.

Tshogpa (DPT) led by the father-in-law to one of the princesses, the incumbent Prime Minister Jigme y Thinley."[23]

As to the judiciary, Article 21 (1) of the Constitution states that the judiciary shall safeguard, uphold, and administer justice fairly and independently without fear, favour, or undue delay in accordance with the Rule of Law to inspire trust and confidence and to enhance access to justice.[24] In December 2009 the Human Rights Organization of Bhutan (HUROB) reported that "the judiciary in Bhutan is not independent of interference by the monarchy, especially in matters relating to the royal family members and high level officials. Claims that the Bhutanese judiciary system is independent and guarantees fair trials is questionable when its High Court (the highest house of justice) could not secure the conviction of a chief district officer, who at point-blank shot dead a monk in 1997 and committed many similar offences against southern Bhutanese. Instead, the officer was set free, his authoritative position uncompromised, but awarded all emoluments as may be enjoyed by a chief district officer."[25]

E. National Council and National Assembly

As per the Constitution there are two houses, the National Council (the upper house) and the National Assembly (the lower house). However, unlike a true democracy where the members of both houses are from political parties the lower house members are from the political parties but the members of the National Council (the upper house) are apolitically elected independently from their respective districts. There are 20 members in the upper house representing their districts with five additional members nominated directly by the King. This kind of arrangement leaves room for manipulation of the Council as the King chooses. There is a risk of power clashes and ego conflicts between the members of the assembly and the council, as they perform on totally different perspectives. Moreover the local bodies which look after the day to day affairs in blocks[26] and villages are elected and on the payroll of the government. In addition, the political parties and their elected representatives who are members of the national assembly (lower house) have no direct control over them.

The King has maintained parallel offices in three regions covering all 20 districts and has mandated them to look after the welfare of the general public, separately from the civil authorities. In the event of power clashes, the King's officials will prevail as they are directly appointed by the King and are the final instance of authority.

F. The Citizenship laws of Bhutan

The Citizenship Act of 1985 states that any citizen of Bhutan who has acquired citizenship by naturalization may be deprived of his/her citizenship at any time if that person has shown by act or speech to be disloyal to the King, Country and People of

---

23 Report by the Human Rights Organization of Bhutan (HUROB), report to Human Rights Council Working Group, December 2009.

24 See Article 21 (1) of the Constitution of Bhutan.

25 Report by the Human Rights Organization of Bhutan (HUROB), *op. cit.*, note 23.

26 A block, '*gewog*' in the Dzongkha language, is a group of villages.

Bhutan.[27] Such citizens who have been deprived of citizenship must dispose of all their property and leave Bhutan forever. Most of the refugees fall under this category. This particular Citizenship Act was passed in 1985 and implemented in 1988. In 1988, a census was carried out in the southern districts of Bhutan and people who had been recognized as Bhutanese were arbitrarily declared illegal immigrants; they were deemed Bhutanese citizens under the 1958 Nationality Law and 1977 Citizenship Act of Bhutan. However, using the criteria of the 1985 Citizenship Act, the census required ethnic Nepalese to provide documentary evidence, e.g. the land tax receipt of their residence in the country in 1958. The census team thus demanded the land tax receipt of 1958 in the year 1988 (after 30 years) to prove their residence in Bhutan on or before 1958. Based on it the census team categorized the southern Bhutanese into seven groups from F1 to F7.[28] Those who were able to produce the land tax receipt of 1958 were considered Bhutanese and those who could not produce it were declared non-nationals. However, even those families who produced the document of 1958 are living in exile today.

As stated by Amnesty International "the 1985 Citizenship Act of Bhutan contains a number of vague provisions, and appears to have been applied in an arbitrary manner. It contains provisions which could be used to exclude from citizenship many people who are not members of the dominant ethnic group, as well as those who oppose government policy by peaceful means."[29]

As to the 1958 Nationality Law of Bhutan: it was under this law that full citizenship status was granted to the southern Bhutanese. According to the 1958 Nationality law, a person born to a Bhutanese father and resident in the Kingdom was considered Bhutan's natural citizen.[30] Also, a child born within or outside the kingdom upon coming of age would be granted citizenship if the father was a Bhutanese at the time of the child's' birth.[31] Foreigners resident in Bhutan for a period of at least 10 years and owners of agricultural land (5 years for those in government service) were eligible for Bhutanese citizenship.[32] A non-Bhutanese woman married to a Bhutanese man was to be granted Bhutanese citizenship upon taking an oath of loyalty and provided she has reached the age of majority.[33] The amendment incurred through the adoption of the 1977 Bhutan Citizenship Act increased the period of residential requirement up to 15 years to those in government service and 20 years for others;[34] the 1977 amendment also added other specific requirements.

Over two decades after the enactment of the 1985 Citizenship Act the Constitution of Bhutan was approved. The provision under Article 6 (1) of the Constitution, according to which a person whose parents are Bhutanese is a natural Bhutanese citizen, invalidates the citizenship rights of all those Bhutanese refugees who had acquired citizenship under the 1958 Nationality Law for which the father's citizenship

---

27 See Article 6 (c) of the Bhutan Citizenship Act of 1985.

28 For a detailed analysis of the F1-F7 groups please refer to note 17.

29 See Amnesty International, *"Bhutan: Forcible Exile"*, (Amnesty International Doc. ASA 14/004/1994, July 1994), 4.

30 See Article 3 (a) of the 1958 Nationality Law of Bhutan.

31 *Ibid.*, at (b).

32 See Article 4 (1) of the 1958 Nationality Law of Bhutan.

33 *Ibid.*, at (2).

34 See 1977 Citizenship Act, Conditions Required for the Grant of Citizenship Article 1 and 2.

of the applicant was a sufficient requirement.[35] In addition, Article 6(2) of the Constitution is inherent with greater foul-play. The Article envisages a two-fold requirement: (a) that one was a resident of Bhutan prior to the year 1958 and (b) that your name is registered in the official record of Bhutan.[36] The requirement of the pre-1958 residential proof is arduous for the largely rural population that constitutes the majority of the refugees. The malicious intent inherent in the provision is clear and manifest as the RGOB only began a mandatory census and kept land tax records at a much later date. Furthermore, the records of a majority of the refugees were confiscated by the government prior to their eviction. This provision also deprives the citizenship rights of those who would have acquired citizenship under the 1958 Nationality Law by having fulfilled the residential requirement of 10 and 5 years demanded for those holding agricultural lands and government services, respectively.[37]

The requirements of Article 6 (2) of the Constitution, namely not only to have been a resident of Bhutan prior to 1958 but also to have the name registered in the official government record reveals the RGOB's plan to denationalize even those persons in possession of Bhutanese citizenship and which have a legitimate generational right to it, as per the first Nationality law of Bhutan. This is provided with a criminal intent after a systematic obliteration of records of Southern Bhutanese, now refugees, was earlier maintained by the RGOB. The notification dated 17 August 1990, issued by the then Deputy Home Minister of Bhutan, Dago Tshering, underlines the nexus between RGOB's denationalization agenda and the draft constitution by stating: "Any Bhutanese National leaving the country to assist and help the anti-nationals shall no longer be considered as a Bhutanese citizen. It must also be made very clear that such people's family members living under the same household will also be held fully responsible and forfeit their citizenship."[38] With the expulsion of about one hundred thousand citizens completed, evidence from government records was removed, evacuated houses destroyed, names of places changed and the resettlement of northern Bhutanese into southern Bhutan undertaken. Therefore, the second part of Article 6 (2) relating to the existence of their names in RGOB's official record is intended to prevent those refugees who qualify under the other requirements from claiming citizenship rights. The RGOB is fully aware of the fact that the refugees cannot fulfil this requirement as it has ensured the deletion of the names of the Bhutanese refugees from its' official records. Furthermore, Article 6 (3) (e)[39] of the Constitution is intended to strip citizenship from dissidents accused of anti-governmental activity. Article 6 (3) (c)[40] and (d)[41] to deprive children born to refugees in the camps and

---

35 Article 6 (1) of the Constitution of Bhutan states that "A person, both of whose parents are citizens of Bhutan, shall be a natural born citizen of Bhutan."

36 According to Article 6 (2) of the Constitution of Bhutan "A person, domiciled in Bhutan on or before the 31 December 1958 and whose name is registered in the official record of the Government of Bhutan shall be a citizen of Bhutan by registration."

37 See Article 5 (1) of the 1958 Nationality Law of Bhutan.

38 See Bhutanese Home Ministry circular of 17 August 1990.

39 Article 6 (3) (e) affirms that "A person who applies for citizenship by naturalization shall have no record of having spoken or acted against the Tsa-wa-sum."

40 According to Article 6 (3) (c) "A person who applies for citizenship by naturalization shall be able to speak and write Dzongkha."

those who left Bhutan as children from citizenship. This leaves almost no refugee qualified for Bhutanese citizenship.

The effect of Article 6 of the Constitution is therefore calamitous. The Article contains the potential to effectively marginalise the refugees as stateless persons which carries grave humanitarian and security implications. The Constitution has centralized the power in the King in such a manner that the elected government has no authority to grant citizenship to Bhutanese.[42] Moreover, the constitution denies citizenship to any individual Bhutanese who has spoken against Tsa-Wa-Sum (King, Country and People).[43] The present Constitution contains many shortfalls and needs amendments to devolve power from the King to elected representatives and thereby the people.

G. Political Prisoners, custodial deaths and disappearances

According to the DNC "there are more than 200 political prisoners incarcerated in various prisons since 1990 and 1997 after the peaceful demonstrations in southern and eastern Bhutan."[44] They have not been released even following the proclamation of democracy. The International Committee of the Red Cross (ICRC) conducts annual visits to the Chemgang jail in Thimphu and a few visits to the Lodrai jail where political prisoners are kept. No other organisations have access to the facilities in order to ascertain the conditions. Moreover, the DNC reports that "to show the outside world and foster a good rapport with the ICRC, Chemgang jail in Thimphu is well maintained, even with a proposed conjugal room for married prisoners. The condition of prisons and prisoners in other jails in the twenty districts are sub-human and many prisoners are kept in solitary confinement and incommunicado, and subject to harsh mental and physical suffering".[45] There were many deaths in custody in the period of 1990-1999. Reportedly the causes of deaths were due to starvation, lack of water, torture and lack of medical treatment.

H. Education policy in Bhutan

There is no accurate information on the number of schools which have been reopened in Southern Bhutan till date. Most of the schools in southern Bhutan have remained closed since 1990. According to the Kathmandu Post of 28 December 2004 there are an estimated 40.000 children in Bhutan who have been denied their right to education.[46] For instance, a nine–year-old girl from Chukha, Bhutan, arrived in the

---

41 According to Article 6 (3) (d) "A person who applies for citizenship by naturalization shall have a good knowledge of the culture, customs, traditions and history of Bhutan."
42 See Article 6 (4) of the Constitution of Bhutan: "The granting of citizenship by naturalization shall take effect by a Royal Kasho (a written order) of the Druk Gyalpo (the King)."
43 As stated by Article 6 (3) (e) "A person who applies for citizenship by naturalization shall have no record of having spoken or acted against the Tsa-wa-sum."
44 See Druk National Congress (DNC), *op. cit.*, note 17.
45 *Ibid.*
46 See "Denied in Bhutan she finds school in Nepal", in *Kathmandu Post* of 28 December 2004, available at:
http://www.ekantipur.com/the-kathmandu-post/2004/12/28/top-stories/Denied-in-Bhutan-she-finds-school-in-Nepal/27152/

Beldangi refugee camp in Jhapa after she was deprived of education by the Bhutanese government. According to her, she tried to enrol in an elementary school for the past three years, but every time school authorities refused to register her.[47] A Non-Objection Certificate (NOC) from the police is a pre-requirement for a child's admission to school in Bhutan. It is very difficult to get NOCs for those whose relatives are in the refugee camps or who personally or whose family and relatives participated in the 1990 peace movement. In this context it is worth recalling that Bhutan has ratified the Convention on the Rights of the Child without reservation and declares itself committed to international human rights principles.[48]

I. The land re-settlement policy and property restitution

The government of Bhutan is implementing a programme of transferring parts of the population - from Northern to Southern Bhutan. The land and the houses vacated by the Southern Bhutanese are being given to the people from the hills and from the central and eastern regions. The Habitat International Coalition, an NGO based in The Hague, sent a fact-finding mission to South Bhutan from September 23 to October 1 2001. The aim of the mission was to verify the claims of the Bhutanese refugees that their lands were being given away to northern Bhutanese settlers under the Bhutanese government's resettlement programme. Besides interviewing 25 refugee families from the camps in Nepal, the team visited selected villages in Bhutan to verify the claims. In their preliminary findings, the team indicated that they came across cases where the Royal Government of Bhutan settled north Bhutanese on the lands of the south Bhutanese who were evicted since 1990. They have also stated that not all the North Bhutanese settled in the southern districts were, as the government claims, landless persons. Land was being given to army and police officers and/or their relatives.[49]

The Royal Government of Bhutan, in the guise of rehabilitating landless people, has been ensuring the impossibility of the evicted citizens returning by re-distributing their land. It has been reported that the northern Bhutanese persons have often been coerced into settling on land belonging to the evicted Lhotshampas. This is demonstrated by the notice that appeared in the Kuensel Editorial below.

"Landless people from other Dzongkhag who got land allotment in Tsirang Dzongkhag under resettlement programme have failed to report despite repeated requests by Dzongkhag. Therefore, the Tsirang Dzongkhag administration once again requests them to report immediately as the cultivation season is already set in. Non-compliance shall be viewed very seriously and Dzongkhag administration shall not be held responsible if any complication arises in future on the matter".[50]

"All the Shi-Sarps (Re-Settlers) of phase one and two from different Dzongkhags should report to their respective areas under Sarpang Dzongkhag within April 1999.

---

47 *Ibid.*

48 For an overview on the status of ratification, declarations and reservations please visit: http://treaties.un.org/Pages/ViewDetails.aspx?src=TREATY&mtdsg_no=IV-11&chapter=4&lang=en

49 See Habitat International Coalition (HIC), "Resettlement on Land of Bhutanese Refugees. A report on new threats to repatriation", HIC Fact-Finding Report No. 4, 2002.

50 See *Kuensel OnLine* newspaper editorial of 20 March 1999, in Jagatmani Acharya, *"Bhutanese Refugee Situation"*, (South Asian Forum for Human Rights (SAFHR), E-Briefs Vol.1 Issue 1, February 2000).

Failure to report within the above dateline, this Dzongkhag Administration would consider the lands to have surrendered by the Shi-sarps (Re-settlers) to the Government. The concern Dzongkhags are also requested to kindly inform their respective Shi-sarps (Re-settlers), to report within the above dateline. For convenience of the Dzongkhags the list of Shi-sarps will be faxed to the individual Dzongkhag within the week".[51]

In order to make this program attractive and acceptable to families from the North, the government supplied free building materials and financial assistance. Furthermore, in the same areas, the Government reopened most of the basic facilities like schools, health centres and other social service schemes, previously closed since 1990. There are reports that the remaining Lhotshampas face harassment and humiliation at the hands of the new northern settlers and government officials.

In March 2008, the Centre on Housing Rights and Evictions (COHRE) reported that "the right to return and the right to housing, land and property restitution as set out/enshrined in the 'United Nations Principles on Housing and Property Restitution for Refugees and Displaces Persons', in short the Pinheiro Principles,[52] provide the Bhutanese refugees and displaced persons with a distinctive and genuine right to return and claim back their property, their land, and their houses in Bhutan. If Bhutanese nationality is not restored, the refugees remain entitled to housing, land and property restitution as long as they can prove that they owned, used or occupied a certain home, land and/or property before being displaced".[53]

J. Bilateral negotiation and the verification process

The Bhutanese government has not shown any intention to repatriate the verified Bhutanese refugees from one of the seven camps, namely the Khudunabari refugee camp in the Jhapa district of Nepal. Fifteen rounds of talks between a joint Nepalese-Bhutanese Ministerial committee have been held with no results. The bilateral process is a total failure. As reported in 2003 "It was agreed in the 15th ministerial meeting to repatriate all refugees of categories one, two and four from the Kudenabari camp".[54] It was also understood that the refugees would return with honour, safety and dignity. Bhutan has successfully fooled the refugees, the government of Nepal and the international community. The verification of 12.183 refugees started on 26 March 2001 and was completed on 14 December 2001.[55] The governments of Bhutan and

---

51 See Kuensel OnLine newspaper editorial of 27 March 1999, in Jagatmani Acharya, *op. cit. supra* note 49.

52 See Office of High Commissioner for Human Rights (OHCHR), *"Handbook on Housing and Property Restitution for Refugees and Displaced Persons Implementing the 'Pinheiro Principles'"*, (OHCHR March 2007), available at: www.ohchr.org/Documents/Publications/pinheiro_principles.pdf

53 See Centre on Housing Rights and Evictions (COHRE), *"Hoping to Return Home: Housing, Land And Property Restitution Rights for Bhutanese Refugees and Displaced Persons,"* (COHRE Country Report March 2008), 33.

54 See Dr. S. Chandrasekharan, "Bhutan: 15th Ministerial meeting at Thimphu on refugees: *Break through?"*, (South Asian Analysis Group, Note No. 201, Update 35 of 27 October 2003). Available at: http://www.southasiaanalysis.org/notes3/note201.html

55 The verification process was carried out by a Bhutan-Nepal Joint Verification Team (JVT) composed of five members each from the two countries.

Nepal on 18 June 2003 finally announced the results of the verification of refugees. Out of the 12.183 refugees interviewed in Khudunabari:

- Two and a half percent of the refugees (only 293 people) were placed in Category I: bonafide Bhutanese citizens who would be eligible for repatriation to Bhutan;
- 70 percent were placed in Category II: refugees who "voluntarily emigrated" from Bhutan and would be required to reapply for Bhutanese citizenship;
- The claims of about 24 percent were rejected as they were placed in Category III: non-Bhutanese;
- Three percent of the interviewees were classified as criminals and were placed in Category IV who were to be repatriated and tried in Bhutanese courts.[56]

The issue of return was further complicated after 22 December 2003 when the delegation of the Government of Bhutan announced harsh conditions for returning refugees. The Bhutanese delegation emphasized that inside Bhutan the refugees belonging to different categories would get different treatment. For instance, refugees classified as Category I (Bonafide Bhutanese, evicted forcefully) would be repatriated to Bhutan in the first phase. They would be returning as citizens and would enjoy all rights as other Bhutanese citizens. People belonging to Category II (voluntary emigrants) would be treated like other foreigners for a period of two years. They would not be eligible to reclaim their property until they proved their loyalty to the Bhutanese crown, culture, language and tradition. Furthermore, to regain their citizenship, they would have to learn to speak the Bhutanese language. Furthermore, those persons belonging to Category II would be taken to Bhutan and kept in the camps. During this period one member from each of the repatriated families would be employed as a labourer in road construction. They would not be allowed to move freely inside Bhutan until they were granted citizenship. The appeals of persons who were classified as Category III (non-Bhutanese) were rejected, however, numerous refugees in this category have claimed that they have documents to prove that they are Bhutanese citizens. Persons classified as Category IV (alleged criminals) were to be handed over to the police in Bhutan. Around 85 families were categorised as criminals, including babies and young children born in the camps.[57]

The governments of Bhutan and Nepal have violated the rights of refugees by carrying out a verification and categorization process lacking transparency and fairness, thus affecting the refugees' ability to exercise their right to return home. The whole process of verification was a waste of time and public funds. The bilateral process is not going to resolve this problem nor provide a durable solution to the Bhutanese problem. Following the 22 December 2003 Khudanabari evaluation it would appear what has long been suspected has come true: the government of Bhutan looking for an excuse not to take back a single refugee.[58] To end the misery of the

56 See Jagatmani Acharya, *"Verification of refugees and the question of return to Bhutan"*, (South Asian Forum for Human Rights (SAFHR), E-Briefs Vol.2 Issue 1, December 2003).

57 *Ibid.*

58 On 22 December 2003, the people in the camps in eastern Nepal physically assaulted and verbally abused the Bhutanese Joint Verification Team. For further information please see "Proceedings of the

refugees, the international community should provide resettlement options until they can return to Bhutan with dignity and honour.
The result of the Joint Verification Team of the Bhutanese refugees in Khudunabari has revealed the absence of a clear will to resolve the issue. It has only demonstrated to the world that the refugees have been verified and are to be repatriated. However, few are aware that families have been divided, children categorized as criminals, citizens in possession of citizenship cards declared non-nationals and those forcefully evicted categorized as having left the country willingly. Bhutan has at least accepted that it forcefully evicted 1.5 percent of the total families in Khudunabari. The large proportion of people in Categories II and III who have no documents to prove the terror tactics of the government of Bhutan, have unnecessarily been victimized. The causes of the refugee crisis are important to understand the situation. The international community must understand the causes and unite to undo the grave injustice that Bhutan has committed against its' people in the name of Bhutanisation.

III. BHUTANESE REFUGEES IN NEPAL

Nineteen years in exile is a long time and the situation inside the camps is not very encouraging. Each family member lives a miserable life in a 12ft by 18ft bamboo hut.[59] "They don't get all the basic needs for daily survival, legally they are not allowed to work, many of the refugees have become victims of the locals and the state administration. Housing, health and the education system are poor. There is no electricity. As the amount of coal briquettes and one litre of kerosene per month for each family supplied by the relief agency is often not enough for cooking and light in the night, many refugees go out into the surrounding forests to cut firewood. This has led to clashes between the refugees and local people on several occasions. The refugees are provided with a basic assistance package which is not enough for survival. As the refugees have no right to work and therefore are in no position to earn a living for meeting the extra costs for care of the young children or old people. Nevertheless, many of them do go out of the camps to work as manual labourers or take small jobs. The local communities have also raised objections to their 'taking over' many of the jobs and work that would under normal circumstances be available to local people".[60]
There was hope that the crisis would be resolved quickly and Bhutan would take back the people it had thrown out. As time went by and the repatriation efforts stalled, Bhutanese refugees became less visible as some of its major backers slowly withdrew their material support. The aggressive campaign organised by Bhutanese government representatives since the 1990's and the failure of the Government of Nepal to take the issue of the Bhutanese refugees to official international forums has also contributed to the invisibility of the Bhutanese refugee issue. The RGOB, in its

---

82nd National Assembly session June-July 2004" in *Information Bhutan International* available at: http://www.freewebs.com/bhutaan/bhutannationalassembly.htm

59 A family of up to nine members stays in a 12x18 foot straw/plastic roof and bamboo-fenced hut. When a family becomes larger than nine members, two plots are allocated. The plot contains a kitchen, bedroom, sitting room and guest room.

60 Jagatmani Acharya, Goldhap Bhutanese refugee camp, Sector C, Unit 1, hut no. 59, I am a refugee myself and it is based on my own experience.

publication *"Southern Bhutan Problem: Threat to a Nation's Survival"*, states that "the southern Bhutan problem is neither a movement for democracy nor an issue concerning human rights. It is simply an attempt by a minority ethnic community to turn themselves into a majority through illegal immigration in order to take over political power."[61] In these years, the UNHCR has been the main or rather the only international agency caring for the Bhutanese refugees in Nepal. However, the UNHCR has had to reduce the level of relief supplies and other facilities as it has faced donor fatigue, resulting in the reduction of funds.[62] As reported by Human Rights Watch "The support system in the camps has come under increasing strains, with budgetary constraints necessitating cuts in the provision of essential services, including food, fuel and medical care. [...] The Bhutanese refugees in Nepal are trapped between their forced dependency on international assistance and the increasing reluctance of the international community to keep providing for their needs".[63] Camp life was never ideal. As a matter of fact, of the refugees who have been offered third-country resettlement options, as of December 2009 some 25.000 refugees have chosen to be resettled.

A. Social services: Health and Education for refugees in Nepal

As the resettlement process began, the quality of education decreased leading to an increase in the number of children dropping out of school . Teachers face an increased workload as colleagues leave under the resettlement programme. CARITAS Nepal, who are responsible for the education programme in the Bhutanese refugee camps, are now adjusting plans and policies to run the schools in the best possible manner despite the additional strains. Bhutanese refugee children are granted education until grade/year ten, following which they have no further access to education. Very few can afford to continue studying. Those that do are supported by their parents and relatives. Some of them go outside the camps to find jobs, and many of the refugees are victimized as they are not legally allowed to work. Those who want to study engineering, medicine or other professional subjects often have to pay the higher fees commanded from foreign students. Furthermore, avenues for getting scholarships for higher education beyond the 10th grade/year have been closed. While India provides scholarships for admission to government institutions and universities for Bhutanese and Nepalese, the refugees come under neither category and higher education is thereby denied to them. This is going to create a major social problem and is a reason for India and Nepal to relax the rules and admit them to scholarships. The Nepali and Indian governments and agencies working in the field of education should provide scholarships for refugee students who have completed the School Leaving Certificate. UNHCR used to provide education up to the university level but ceased offering this

61 See Royal Government of Bhutan (RGOB) Ministry of Home Affairs, *"The Southern Bhutan Problem: Threat to a Nation's Survival"*, (RGOB, Thimphu, May 1993).
62 See "Absence of funds threatens UN Efforts to feed 106,000 Bhutanese refugees in Nepal" in *UN News service* of 22 December 2006, available at:
http://www.un.org/apps/news/printnewsAr.asp?nid=21084
63 See Human Rights Watch (HRW), *"Last hope: the need for durable solution for Bhutanese refugees in Nepal and India"*, (HRW Volume 19, No. 7 (C), May 2007), 3 and 19.

opportunity after just two or three years, leaving young refugees with access to primary and secondary level education only.
As to the health facilities in the camps, only primary health care is provided at the camp level. Patient referral services to the nearest hospital are done according to need; emergencies are dealt with by ambulance. Referral to specialised or better medical centres is limited due to insufficient funds available in the UNHCR referral process. It has been found, however, that the referral cases from the refugee camps are not treated as local patients. In areas hosting refugee populations, funds have been specially allocated to local hospitals with an understanding that refugees would get treatment from these hospitals. Though the funds were allocated it is a matter of concern why refugees are not treated as locals. Many cases deemed expensive are not referred because of the lack of funding for treatment by the concerned organizations. Few people go begging for treatment. Most of them go without adequate medical treatment.

B. Un-registered refugees

Many Bhutanese asylum seekers have been denied the status of refugee. This is a grave international humanitarian crisis, requiring that unregistered Bhutanese asylum seekers be formally recognized and protected consistent with accepted international standards of human rights. There might be around twenty-five to thirty thousand non-registered refugees' asylum seekers in Nepal and India relying on close or distant family members and begging in the camps and nearby villages. The persistent strain of daily life thus creates an atmosphere of humiliation amongst the unregistered. Unregistered refugees face glaringly limited options: without travel documents movement proves to be an onerous and dangerous task so that even those forming advocacy groups cannot make their voice heard. Considered as illegal migrants, they are banned from working, owning property and receiving protection from UNHCR or HMG of Nepal. This creates a very turbulent and vulnerable environment for unregistered asylum seekers who desperately seek temporary livelihoods to sustain their families. Without official status and thus without rights, they lack the provision of security and are highly vulnerable to exploitation and ill treatment.
During the 2006-2007 census undertaken jointly by UNHCR and the Government of Nepal, many refugees applied for registration. Many applications were considered, but there are still many pending cases. There are doubts if these cases will be considered as till date nothing has been done. There are thousand of new applicants who arrived after the resettlement process started. These later applicants do not know what will happen because there are no proper authorities to handle their demands. They are under tremendous strain as family members are separated and/or resettled. An additional burden is that once registered members leave, the huts are dismantled and unregistered family members remaining are forced to leave the camps.

C. Nepalese Law and Refugees

Although Nepal does not have specific provisions for safeguarding refugees, it has housed large numbers of Bhutanese exiles. Treated as aliens under existing Nepalese law, the registered refugees enjoy the same basic rights as Nepalese citizens according to the Nepalese Constitution, which makes no distinction between citizens and legal aliens. In practice, however, it is very different and refugees face problems at every step they take. They are not allowed to work, own property and the freedom of movement is restricted. The Citizenship Act of 1964, Section 3, permits the naturalization of refugees, although this practice is rare and requires the approval of government authorities. Furthermore, the Immigration Act of 1992 retains the power to expel aliens based on national interests.[64] The Extradition Act of 1988 supports the principle that political offenders are not to be extradited, which coincides with international refugee law.[65] Without specific legislation for regulating refugee inflow, Nepal confronts refugee issues on an ad hoc basis.

The citizenship law of Nepal has been instrumental in integrating and assimilating some of the older refugees like Sindhis, Tibetans and Burmese of Nepali origin. Citizenship by naturalization might be provided under the 1964 Citizenship Act, Section 6. Under this section any foreigner who fulfils the terms and conditions may apply for Nepali citizenship to the government through the Chief District Officer.

Many refugees have left their country with certain skills, but there is no place to sell their skills once in Nepal. Refugees produce goods but they are not allowed to sell them in the local market and they are not allowed to do any type of business in Nepal. Many refugees who try to sell their skills and do business often become victims of the authorities and the locals. The government of Nepal should clarify policies and laws pertaining to Bhutanese refugees. Until and unless the problem to these problems are resolved, the government should make the necessary arrangements for granting long term residence permits to enable refugees to work, own property and do business in Nepal.

D. Bhutanese refugee women and children

Bhutan has signed and ratified the Committee on the Elimination and Discrimination against Women (CEDAW) and the Committee on Rights of the Child (CRC) in 1981 and 1990, respectively. Although Bhutan has committed to improve the status of the women for almost 30 years and protect the rights of the child for 20 years, the reality of the rights of women and children is unacceptable. The situation of Bhutanese refugee women and children is appalling. In the cultural sphere the southern Bhutanese women bore the brunt of the government's cultural policy. The Bhutanese government has done little to improve the status of women and deliberately preyed upon the vulnerability of women in its campaign of ethnic cleansing. Southern Bhutanese women were deprived of the right to wear their traditional dress; their ceremonial marriage necklaces were stripped from them and they were forced to cut their hair short. They were forced to adopt the dress and culture of the northern Bhutanese. The women have been always the worst affected victims of government repression. In most cases, their husband were imprisoned or had to flee the country for fear of persecution. The security forces plundered their homes, tortured, intimidated and raped these helpless women.

There are even cases where women and girls were to be forcibly taken to the Army, "My father was born in Bhutan and his age is 63. Every day the office bearers used to

---

64 See Article 9 of the Immigration Act of Nepal, 1992.

65 See Article 12 of the Extradition Act of Nepal, 1988.

come and threaten me to leave the village. They not only intimidated me, but the Bhutanese army one day suddenly came and burnt all the 27 houses of the village. They accused me of being a Nepali citizen and asked us to hand over our girls and wives to serve them. They demanded 15-20 ladies to be handed over. In these circumstances we left our village. Our relatives are still there and we have our registered land there."[66]

Women and children in the camps continue to be subjected to various forms of torture and suppression. Many women have become the victims of the authorities working in the camps.

As reported by Human Rights Watch: "Nepal's system of refugee registration discriminates women by distributing rations through male heads of household. [...] This policy denies women equal and independent access to food, shelter and supplies, and imposes particular hardship on women trying to escape abusive marriages. Either these women must stay in violent relationships, leave their relationships (and thus relinquishing their full share of aid packages), or marry another man; in such a case they lose legal custody of their children."[67]

Ethnic Nepalese women and children who managed to avoid expulsion face persistent discrimination and ongoing threats to their citizenship status. Moreover, as indicated by Human Rights Watch in 2007 "Bhutanese Nepali speakers who still live in Bhutan continue to suffer discrimination in almost all aspects of their daily lives, including in education, health, employment, and land ownership. Some have been denied citizenship cards following the latest census in 2005 and are now effectively stateless in their own country."[68] The same report further highlights the denial of the right to return to one's own country, the discrimination against ethnic Nepali children in Bhutan including access to education health care, right of ethnic or linguistic minorities to enjoy their own culture and use their own language as well as sexual violence and other abuses against girls and women.[69]

IV. Bhutanese Refugee Resettlement Programme

The Core Working Group on Bhutanese Refugees in Nepal in its Joint Communiqué of May 2007 stated that it is "committed to working with the United Nations High Commissioner for Refugees, the Royal Government of Bhutan and the Government of Nepal towards a comprehensive and sustainable solution for this refugee population that best meets the individual needs of the refugees."[70] In 2003, Bhutan reportedly agreed to take a certain number of refugees. It is nineteen years now since the refugee camps were established but not a single individual has been repatriated. As stated by

---

66 A statement by Mr. A. in *"Voices of Pain/The Bhutan tragedy when will it end - report of the SAARC jurist Mission on Bhutan"*, May 1992.

67 See Human Rights Watch (HRW), *"Nepal/Bhutan: Refugee Women Face Abuses"*, HRW News of 24 September 2004.

68 See Human Rights Watch (HRW), *"Discrimination against Ethnic Nepali Children in Bhutan. Submission to the Committee on the Rights of the Child"*, 3 October 2007 available at: www.hrw.org/legacy/backgrounder/crd/2007/bhutan1007

69 *Ibid.*

70 See Communiqué of the Core Working Group on Bhutanese Refugees in Nepal, 16 May 2007, § 3 available at: http://www.international.gc.ca/genev/new-nouveau/20070516.aspx

UNCHR in December 2009: "While resettlement offers a way out for refugees who see no future in the camps, UNHCR continues to advocate for voluntary repatriation for those who are willing to wait in the camps."[71] In this context, the United States announced that it would resettle approximately 60.000 refugees. Other members of the Core Working Group including Australia, Canada, Denmark, the Netherlands, New Zealand and Norway expressed their desire to take their share of refugees. Canada has announced that it plans to resettle 5.000 refugees. The United States has further pledged that it will continue the resettlement program until all refugees who are interested in resettlement are considered for the program, even if that number exceeds 60.000.[72]

The Bhutanese refugee resettlement programme began in November 2007. Bilateral negotiations for a return to Bhutan failed and in September. 2007 the Nepalese government signed a Memorandum of Understanding with the International Organisation for Migration (IOM), to carry out resettlement activities in Damak, a small town in eastern Nepal. IOM works with the resettlement countries and UNHCR to facilitate refugee departures. It processes cases for resettlement countries, conducts health assessments and cultural orientation courses based on the requirements of each resettlement country and organizes all transportation from the refugee camps to the final destinations. IOM organizes some 1.500 refugee departures every month by charter flight from eastern Nepal to Kathmandu. It then takes the refugees from Kathmandu to their final destinations on commercial flights.

According to the UNHCR, as of December 2009 the total number of Bhutanese refugees resettled in the third countries has exceeded 25.000 persons. Of the total 107.017 refugees living in the seven UNHCR-administered camps in eastern Nepal in 2007, 25.000 have now left for third countries to begin entirely new lives. Among the seven core group nations resettling Bhutanese refugees under one of the UNHCR's largest ever refugee resettlement programs, the United States has welcomed the highest number, with 22.060 resettled. The other countries accepting refugees are Australia (1.006), Canada (892), Norway (316), Denmark (305), New Zealand (299) and the Netherlands (122). Finally, more than 86.000 refugees from Bhutan still remain in the eastern camps in Nepal.[73]

A. Resettlement a challenge for Bhutanese refugees

When refugees resettle to new countries, the population left behind is affected. When large numbers leave the camps the families, relatives and friends are divided, the quality of services like health education is affected as more and more experienced, educated and skilled manpower leaves the camps. Remittances have increased as the refugees are resettled in richer countries but the income from local sources has decreased. For local residents living near the refugee camps in Nepal, the departure of large numbers of refugees will lead to a decrease in competition for local resources

---

71 See UNHCR, "Number of refugees resettled from Nepal passes 25,000 mark", UNCHR *News Stories* of 11 December 2009, available at: http://www.unhcr.org/4b22462e6.html

72 See Asian Centre for Human Rights (ACHR), "US clarifications on the Bhutanese refugees", ACHR Weekly Review 168/07 of 23 May 2007 available at:
http://www.achrweb.org/Review/2007/168-07.htm

73 See UNHCR, "Number of refugees resettled from Nepal passes 25.000 mark", *op. cit.*, note 68.

and employment. Local residents, however, will not find such an abundance of cheap labour.

Resettlement of Bhutanese refugees into some of the most developed countries is full of challenges. The culture and way of life of the Bhutanese refugees in Bhutan and camp life in Nepal is very different from the technologically driven societies in the West. In these countries life revolves around the clock. Bhutanese refugees come from a culture that values social norms, traditions and rituals more than work. Bhutanese refugees know the plough and the field, the crops, orchards, cattle, temples, monasteries, dzongs, extended families, the ritualistic life, traditions, festivals and celebrations - none of these will be part of their social life any more. "The west works, learns and communicates through technology. The centrally heated houses, bath showers, the western toilet system, air filters, smoke alarms, vacuums, dish washers, microwaves, barbecue grills, washing machines, dryers, home computers, online payment systems, traffic rules, riding a public bus system and trains, paying by credit cards, lifts and escalators, drug bottles with child lock systems, assembling ready-made (packed) furniture, child seats, seat belts, pumping gas, school admissions, tax filing, vending machines, cell phones or registers at work – for the Bhutanese people everything is an absolutely new experience. From food habits to work habits, from customs to culture, from ways of life to personal habits and etiquette – the need for change is absolutely pervasive and ubiquitous".[74]

Furthermore, as Guragain reported "Refugees are finding it difficult to adjust to life in Europe and separation from their extended families, but their children have fit right in. They are learning the local languages and making friends fast. It is the older family members who bear the brunt of culture shock and find their new environment difficult to get a handle on. But all agree that they are willing to go through it for the sake of their children. Ramesh Gautam, 26, who arrived in Norway in September. 2009 has picked up Norwegian so rapidly that his teacher, Ina Jacobsen was impressed. "They are so fast with the language it is amazing," Jacobsen said, "but I must say we language instructors have learnt much more from our students about Bhutan than they have from us." The Bhutanese refugees say it is the first time in a long time they are treated with respect. Naturally, there is the sorrow of separation from their extended families back in Bhutan and Nepal. "We now have everything we want, the only worry is about the relatives we left behind," says Kebalram Rijal, 55, who arrived in Utrecht from Goldhap refugee camp. In the west Norwegian town of Tysuar Rohit Pokhrel, 68, and his wife are worried about their family as well, and say the only thing missing in their life is a Hindu priest to do saradhha and other ceremonies.[75]

Guragain, in his 2008 report from the Amsfoort Transit Centre, quotes "As a refugee, we had no status. No one gave us any respect," recalls Kamala Rizal, who used to be a teacher at the Sanischare Camp in Morang. "Suddenly, the opportunities for us are limitless." Kamala wants to continue her teaching profession in the Netherlands after

---

74 See R.P. Subba, "Bhutanese Refugees: Transition, Transformation and Vision for the Diaspora," in *ApfaNews.Com* of 10 July 2009 available at:
http://www.apfanews.com/commentary/transition-transformation-and-vision-for-the-diaspora/

75 See Gopal Guragain, "Euro Bhutanis. Refugees no more Bhutani families adapt to life in Europe", in *Nepali Times* of 11 December 2009, available at:
http://www.nepalitimes.com.np/issue/2009/12/11/Nation/16591

she learns the language. The Bhutanese are all learning Dutch and while at the Transit Centre they get free lodging and 53 Euro pocket money every week for food. Rohit Acharya is still in a state of culture shock. He proudly shows a visitor the kitchen and bedroom in his apartment, and says it is difficult to get used to this after the collective camp life where there was never any privacy. Also for Acharya, the most remarkable thing is that he has respect. 'I am now treated like a human being again, people treat you as an equal. They don't look down on you because you are a refugee."[76]
In addition, Promod Rizal on the employment possibilities of resettled Bhutanese refugees in the U.S. explains that "Upon arriving in a land so different with its new culture, Bhutanese refugees are facing with new sets of challenges in the US labour market. Their skills and education are hard-to-be-considered. However, many of the refugees have the advantage of speaking English. Colorado has hosted some 1500 Bhutanese refugees. For most of the families, their suburban relocation has made it easier for both job hunting and housing. [...] After eight months of assistance from the resettlement agencies, refugees face hard challenges to find job in the competitive labour markets. [...] Majority of these people are working at the Denver International Airport or at Hyatt and Casinos at Rocky rank next to the airport. Another small number of these people are employed in meat processing plants located in Greeley in Northern Colorado, hotels around Denver, Old care centres and shopping complexes around their habitations. U.S. is a nation that still believes that opportunities should be taken and hard work rewarded."[77]
An example of this resettlement policy comes from the story of the separated families of Krishna Maya Darjee. Resettled in 2009 to New York, she talks about the pain suffered due to the separation from her family members and her illiteracy. Darjee says she has hard times in New York and wants to return to Nepal if her son continues to remain in the refugee camp. They are four family members resettled in the US. Her husband was employed for two and a half months but is now unemployed, her son has joined the school, her daughter is the only one who is working and earns US $ 1000 per month which is just enough to pay the rent. Her life is limited to a room, she recounts that life has become very difficult: "we see only buildings, neighbours do not talk with us, I cannot go out alone because I am scared. [...] Whilst in Nepal, during the interview I was informed by them (IOM/UNHCR) that I will not go without my son, they said to me 'your son will follow you very soon but till date his case has to be forwarded for resettlement from the UNHCR office to the IOM." [78] Her son could not go with her mother because he is married to a local girl. There has been an announcement by the receiving countries that they would take anyone willing to resettle, but it is sad that UNHCR is separating the family on the grounds that he is

76 See Gopal Guragai, "Refugees finally find respect", in *Nepali Times* Issue 409 (18-24 July 2008) available at: http://www.nepalitimes.com.np/issue/2008/07/18/Nation/15045
77 See Promod Rizal, "Job hunting – a greater challenge for Bhutanese in Colorado", in *'Chhitiz' – A Bhutanese Clud in California* of 23 November 2009, available at: http://chhitiz.wordpress.com/2009/11/23/job-hunting-a-greater-challenge-for-bhutanese-in-colorado/
78 See TP Mishra interview with Krishna Maya Darjee, "Agony of Family Split" in *Radio Bhutan Online* of 27 November 2009, available at: http://www.radiobhutanonline.com/2009/11/agony-of-family-split/

married to a local girl. There are many families who have married to local girls that have been resettled.[79]

B. Resettlement and mix marriages

There are more than 1.000 cases of mixed marriages, for instance Nepalese and Indian girls married to Bhutanese refugees are still waiting for their case to be forwarded for resettlement. It is not only Darjee's families whose family members are being separated; there are hundreds of other cases like that. I have come across many Bhutanese refugee women who have been married to non-Bhutanese and are either divorced or have no more relations with their husband. These women are going through lot of pressure and are having tough time in the camps, some of these women even do not get the camp facilities because some of their parents and relatives have already left under the resettlement programme.

As per the UNHCR resettlement bulletin, "A refugee woman married to a Nepali man may not be eligible for resettlement because she is able to naturalize in Nepal, [...] She would therefore no longer be a refugee."[80] According to UNHCR, such women do not require international protection and resettlement as a durable solution. However, if an exiled man marries a Nepali woman, he may be eligible to apply for residency status in Nepal. "It is UNHCR policy, however, to conduct a thorough assessment of the entire family to determine the refugee family's situation and whether they should be referred for resettlement to a third country together due to the nature of dependency bonds between family members."[81] Furthermore, regarding marriages between exiled Bhutanese and Indian citizens UNHCR has said that if an exiled Bhutanese has married an Indian national, the former may be entitled to residency status in India, and even citizenship.[82]

V. CONCLUSION

The refugees resided in Bhutan for generations; they faced discrimination and persecution by the Royal Government of Bhutan. The citizenship issue is the key question affecting their fate. The Bhutanese government does not recognize them as Bhutanese citizens. Who are they? They are people without a state. They are landless people who have lost their lands in Bhutan. They lived in their lands, cultivated them for generations and made a living from them. But a piece of paper - the Bhutanese Citizenship Act of 1985 - disowned them. In 2008 Bhutan began the transformation from absolute to constitutional monarchy. The transformation prompted criticisms: Bhutan "faced a range of questions and recommendations from nearly 60 countries on poverty reduction, gender inequality, child labour, minority rights, citizenship regulations, and on the people in the camps in Nepal, when it presented its Universal Periodic Review (UPR) to the UN Human Rights Council working group on 4

---

79 *Ibid.*

80 See UNHCR Resettlement Bulletin of 18 August 2008 in "UNHCR says mixed marriage cases unlikely for TCR", in *ApfaNews.Com* of 23 September 2008 available at:
http://www.apfanews.com/stories/unhcr-says-mixed-marriage-cases-unlikely-for-tcr/

81 *Ibid.*

82 *Ibid.*

December 2009 in Geneva, Switzerland."[83] During the 2005 census, Bhutan again created 37.453 so-called "non-nationals".[84] There is a high risk that they may be forced to leave the country and even if they remain inside they will be forced to live as a displaced population without any rights as citizens of Bhutan.

Bhutan's claim that people in the refugee camps are not all Bhutanese citizens is a baseless argument. Bhutan undermines the credibility of the UN which is working globally to address the issues of international concern. The third country resettlement program started only after UNHCR and the government of Nepal jointly conducted a census of the people in the camps and found that the people in the camps are all Bhutanese citizens and deserve UN intervention for a solution. Bhutan is not upholding the UN Charter and its' obligations as a member state. It needs to be questioned about its' conduct and condemned internationally.

The Government of India (GOI) has been silent on all negotiations concerning Bhutanese refugee issue. This is interesting, because Article 2 of the 1949 Treaty of Friendship states that "the Government of Bhutan agrees to be guided by the advice of the Government of India in regard to its external relations."[85] Despite the fact that the Bhutanese refugees streamed across its borders in the early 1990s and today reside only an hour's drive from the Indo-Nepalese border, India has thus far not exercised its right to offer advice, something that could have helped resolve the crisis. Why it has not done so has been the subject of much speculation and debate, although it is clear that India has taken sides with Bhutan for economic and geo-political reasons. India provides substantial economic assistance to Bhutan and similarly plays a large part in financing Bhutan's five-year plans. The New Delhi government contributes almost one-third of the total Bhutanese budget. A recent newspaper article stated that: "[The] Indian Ambassador to Nepal, Rakesh Sood, clarified that the long-standing Bhutanese refugee problem is a bilateral issue between Nepal and Bhutan which the two countries should resolve mutually and that India will not intervene in the matter. He said that the Bhutanese refugee problem is very much on the way of being resolved thanks to the third-country resettlement option. He also said that Indian mediation is not required for repatriation of Bhutanese refugee in their country as it is a bilateral issue to be sorted out between Nepal and Bhutan and that his country won't play any role in it."[86]

Refugees in the camps in eastern Nepal live a miserable life where they do not receive the basic needs for daily survival. There are another 30.000 people in Nepal and India who are not registered and are forced to live a miserable life. There is a high risk that these populations may not be included in a durable solution. They are not included in the ongoing resettlement programme. The challenge for the international community,

---

83 See Gyalsten K Dorji , "Bhutan presents human rights report", in *Kuensel Online* of 8 December 2009, available at: http://www.kuenselonline.com/modules.php?name=News&file=article&sid=14168

84 See Centre on Housing Rights and Evictions (COHRE), *op. cit.*, note 52, 24.

85 See Article 2 of the Treaty of Friendship between India and Bhutan, 8 August 1949 available at: http://www.unhcr.org/refworld/docid/3ae6b4d620.html

86 See "India can't assist in resolving Bhutanese refugee problem: Indian envoy", in *Nepal News* of 9 December 2009 available at: http://www.nepalnews.com/main/index.php/news-archive/2-political/2823-india-cant-assist-in-resolving-bhutanese-refugee-problem-indian-envoy.html

particularly for the resettlement countries and the government of India who maintain diplomatic relations with Bhutan, is to put pressure on Bhutan to ensure a dignified return of the Bhutanese refugees. The Government of Nepal should come up with an open policy for local integration for those who would like to stay in Nepal.

CHAPTER 3

Human and minority rights in Sri Lanka

Anton Piyarathane*

I. INTRODUCTION

Sri Lanka is a multi-ethnic and multi-religious society. Nearly 77 percent are Buddhists, eight percent are Hindus, eight percent are Islamic, six percent are Roman Catholic and one percent are other religious groups. According to ethnic distribution, there are 82 percent Sinhalas, 4 percent Sri Lankan Tamils, five percent Indian Tamils, eight percent Sri Lanka Moors and nearly one percent Burghers, Malays and Sri Lankan Chetties and Bharathas.[1] There are two main languages used by Sri Lankans: Sinhala and Tamil . The Sinhala language is used by the majority identified as Sinhalas[2] while the Muslims and Tamils mainly speak Tamil .[3] A small percentage of these two communities use English as their mother tongue.

In this discussion whether one can lead a peaceful life and work for personal improvement with a sense of dignity without disturbance by other persons or institutions is a crucial question. In this context, we have to assess whether all Sri Lankans are afforded human rights or if some groups have more rights than other groups. In general, there are a significant amount of publications suggesting that Sinhalas, who represent the majority of Sri Lankans, are afforded more rights than ethnic minorities such as Tamils or Muslims. However, it is possible to argue that only a certain class or elite group of Sri Lankans enjoys all rights whereas the majority is not afforded such rights. Summarily, the conclusion is that there is a problem in ensuring equal human rights for all citizens.

This paper discusses human and minority rights issues in Sri Lanka based on available literature and research, as well as the writers' experience. The modern concept of human rights is still new to Sri Lankan society. It is a country influenced by major global changes, but the policies of the political regime have not consistently reflected these changes, , resulting in uneven social development.

II. THE EXISTING FRAMEWORK TO PROTECT HUMAN RIGHTS IN SRI LANKA

In addition to the pledge of human rights given by the 1978 Constitution of the Democratic Socialist Republic of Sri Lanka under fundamental rights, a few institutions have additionally been established in order to protect human rights.[4] Were

---

* PhD Candidate in Anthropology at the Macquarie University of Sydney and Senior Lecturer, Open University of Sri Lanka, Department of Social Studies.

1 National Census of Population and Housing 2001. For further information please refer to: http://www.statistics.gov.lk/PopHouSat/Pop_Chra.asp

2 *Ibid.*

3 They are identified as Sinhalese in most of the writings.

4 See 1978 Constitution of the Democratic Socialist Republic of Sri Lanka, available at: http://www.parliament.lk/about_us/constitution.jsp

the fundamental rights provided by the constitution secured for all, Sri Lanka would be a beacon for the respect of fundamental rights.. However, we hardly find application of these statements in the practical world – and this is where the problem emerges. In 1996 the government of Sri Lanka established a Human Rights Commission in Sri Lanka (HRCSL) under the parliamentary Act No. 21. The head office of HRCSL is located in Colombo while branches are situated in Kandy, Matara, Batticaloa, Anuradhapura, Trincomalee, Vavuniya, Badulla, Ampara, Jaffna and Kalmunai. The vision of HRCSL is to ensure human rights for all and promote and protect the rule of law. Its stated mission is to "develop a better human rights culture in Sri Lanka through protecting and promoting human rights for all in law, policy and in practice, adhering to universally recognized human rights norms and principles with a special emphasis on the fundamental rights guaranteed under the Sri Lankan Constitution for the citizens of Sri Lanka, with the coordination and corporation of all stakeholders that work towards protecting and promoting human rights for all".[5]

Table 1. Distribution of Complaints received by the main office of Human Rights Commission of Sri Lanka in 2006 and 2007[6]

Category of complaints	*2006*			*2007*		
		Backlog (pending)	Total		Backlog (pending)	Total
Non violations	166	788	954	208	667	875
Disinterested	373	1330	1703	396	1629	2025
Recommended	56	830	886	36	357	393
Settled	82	195	277	100	189	289
Relief granted	44	181	225	119	191	310
Withdrawn	138	177	315	118	170	288
Referred to other authorities	481	8	489	436	36	472
Others	293	497	790	427	1321	1748
Total	1633	4006	5639	1840	4560	6400

The above table indicates that in the year 2006-2007 the number of complaints received by the commission progressively increased. However, there is a considerable backlog of cases that the organization has yet to address. It is of interest to ascertain why people who made complaints to the commission have not shown adequate interest in pursuing their cases as labelled in the category 'disinterested', especially due to the proportionately high number. Among the numerous reasons which may contribute to this situation the following is worth noting: the people's lack of trust in the justice procedure, caused in part by the unnecessary delays and problems faced by the HRCSL in the early days of its' existence.. In order to address the number of cases brought before the commission, the commission would have to work very efficiently. Unfortunately, the table indicates that the HRCSL's efficiency and thereby affectivity

5 For further information about the HRCSL please visit the dedicated website at http://www.hrcsl.lk/english/index.html

6 Human Rights Commission of Sri Lanka, *"The Annual Report of Human Rights Commission of Sri Lanka 2006-2007"*, HRCSL Colombo 2008, 19-20, available at: http://www.hrcsl.lk/PFF/2006%20&%202007%20%20HRC%20Annual%20Report.pdf

is left wanting. A slight increase in the number of settled cases could be construed as a positive trend in the work of the HRCSL, taking into account the lack of dedicated resources available amongst other problems.
Apart from the HRCSL, in Feb. 2006 the government of Sri Lanka created a new cabinet seat: the Ministry of Disaster Management and Human Rights. This can be considered as one of the more progressive steps taken by the Sri Lankan government in the field of human and minority rights. Among the responsibilities assigned to the Ministry are areas with directly human rights relevance. These include the supervision of Non-Governmental Organisations (NGOs) and voluntary social welfare agencies in relation to the provision of relief work and the promotion of human rights; facilitation of and assistance to NGOs and voluntary social welfare agencies in the fields of disaster management and human rights; promotion of human rights, and the co-ordination of activities with the United Nations High Commissioner for Human Rights' and other international and regional human rights institutions. In addition to the above named responsibilities, the Ministry is also entrusted with the role of coordinating activities related to Internally Displaced Persons (IDPs) in the North and East of Sri Lanka since June 2006.

III. Main Instances of Human Rights Violations

Discussion about human rights in Sri Lanka needs to be contextualized. In the history of the country there are many contexts where human rights related issues have been discussed at the national and international level. For instance, the majority Sinhalas feet that their rights were violated during the youth insurrections, led by the Peoples Liberation Front (JVP – Janatha Vimukthi Peramuna), that took place in the years of 1971 and 1988-1989. High rates of unemployment and other forms of social injustices such as discrimination based on caste, class and language also contributed to such conflicts. At the time, Britain's "divide-and rule" colonial policies in favouring the Jaffna Tamils at the expense of the Sinhalas resulted in the Sinhalas attempting to re-establish their language and culture to "its rightful place of prominence and dominance."[7] Therefore, the Sri Lankan government approved a number of laws that eased the way for Sinhalas into positions formerly held by Jaffna Tamils and restricted the ability of Jaffna Tamils gaining others. The consequence was of perceived discrimination felt by the Tamils and also contributed to the ethnic conflict in Sri Lanka.[8] During the civil war the Liberation Tigers of Tamil Ealam (LTTE) attempted to evict Muslims from Jaffna and launched attacks against Muslims in the northern and eastern areas leading to an exodus of IDPs. The LTTE appeared as the main political force representing Tamil interests before the 2009 killing of the leader of the LTTE, Velupillai Prabhakaran, by government forces. Up until the death of the LTTE leader in 2009, the war cost lives, created casualties and wasted resources that could have been used for other purposes, such as on the country's economic development. Due to the war between the government and the LTTE, many lives were

---

7 See Neil De Votta, "Control Democracy, Institutional Decay and the Quest for Eelam: Explaining Ethnic Conflict in Sri Lanka", *Pacific Affairs*, Vol. 73, No. 1 (Spring 2000), 58.
8 See Brian Blodgett, "*Sri Lanka's Military: The Search for a Mission*", (Aventine Press, San Diego 2004).

lost on both sides. According to the Internal Displaced Monitoring Centre (IDMC), Sri Lanka is a country which still has around 400,000 IDPs in welfare camps.[9] Apart from the physical and human damage caused by the war, the militarisation of Sri Lankan society has come at the cost of civil life. Militarisation can be described as "a process by which a person or a thing gradually becomes controlled by the military or comes to depend for its well-being on militaristic ideas."[10] At the peak of this process, the military could take over civilian institutions.[11] As a result of the cultural militarization, people started using terms such as *deshapremiya* (patriot) and *dehsdrohiya* (traitor) to label members of their own communities – an example of the narrow-mindedness that overcame the society.. This really shows the danger of militarisation of a society and the loss of human rights in such a context.

Despite the cessation of hostilities, police and army checkpoints litter the city of Colombo. Buses are stopped and passengers questioned regardless of their ethnicity, but to an extent which severely test the patience and tolerance of a normal person.[12] Resolving issues at the checkpoints depend on the personality of both officers of the forces or police and the persons being questioned. Whatever action the forces take is taken under the guise of national security or to prevent a betrayal of the country. In this a kind of charged atmosphere the protection of human rights is a complicated task.

The relationship between majority and minority groups is, generally speaking, not equal. Similar to other societies, minority groups in Sri Lanka face exclusion, less recognition and less privileges, etc. A consensus or a sense of unity amongst the minorities against the dominance of the Sinhalas is not tangible: they too work against each other, violating each others rights. The best examples of such demarcations between minorities are the actions taken by LTTE, fighting for the liberation of Tamils. The LTTE expelled the Muslims who traditionally lived in Jaffna. Furthermore, there are ongoing tensions between Muslims and Tamils in the eastern province. Minority groups also have competing factions within themselves, for instance the Tamils in Sri Lanka are divided into Jaffna Tamils, Colombo Tamils, Batticaloa Tamils and Estate Tamils.[13] In addition, they face difficulty in interacting with the main society dominated by the privileged groups.

---

9 See Internal Displacement Monitoring Centre (IDMC), country profile Sri Lanka available at: http://www.internal-displacement.org/

10 See Neloufer De Mel, *"Militarizing Sri Lanka: Popular Culture, Memory and Narrative in the Armed Conflict"*, (Sage Publication, New Delhi 2007), 12.

11 *Ibid.*

12 See, "Sri Lanka: Checkpoints in Paradise", in *Lanka Journal Newspaper* available at: http://www.lankajournal.com/?p=11178

13 See Jayaratnam A. Wilson, "The Colombo Man, the Jaffna Man, and the Batticaloa Man: Regional Identities and the Rise of the Federal Party" in, Chelvadurai Manogaran and Bryan Pfaffenberger, (eds.), *The Sri Lankan Tamils: Ethnicity and Identity*, (Westview Press, Colorado 1994).

IV. CONCEPTUAL FRAMEWORK

The discussion on human rights (HR) and minority rights (MR) can be focused on four aspects. *A*) The Constitutional framework, *B*) role of the state and its institutions, *C*) awareness and attitude of the people, and *D*) role of the social institutions and civil society organizations.

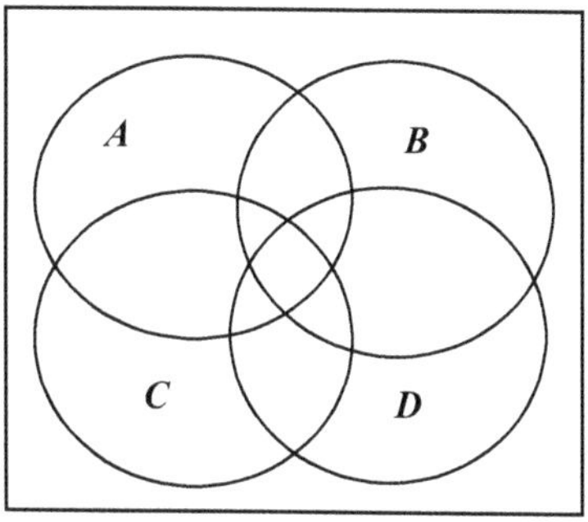

- *Constitutional Framework*
- *Role of the state and its institutions.*
- *Awareness and attitude of the people*
- *The role of the social institutions and civil society organisations.*

A. Constitutional provisions relating to Human and Minority Rights

The 1972 constitution mainly tried to give prominence to Sinhala Buddhists, who are the ethnic majority in Sri Lanka. This attempt resulted in agitation by educated Tamils against the government of Sri Lanka. This step contributed to the military struggle engaged upon by the youth Tamils.[14] Furthermore, the 1958 government language policy in giving more prominence to the Sinhala language bestowed an advantage upon Sinhalese educated persons over the Tamil or English speakers. This situation then resulted in the English educated Sinhalas and Tamils leaving the country.[15] Tamils who did not have great Sinhalese skills were thereby compelled to deal in Sinhala.[16] When Sinhala was made the official language of the country in 1956, 50 percent of the positions in the clerical service, 60 percent of the professional and technical services, 40 percent of army, navy and police, and 30 percent of the administrative service were held by Tamils. By 1970, the percentage of Tamils who held these positions was reduced drastically. The percentage of Tamils holding

14 See Thangarajah C.Y., "Youth, Conflict and Social Transformation in Sri Lanka" in Hettige S.T. and Mayer Markus (eds.), *"Sri Lankan Youth: Challenges and Responses"*, (Friedrich Ebert Stiftung-Colombo in collaboration with the University of Heidelberg South Asia Institute (SAI) and the Development Studies Institute University of Colombo (DSIUC), Friedrich Ebert Stiftung 2002), 189. Available at: http://www.fessrilanka.org/pdf/sly1.pdf

15 *Ibid.*, 189.

16 *Sinhala* is the language of Sinhalas (popularly known as Sinhalese), the majority ethnic group in Sri Lanka.

positions in the administrative services came down to five percent while the percentage of professional and technical services reduced up to ten percent, the clerical services were also limited to 5 percent.[17] Fortunately this situation has been rectified.

The existing 1978 constitution of Sri Lanka adopted specific provisions to safeguard the interests of minorities . These provisions were adopted to mitigate the discrimination of minorities.. Two chapters of the constitution include detailed provisions to safeguard the rights of minorities: the chapters on Fundamental and Language Rights, respectively.[18] Moreover, there are other provisions, such as the provisions contained in the Thirteenth Amendment to the Constitution which attempt to safeguard minority rights. The aforementioned amendment established Provincial Councils with power devolved to the Provinces.[19] In this context, the introduction of a Proportional Representation Scheme into the Constitution, abided by during parliamentary and local government elections, is another means by which the adequate representation of minorities is ensured. This measure redresses the representative imbalances of the voting system prior to 1978.[20]

Some writers, however, have pointed out the weaknesses of the 1978 Constitution. For instance, Sivathamby argues that the role and function of the Sri Lankan Tamils as a political group should be closely defined in the constitution.[21] This would not be a practical suggestion as the constitution has to ensure equal attention to all minority groups. Making matters worse there are some Sinhala groups who question what they have gained as a majority

Amendments introduced to the existing Constitution have, for various reasons, yet to be fully implemented. For example, the full implementation of the Thirteenth Amendment to the Constitution is still an issue being debated amongst the members of the ruling party as well the parties of the coalition government. Furthermore there is no common agreement amongst the other political parties of Sri Lanka in this matter. The intention of the Thirteenth Amendment was to empower provinces of Sri Lanka; it included provisions to establish provincial councils for each province, thereby allowing the communities to use their own language in administrative affairs and for the people of the region to make decisions without the interference of the central government. Though the provincial councils have been established and are now functioning, some issues such as security, finance, trade and commerce have not been devolved to the provincial councils. The devolution needs to be addressed soon in order to ensure all rights are afforded to minorities in Sri Lanka.

---

17 See Chalvadorai Manogaran, *"Ethnic Conflict and Reconciliation in Sri Lanka"*, (University of Hawaii Press, Honolulu 1987), 129.

18 See respectively Chapters III and IV of the Constitution of the Democratic Socialist Republic of Sri Lanka.

19 See the thirteenth amendment to the Constitution of 14 November 1987 to make Tamil an official language and English a link language, and for the establishment of Provincial Councils. For further information please visit: http://www.priu.gov.lk/Cons/1978Constitution/ConstitutionalReforms.htm

20 See Article 99 of the Constitution of the Democratic Socialist Republic of Sri Lanka.

21 See Karthigesu Sivathamby, *"Being a Tamil and Sri Lankan"*, (Aivakam, Colombo 2005).

The Seventeenth Amendment to the Constitution has also been passed by the Sri Lankan parliament but not yet implemented.[22] This Amendment has broad support across the entire political spectrum and has been applauded as one of the very good changes in order to create a state mechanism through which the rights of the people are ensured. The amendment recommends appointing commissions such as the Election Commission, Public Service Commission, the National Police Commission, Human Rights Commission of Sri Lanka, Permanent Commission to Investigate Allegations of Bribery or Corruption, Finance Commission and Delimitation Commission.[23] The implementation of this amendment would be a remedy to the acute politicisation in public sector organisations. On the whole the officers attached to government institutions are today trapped because of ministers or head of state's power to take decisions about their positions. This is a negative consequence of the evolution of the public administration system in Sri Lanka.[24]

B. The role of the state and its institutions

Writers such as Bopage believe that the post-colonial Sri Lankan state never considered the importance of protecting the dignity and security of marginalized and disadvantaged social groups.[25] Various local issues were considered a threat to the state and were dealt with in a conflict paradigm mindset . Peaceful demands for social equity, justice, security and dignity went unnoticed and when they became visible, were unceremoniously quashed by the State. This behaviour and the suppression of peaceful demands of marginalised groups became a motivation for marginalized individuals and groups to take up arms.

The state institutions have conveniently forgotten the causes that contributed to the youth insurrections in Sri Lanka. The Presidential Commission on Youth appointed following the suppressed youth movement of 1989 presented their recommendations to the government in 1990.[26] The mandate of the Commission was to examine the causes of youth dissatisfaction and unrest. Recommendations were made on how to discourage the use of violent measure while encouraging the fulfilment of youth needs and aspirations through the use of legitimate, peaceful means. The report tabled by the Commission made a number of constructive and reasonable recommendations for broader changes in society and for the effective democratization of the State. The members of the Commission specifically warned against the over-politicisation of society, the misuse and abuse of political power and the arbitrary political interventions in public institutions. Furthermore, the Commission recommended

---

22 See the Seventeenth Amendment to the Constitution of 3 October 2001 to make provisions for the Constitutional Council and Independent Commissions. For further information please visit: http://www.priu.gov.lk/Cons/1978Constitution/ConstitutionalReforms.htm

23 See Chapter VIIA of the Seventeenth Amendment. For further information please visit: http://www.priu.gov.lk/Cons/1978Constitution/SeventeenthAmendment.html

24 See K.M. De Silva, "The Bureaucracy" in K.M. De Silva (ed.), *"Sri Lanka: Problems and Governance"*, (International Centre for Ethnic Studies, Konark Publishers, Delhi 1993); and B.S. Wijeweera, *"A Colonial Administrative System in Transition: The Experience of Sri Lanka"*, (Marga Publications, Colombo 1988).

25 See Lionel Bopage, Political Violence in Sri Lanka, in *Sri Lanka Guardian*, 4 August 2009, available at: http://www.srilankaguardian.org/2009/08/political-violence-in-sri-lanka-part_06.html

26 See Hettige S.T. and Mayer Markus (eds.), *op. cit.*, note 14, 5-8.

specific reforms in the education and employment sectors as they are considered priorities to youth development and to youth participation in society and mainstream politics.

The state and its institutions have to work to protect the fundamental rights of people from heterogeneous background. Unfortunately, the country is still run under the emergency law promulgated during the civil war and the youth insurrections led by Sinhala in 1971 and the 1988-1989 periods. Furthermore, due to the Prevention of Terrorism Act (PTA) passed in 1979, Sri Lanka has operated under emergency regulations. According to the current emergency regulations suspects can be arrested without warrant and held for 18 months without formal charges or access to legal representation.[27] Under the emergency regulations the head of the state is given extraordinary powers enabling him/her to act arbitrarily by amending, revoking or applying any law deemed necessary.[28] Even following the victorious war of the Sri Lankan forces against the LTTE the government has sought parliamentary approval for the ongoing invocation of emergency regulations. Almost all civil activities including the recently held presidential election and the forthcoming parliamentary elections are held under these regulations. These measures exemplify the problems and limitations Sri Lankan citizens have in exercising their human rights.

Though the best constitution in the world can exist on paper, it is the implementation thereof that is crucial. Any government must ensure that careful attention is paid to the implementation of the constitution. Due to the well-known tensions and history of misunderstandings with its' minority groups, the Sri Lankan government has to pay much more attention to ensuring socio-economic, cultural and political rights of tits' citizens and its' minorities in particular.

In general the state must have policies for education, health, other infrastructures, economic development and electoral processes applicable to the entire country. According to Manogaran existing policies are very unfavourable towards the Tamils.[29] The low enrolment of Tamil students from plantation areas in the universities is a case in point as is the rural-urban disparity in education-related issues. Furthermore,, schools attended by Sinhala also have very poor facilities. All these differences are the result of an unclear policy regime.

There are instances to prove that the government adopted discriminatory employment policies. For instance, in 1962 the government adopted a policy of recruiting exclusively from the Sinhala Buddhist community to the armed forces. This led Tamils and other ethnic groups to believe that they were viewed as second-class citizens who cannot be trusted to guard the country.[30] According to Manogaran f Tamils made up 40 percent of the army, navy, and police in 1956 and by 1970 there were none.[31] In a context where there was a war between government forces and the

---

27 See Maura R. O'Connor, "How Sri Lanka governs through detentions: Sri Lankan officials defend the country's post-war use of anti-terrorism rules" in *Global Post*, 15 September 2009 available at: http://www.globalpost.com/dispatch/asia/090909/sri-lanka-emergency-regulations.

28 See Raisa Wickrematunge, "State Of Emergency — Here To Stay?" in *The Sunday Leader*, 7 February 2010 available at: http://www.thesundayleader.lk/2010/02/07/state-of-emergency-—-here-to-stay/

29 See Chalvadorai Manogaran, *op. cit.* note 17.

30 See Brian Blodgett, *op. cit.*, note 7.

31 See Chalvadorai Manogaran, *op. cit.* note 17.

Tamil LTTE, this can be justified, but the state now has to reconsider and review its' policy in this regard. There were attempts by the government to recruit Tamils from northern and eastern areas to the police forces which is an admirable effort that needs to be expanded to include the armed forces as well. It would be a first step in convincing minority groups that the Sri Lankan state respects them and expects their cooperation for the development of the country. The presence of Tamils in the administrative services, clerical positions technical as well as professional positions were also drastically reduced by 1970 according to Manogaran.[32] This situation not only leads to a reduction in the number of employed Tamils but constitutes a violation of the Tamils freedom to self-development and right to access and interact with state organisations in their own language. Furthermore, it alienates Tamils, many who grow up believing that there is no future for them in Sri Lanka.

In this context, State institutions have not shown enough interest in protecting human rights of the people in general and minorities in particular. Thangarajah reports how human rights activists in the east became very vulnerable when the Sri Lankan military forces captured some of the villages: "*The military operations of 1990 to recapture the area under the control of the LTTE even after they had abandoned the area, led to thousands being killed by the Sri Lankan army. Entire villages were wiped out during this campaign of mass terror. Community leaders who were involved in human rights work and other public interest activities were systematically targeted and eliminated and civic activity became a life-threatening vocation*".[33]

Ideally the government forces ought to have worked cooperatively with civil society members and activists in protecting human rights. For example, at the time of writing there was news about three army soldiers raping a nine year old girl in Batticaloa. According to the Lanka-e-News, under the heading of "War ends rape begins: a schoolgirl the victim –body of a villager who went to the camp to protest was found in a pond", a nine year old school girl was abducted and raped by three army soldiers when she was returning home after school.[34] The parents of the girl lodged a complaint against the soldiers with the police. Galvanised by the incident, villagers protested against the culprits. Shortly afterwards villagers found the body of Chandrasekeran Sugabalan (31) who participated in the protest in a pond at Digilivedai the following day. According to the news not only did the soldiers commit the crime, they were also attempting to disturb the process of seeking justice for the child, parents and villagers. Obviously, there can be individuals with deviate tendencies in every institution, but justice needs to be served in order to ensure public trust in the law and order in the country. Following the hardships of the war between the LTTE and the government forces, this should not be the plight of the people in those areas. This is not an isolated incident in the history of the conflict. It is the duty of any government to take prompt actions against those who committed the crime and make sure such things are not repeated in the future. Officers of the forces also have

---

32 See Chalvadorai Manogaran, *op. cit.* note 17.

33 See Thangarajah C.Y., *op. cit.*, note 14.

34 See Lanka-e-News, "*War ends rape begins :a schoolgirl the victim –body of a villager who went to the camp to protest found in a pond*" available at: http://www.lankaenews.com/English/news.php?id=9133

to be mindful of their activities, show sensitivity to the people and ensure a feeling of safety and protection for those who suffered a lot during the war.

There are many acts of political violence in Sri Lanka and the victims are not given proper support by the law enforcement authorities. A study conducted in the district of Kandy, shows how people in a village of Sri Lanka suffer due to election violence.[35] The study was conducted in the year 2007 in order to shed light on the nature of election violence which took place during the parliamentary elections in the years 2000-2001. The study shows how members of the opposition were suppressed by the winning party with direct state support. The police did not uphold justice as the officers were afraid of transfers as punishment for acting upon the crimes committed by members of the ruling party including the Members of Parliament (MPs) and Ministers. Even during the recently held presidential and parliamentary elections violence and malpractices occurred around the country. Election monitors as well as the election commissioner stated that there were numerous instances of malpractice in the election process, but no action was taken against the culprits. In a reversal of the roles they should play, institutions meant to uphold and protect law and order are used to punish people who hold different opinions.

The acute politicisation of almost all state institutions has resulted in people losing trust in government organisations. For instance, there is a lot of discussion about the professionalism of the police department.[36] Of course one could ask *"why don't people seek the support of the courts?"* In practice going to court requires a lot of money to retain the services of a good lawyer. The anthropological comprehension of the legal procedures would be useful in understanding how poor innocent persons have become more vulnerable in the court system. Recently, there was BBC news report(2008) reporting the release of a man identified as P.P. James from prison in Sri Lanka after being held on remand for 50 years without conviction. He was arrested for stabbing his father at the age of 30 and released at the age of 80.[37] He seems to have been forgotten by the administration of the court. The lawyer who appeared on behalf of James explained the reasons why James did not take up this matter with the relevant authorities by saying that "the *client did not complain because he was from a village and ignorant of the law.*" This incident shows the plight of the vulnerable people in the legal system of the country.

Citizens of Sri Lankawould have faith in law enforcement authorities if they upheld the law. The national youth survey data proves that youth do not have high levels of trust in state institutions such as the military, judiciary or police.

Table 2: Level of trust: state institutions[38]

Level of trust	*Military*	*Judiciary*	*Police*	*Bureaucracy*	*Average*
Great deal	41.6	38.9	16.5	8.1	26.3

---

35 See Kristine Hogland and Anton Piyarathne, "Paying the Price for Patronage: Electoral Violence in Sri Lanka" in *Commonwealth & Comparative Politics* Vol. 47, No. 3, July 2009, 287–307.

36 See *Daily Mirror*, Editorial of 12th March 2010, available at: http://www.dailymirror.lk/print/index.php/editorial/106-editorial/5783.html

37 See Roland Buerk, "Sri Lankan remanded for 50 years" in *BBC News*, 13 January 2008 available at: http://news.bbc.co.uk/2/hi/south_asia/7186063.stm.

38 From Fernando Laksiri, "Youth and Politics: Why They Rebel?" in Hettige S.T. and Mayer Markus (eds.), *op. cit.*, note 14, 137.

Somewhat	43.8	47.2	56.8	60.8	52.2
Not at all	13.7	12.6	29.7	29.7	20.4
Don't know	0.0	1.3	1.4	1.4	1.1

According to the data presented in the table above none of the organisations were able to count on more than 50 percent of respondents having a "great deal" of trust in them, demonstrating the weaknesses of these organisations. Sri Lankans have to be very tolerant when they have an issue that needs to be sorted out with these institutions.

C. Awareness of people about Human Rights

In Sri Lanka, people are generally peaceful and admire a non-violent approach to settling disputes. The majority of them is Buddhist and adopts peaceful means in addressing various issues. Members of almost all the ethnic groups live peacefully in the city of Colombo: Sinhalas, Tamils, Muslims as well as in the suburbs . Even in the plantation areas where the majority is Indian Tamil, they have lived very cooperatively with the Sinhalas or Muslims for years. This was the case even during the war between the LTTE and government forces.

The 2006-2007 annual report of the HRCSL emphasises the need for greater public awareness about human rights.[39] The HRCSL conducted programmes for the general public as well as for government officials including, inter alia, the armed forces, police officers and district child development committee officers. But it is very difficult for the HRCSL to address all the officers and civil society alone. Furthermore, the broadness of the concept of human rights makes the task very difficult for the HRCSL.

One of the key issues in the discussion of human rights is whether people accept the existence of human rights related issues or not. For instance, whether people accept that there is an issue of gender based discrimination. According to the 2001 national youth survey, the majority of youths, some 58.3 percent, feel that both men and women have equal opportunity while 41.2 percent indicated no equal opportunities in Sri Lanka.[40] Among the respondents three percent of them were not aware if this is a human rights issue. Nearly 57 percent of females and 60 percent of males believe that there are equal opportunities for men and women in Sri Lanka. Contradicting the research findings most day-to-day life experience proves this not to be the case. There is a lot of violence against women, they cannot take up certain jobs and they still have no opportunities to partake in higher studies.

The national youth survey data shows if the youth accepts that the country has neglected the needs of the Tamils. Only 46 percent of the total youth sample agreed that the needs of Tamils are being neglected in Sri Lanka with 53 percent disagreeing and only one percent did not know there was such an issue.[41] The majority of youths who agreed that there is a discrimination against the needs of Tamils come from the

39 See Human Rights Commission of Sri Lanka, *op. cit.*, note 6.
40 See Hettige S.T. and Mayer Markus (eds.), *op. cit.*, note 14.
41 See Mayer, Markus, "Violent Youth Conflicts in Sri Lanka: Comparative Results from Jaffna and Hambantota" in Hettige S.T. and Mayer Markus (eds.), *op. cit.*, note 14.

Tamil community. Around 84 percent of Tamils felt so while 56 percent of the Muslim youth and 37 percent of the Sinhala youth agreed with the above response. This brings another dimension in to our discussion which is the need to create awareness for the human rights situation of other ethnic groups.

There are positive results due to the effective awareness-raising programmes jointly created by the government and NGOs. Among these, the rights of children and women and the rights of elders are effectively promoted at present. Currently there is wide social acceptance for not physically punishing children in Sri Lanka; most school teachers used to give physical punishments to children as a disciplinary measure. There are instances of both parents and students filing cases against teachers who physically punished them. There is a women's desk with a female police officer in order to take down complaints made by women at police stations. The Ministry of Child Development and Women's Empowerment has run many programmes with the International Non Governmental Organisations (INGOs) and NGOs on gender sensitive issues. The rights of the elders are also now emphasized by the National Secretariat for Elders set up under the Ministry of Social Services. These aspects can be considered to be positive measures taken by both public and private sector organisations.

D. *The role of the social institutions and civil society organisations*

At this point the writer really would like to highlight the role played by social institutions such as families, schools, the media, religious organisations, peer groups as well as INGOs, NGOs, Community Based Organisations (CBOs), and other groups in working with the people. In this discussion we cannot ignore the role of the political parties, politicians and community leaders. They have a vital role to play in creating a civil society which respects human rights and is dedicated to it. The Chairman's message to the 2006-2007 Annual Report of Human Rights Commission of Sri Lanka also emphasises and recognises the service of the abovementioned groups and organisations in promoting human rights in Sri Lanka.[42] It is essential to create a human rights culture in Sri Lanka. From the family to the various other organisations , all the social institutions have to get together for this task. If the family as a social unit adheres to human rights practices, it could be considered as a foundation of establishing a HR based culture in Sri Lanka. In such a culture there would be no room for the violation of anyone's rights.

V. CHALLENGES OF ESTABLISHING HUMAN RIGHTS IN SRI LANKA

There are challenges that the government and civil society can take into consideration in ensuring human rights in Sri Lanka. The challenges of ensuring human rights in Sri Lanka and creating a society where people respect and abide by human rights could be summarised as follows. Creating a strong constitutional framework which guarantees the right for all the citizens of the country would be the first step in ensuring human rights in Sri Lanka. Then the government has to create a strong institutional framework to protect human rights in its territory. The institutions must

---

42 See Human Rights Commission of Sri Lanka, *op. cit.*, note 6, 2.

be able to work independently without any interferences of any nature and should be in a position to protect those who follow human rights and correct those who do not. Simultaneously, the state must organise effective and efficient public awareness programmes to educate people about human rights. A strong component of human rights could also be incorporated into the school curriculum. There should be programmes to guarantee human rights based environment in both public and private sector organisations. The entire society and public life should follow a strong human rights approach. These aspects are challenging for any government. Initially the government has to give priority to making an honest commitment in creating a society where law and order is re-established and human rights are guaranteed.

VI. Conclusion

The post-Independence governments of Sri Lanka tried to redress the pains and sufferings of Sri Lankans under British rule. This process neglected the rights of minorities as the state was controlled by the ethnic majority following the democratic administrative style introduced to the country by the colonial masters. When the post-Independence Sri Lankan state tried to address the land, livelihood and education related issues of it citizens, the minorities felt that their rights had been neglected. These policies of the Sri Lankan state led to ethnic conflict and to two insurrections. The state response to these movements then paved the way for a violation of rights of those people directly involved in the confrontations and resulted in neglecting the development of civil law. On the other hand, organisations such as the LTTE took to arms against the government for violating the rights of Tamils but are also responsible for violating the rights of thousands of innocent civilians of other ethnic groups. These confrontations resulted in losing a lot of valuable human lives and resources which ought to have used for the development of the country. The three decade long war has come to an end now. We have had the bitter experience of two youth insurrections. The close analysis of these incidents shows that by not protecting the basic rights of these groups contributed to the escalation into violence. Thus, it would be much wiser for the state of Sri Lanka and its civil society to take suitable measures to guarantee human rights for its people with due consideration for ethnicity, gender, age, religion and language, etc. These measures would contribute to ensure the gift of long-lasting peace and development for Sri Lanka.

CHAPTER 4

Human and Minority Rights in Nepal

Som Prasad Niroula*

I. BACKGROUND

Nepal was a closed country till 1990. King Mahendra introduced a Panchayat system which was a one party system where individual candidates used to participate in the election. Political parties were banned. Scores of sympathizers of political parties and civil society leaders were detained at the time. In collaboration, different political parties among them the Nepali Congress and left-wing parties joined together and launched a mass protest movement. As a result of the continuous protests the King was forced to step down as the executive head of the government and introduced a multi-party democratic system. The democratic movement in 1990 provided an opportunity for the people of Nepal to interact with the world. Moreover, the Constitution of 1990 integrated fundamental human rights: the government ratified six major UN treaties and various international instruments on human and minority rights. To date, 16 international instruments on human rights and four humanitarian instruments have been ratified by the government of Nepal.[1]

The objective of this paper is to give an overview of the human and minority rights status in Nepal. The paper will provide information about the demographic status of different minority groups – Indigenous peoples/Janajati, Dalits and Madhesi. The paper does not, however, cover women issues. The research is based on secondary information published by various sources such as: government, non-governmental organizations, journals, news papers (daily, weekly, monthly magazines) and others.

The Communist Party of Nepal Maoists (CPN-M) submitted 40 demands to the government of Nepal on 4 February 1996. The government did not invite CPN-M for the negotiations. The demands contained issues of nationality, people's democracy and livelihood.[2] The CPN- M formally launched armed conflict on 13 February 1996 when their demands were not met by the government. During the internal armed conflict (from 1996-2006) between the government and insurgents Maoists, approximately 13347 Nepalese lives were lost.[3] These included agricultural workers, teachers, police, army, civil servants, journalists, social workers, health workers,

---

* Som Prasad Niroula is a human rights activist and peace educator. He holds a Master's degree in Anthropology from Tribuvan University, Kathmandu, and another Master's Degree from the United Nations Mandated University for Peace in Peace Education. He is currently working with the Nepal Institute of Peace (NIP) as a program officer. His areas of interest are issues on human and minority rights, forced migration, internal displacement and refugees.

1 CERD, ICCPR, ESCR, CRC, CAT, CEDAW and various other instruments – The status of treaties is available at:
http://treaties.un.org/Pages/Treaties.aspx?id=4&subid=A&lang=en

2 See Thapa D. and Sijapati B., *"A Kingdom Under Siege: Nepal's Maoist Insurgency, 1996 to 2003"*, (The Printhouse, Kathmandu 2003).

3 8457 people were killed by government forces and 4733 killed by Maoists.

civilians and Maoists cadres.[4] The human displacement caused by the conflict is estimated between 18.666 and 400.000 persons because of threats and intimidations by both conflicting parties.[5] In addition, physical infrastructure such as schools, health posts and village development committees' offices were destroyed causing financial damage estimated at 39 crores of Nepali rupees.[6] Thousands of people have suffered psychologically having been tortured and/or due to the loss of their family members and/or properties.

The King assumed executive power on 1 February 2005. Media houses were censored, leaders of the mainstream political parties and human rights activists were detained and a state of emergency imposed. In response, the Seven Political Parties Alliance (SPA)[7] and the CPN-M signed a twelve-point understanding on the abolishment of the absolute monarchy, the establishment of people's supremacy, the end of internal armed conflict, the holding of constituent assembly elections and the respect for human rights and democracy. In collaboration the SPA and CPN-M started the so called Jana Andolan II (Peoples movement - II) non-violent protest.[8] The Jana Andolan II began on April 6 2006 by calling a general strike. A total of 25 people were killed and more than 5000 people were injured during the Jana Aandolan II.[9]

As a result of the Jana Andolan II, the House of Representatives was reinstalled. On May 18 2006 the government of Nepal tabled a historic proposal depriving the King and Royal family of all their privileges. Furthermore, the proclamation of the parliament on May 18 2006 declared Nepal a secular country, removed the King as commander of the army and dissolved the Raj Parisad.[10] Meanwhile, the CPN-M declared a three-month ceasefire and signed the comprehensive peace agreement on 21 November 2006. This enabled the CPN-M to join the government. The House of Representatives was also reformulated after the Comprehensive Peace Agreement (CPA).

According to the report of the National Human Rights Commission of Nepal (NHRC) released on the third anniversary of the CPA, in the previous three years 107 people were killed by the Nepalese police, another 26 due to the violence of the Maoists, while at least another 53 persons died by bomb blasts attributed to the so-called militant outfits .[11]

---

4 See Informal Sector Service centre (INSEC), "Human Rights Yearbook", (INSEC, Kathmandu 2007).

5 See Som P. Niroula, "Voiceless Citizens: A case study of Internally Displaced Persons in Nepal", Discussion Paper II in *Refugee Watch Issue* No. 1 to issue no. 32, 2008.

6 See Community Study and Welfare Centre (CSWC), *"A Decade of Disaster: Human and Physical Cost of Nepal Conflict 1996-2005"*, (CSWC Research report, Kathmandu 2006). A crore is a unit in the Indian numbering system equal to ten millions.

7 The seven major political parties are the Nepali Congress (NC), Nepali Congress Democratic (NC-D), Communist Party of Nepal Unified Marxist Leninist (CPN-UML), Nepal Workers and Peasants Party, Nepal Goodwill Party, United Left Front and People's Front.

8 The first Jana Andolan (First People's movement) is the democratic movement of 1990 against the Panchayat System which was a one-party system ruled by the King.

9 See Informal Service Sector Centre (INSEC), *"2007 Human Rights Yearbook"*, (INSEC Kathmandu 2007), 97.

10 *Ibid.*

11 See National Human Rights Commission of Nepal (NHRC), *"Three- Year of Comprehensive Peace Accord"*, (NHRC Kathmandu 2009), 6.

Indigenous/Janajatis have been among the most badly affected groups by the violent conflict between Maoists and the government. Of the 8265 people killed between 13 February 1996 and 31 December 2003, 21.33 percent have been identified as Indigenous/Janajatis (see Table 1 below). Out of those killed, 65 percent are reported to have been killed by the state security forces.

Table 1: Number of victims killed during the conflict between State and Maoists[12]

Caste/Ethnicity	*Total People Killed*	*Percentage Killed*		
		By State	By Maoist	Total
Indigenous / Janajatis	1763	13.78	7.55	21.33
Chhetri / Thakuri	1551	8.19	10.57	18.76
Brahmin	905	5.2	5.75	10.95
Dalit	400	3.53	1.31	4.84
Terai Caste	186	0.83	1.42	2.25
Others	90	0.57	0.52	1.09
Not Identified	3370	33.88	6.9	40.78
Total	8265	65.98	34.02	100

Although more than 40 percent of those killed remain unidentified, the caste and ethnic pattern of the fatalities suggests that victims of state violence were concentrated amongst the Indigenous/Janajatis while Maoist victims were concentrated among higher caste Chhetris, Brahmins, and Thakuris. Table 1, however, shows that Indigenous people have been largely affected by the internal armed conflict between the government of Nepal and the CPN-M.

II. JANAJATIS / INDIGENOUS (NATIONALITIES)

Nepal nationalities are those who have their own languages and traditional culture but who do not fall under the traditional four-fold Varna classification of the Hindu Varna system or the Hindu hierarchical caste structure. Each indigenous group or Janajati has the following characteristics: a) a distinct collective identity; b) own language, religion, tradition, culture and civilization; c) own traditional egalitarian social structure; d) a traditional homeland or geographical area; e) a written or oral history; f) a meaningful sense of belonging; g) no decisive role in the politics and government

12 See Informal Service Sector Centre (INSEC), *"2004 Human Rights Yearbook"*, (INSEC Kathmandu 2004).

of modern Nepal; h) being the indigenous or people native to Nepal; and i) declaring themselves as "Janajatis".

As per the definition of "Janajati" given by the Act enacted by His Majesty's Government of Nepal, it declares that "indigenous nationalities" means a tribe or community in that has its own language and traditional rites and customs, distinct cultural identity, distinct social structure and written or unwritten history.[13] As per the 2002 National Foundation for Development of Indigenous Nationalities Act, his Majesty's Government has identified 59 indigenous nationalities with the above-mentioned characteristics.[14] However, the government omitted Chimtan, Thintan and Shyangtan from the list of indigenous nationalities.

A. Demographic and socio-economic Profile of Janajatis / Indigenous (Nationalities)

For the first time, information on caste/ethnicity was collected in the 1991 census, which identified 26 Indigenous/Janajatis out of 60 ethnic/caste groups. Additionally, the 2001 national census identified 43 Indigenous/Janajatis out of the recorded caste / ethnic groups. 16 Indigenous/Janajatis have not been identified in any of the censuses yet.

According to the 2001 national census, the total population of Indigenous/Janajatis was 8.460041 which is 37.22 percent of the country population.[15] Table 2 below presents the distribution of Janajatis/Indigenous population. The largest group among Indigenous/Janajatis is Magar (7.14 percent), which represent the third largest group after Chhetris and Bramins; these two are not indigenous groups. Followed by Tharu (6.75 percent), Tamang (5.64percent), Newar (5.48 percent), Rai (2.79 percent), Gurung (2.39 percent), and Limbu (1.58 percent). These seven groups comprise 31.77 percent of the total population of the country.

Table 2: Population By Indigenous / Janajati Group and Sex (2001)[16]

Indigenous / Janajati group	*Number*	*%*	*Male*	*Female*
Magar	1622421	7.14	784828	837593
Tharu	1533879	6.75	774924	758955
Tamang	1282304	5.64	641361	640943
Newar	1245232	5.48	620213	625019
Rai	635151	2.79	312363	322788
Gurung	543571	2.39	259376	284195

---

13 See National Foundation for Development of Indigenous Nationalities (NFDIN), *"An Introduction, The Indigenous Nationalities of Nepal"*, (NFDIN, Lalitpur 2003), 7.

14 *Ibid.* The identified 59 indigenous nationalities are: Kisans, Kumals, Kushbadias (Kuhbadias), Kusundas, Gangais, Gurungs, Chimtans, Chepangs, Chhantyals, Chhairottans, Jirels, Jhangads, Thintans, Dolpos, Tangbes, Tajpurias, Tamangs, Topkegolas, Thakalis, Thamis, Tharus, Thudams, Danuwars, Darais, Duras, Dhanuks, Dhimals, Newars, Paharis, Fris, Bankariyas, Baramos, Bahra Gaunle, Botes, Byasis, Bhujels/Ghartis, Bhutias, Magars, Manangays, Majhis, Marphalis, Mugalis, Meches, Rais, Rautes, Rajbanshis, Rajis, Larkes (Nubribas), Limbus, Lepchas, Lhopas, Lhomis (Shingsabas), Walungs, Sherpas, Satars, Siyars (Chumbas), Sunuwars, Surels, Syangtans, Hayus, and Hyolmos.

15 See Central Bureau of Statistics (CBS), *"Population census 2001 National Report"*, (Central Bureau of Statistics (CBS) in collaboration with UNFPA Nepal, Kathmandu 2002).

16 *Ibid.*

Limbu	359379	1.58	174760	184619
Dhanuk	188150	0.83	97507	90643
Sherpa	154622	0.68	77511	77111
Gharti/Bhujel	117568	0.52	58023	59545
Kumal	99389	0.44	48883	50506
Rajbansi/ koche	97241	0.43	48927	48314
Sunuwar	95254	0.42	48065	47189
Majhi	72614	0.32	36367	36247
Danuwar	53229	0.23	26192	27037
Chepang (praja)	52237	0.23	26685	25552
Santhal/Satar	42698	0.19	21515	21183
Dhagar/Jhagar	41764	0.18	20892	20872
Gangai	31318	0.14	15808	15510
Thami	22999	0.10	11392	11607
Dhimal	19537	0.09	9646	9891
Bhote	19261	0.08	9959	9302
Yakkha	17003	0.07	8132	8871
Darai	14859	0.07	7195	7664
Tajpuriya	13250	0.06	6532	6718
Thakali	12973	0.06	6216	6757
Pahari	11505	0.05	5803	5702
Chhantel	9814	0.04	4545	5269
Bote	7969	0.04	3881	4088
Brahmu/Baramu	7383	0.03	3441	3942
Jirel	5316	0.02	2582	2734
Dura	5169	0.02	2377	2792
Meche	3763	0.02	1830	1933
Lepcha	3660	0.02	1935	1725
Kisan	2876	0.01	1382	1494
Raji	2399	0.01	1111	1288
Byangsi	2103	0.01	1094	1009
Hayu	1821	0.01	892	929
Walung	1148	0.01	574	574
Raute	658	0.00	346	312
Yehlmo	579	0.00	281	298
Patharkata/Kuswadiya	552	0.00	286	266
Kusunda	164	0.00	85	79
Other Adibasi/Janajati	5259	0.02	2558	2701
Total Indigenous / Janajatis	*8.460.041*	*37.22*	*4.188.275*	*4.271.766*
Nepal	*22.736.934*	*100*	*11.359.378*	*11.377.556*

Table 3 presents the selected human development indicators by caste/ethnic groups. As shown in the table, in 1998 the average life expectancy of Janajatis was lower than the national average. Furthermore, the average literacy rate of Janajatis was estimated at only 35.2 percent while the national average was 65 percent.

Table 3: Selected Human Development Indicators by Caste / Ethnic Groups (1998)[17]

Caste / Ethnic Groups	*Indicators*		
	Average Life Expectancy (in years)	Literacy Rate (among 6 years and above population)	Per Capita Income (in Rs.)
Brahmin	60.8	58.0	9921
Chhetri	56.3	42.0	7744
Newar	62.2	54.8	11953
Janajati	53.0	35.2	6607
Dalit	42.0	23.8	4940
Nepal	*55.0*	*65.0*	*7673*

Similarly, per capita income of Janajatis was (Rs. 6607) much lower than that of Brahmin (Rs. 9921), Chhetri (Rs. 7744) and national average (Rs. 7673). According to the Nepal Human Development Report of 1998, prepared by Nepal South Asia Centre (NESAC), the incidence of poverty was lowest among the Newars (25 percent) followed by Brahmin (34 percent), Yadav (40 percent) and Chettri (50 percent) and the highest among those in the "lower caste". The incidence of poverty among Gurung, Rai, Magar, Tamang, and Limbu was 45, 56, 58, 59, and 71 percent, respectively.[18]

A. Political participation

The political participation of the Janajati/Indigenous, Dalits and Madheshi was negligible in the parliamentary election and in local governance. However, the Constitutional Assembly (CA) has a more inclusive membership. The table below gives an overview of the current members of the CA.

Table 4: Political participation of Indigenous people[19]

Ethnic Groups	*CA members*	*Percentage (%)*
Indigenous Nationalities	214	35.61
Dalits	50	8.32
Madheshi / Ethnicities	196	28.95
Brahmin / Chetri	163	27.12
Total	601	100

---

17 See Nepal South Asia Centre (NESAC), "*Nepal Human Development Report 1998*", (NESAC Kathmandu 1998).
18 *Ibid.*
19 See Gurung (a), "*Ethnic movement, Constituent Assembly Election and Its result*", paper presented at World Indigenous Day 2008 at Seoul, Korea on 17 August 2008 and Suvash Darnal, S, "*A Land of Our Own. Conversation with Dalits members of Constituent Assembly*", Sasmata Foundation & Jagarn Media Centre, Kathmandu 2009,

According to demographic composition, the number of the representatives in the CA is inclusive. The CA members come from direct and proportional elections; a total of 59 nationalities were recognized. However, the government agreed to include at least one member from the recognized 59 nationalities. In this frame, there are a total of 197 female members of the CA to draft the constitution for the new Nepal; 32.78 percent of the CA members are female.

III. Dalits / Untouchables

The definition of "Dalit" is a person who is culturally, economically and socially marginalized (NHDR, 2001).[20] In Nepal, Dalit means a community or a person who suffers from caste-based discrimination. The practice of the caste-system started to have grown stronger societal roots during the Malla period. Jayasthiti Malla formalized it in law in the 14th century. In the 17th century, King Ram Shah further formalized the caste system. Moreover, the Muluki Ain (National Code) of 1853 enforced the caste system legally; the code further imposed restrictions on the so-called lower caste people or community. In addition, the code included provisions of punishment for violating the code. In this context, Dalits were not allowed to enter the prayer places (temples), touch water or use the same tap as higher castes and were not allowed to enter the houses of higher caste people. For transgressions different punishments for different castes were established.

There is no official definition of Dalit. As a result it is very difficult to identify which group belongs or does not belong to the Dalits. Within the Dalit community, there is hierarchical order: the Kami (blacksmith) are considered higher than the other Dalits such as Sarki (leather worker), Damai (tailor) etc. In 1997, the NGO Dalit Vikash Samiti identified about 23 Dalit groups.[21] However it does not include the Dalits from the Terai regions. The government draft bill of March 2002 has identified 28 caste groups as Dalits; however, similar problems of exclusion of certain groups occurred. The National Dalit Commission (NDC), on the contrary, listed 17 caste/ethnic groups as Dalits.[22]

The 1990 Constitution of the Kingdom of Nepal and the 2006 Interim Constitution of Nepal guarantee the right to equality and prohibits discrimination on the basis of caste, religion, race and political persuasion. These constitutional provisions need to be translated into deeds so as to enable justice to reach all segments of society. Moreover, the government has ratified a number of international instruments which provides a wider legal? framework and space for untouchable people to lead dignified lives.[23]

The Dalits are a severely marginalized group in Nepal. The participation of the Dalits in governance is negligible. The literacy rate is low compared to other groups such as high caste people or indigenous people. The Dalits also face denial of access to public

---

20 See United Nations Development Programme (UNDP), *"Nepal Human Development Report 2001. Poverty Reduction and Governance"*, (UNDP Kathmandu 2002).

21 See Dilli R. Dahal *et al., op. cit.* note 29.

22 NDC listed the following groups as Dalits: Biswakarma (Kami, Lohar, Sunar, Odh, Chunara, Parki, Tamata), Darji (Damai, Pariyar, Suchikar, Ahudke, Dholi), Sarki (Mijar, Charkakar), Badi, Gaine, Dusadh, Chamar, Mushar, Dom, Khatwe, Tatma, Madhasi Dhobi, Halkhor, Bantar, Jhagad.

23 See above note 1.

services such as water, education, health, land, employment, social services and other resources.

A. Demographic and socio-economic profile of Dalits

The demographic and social-economic profile of the Dalits gives an overview of the situation of Dalits in Nepal. According to the 2001 national census, there were 3.030.067 Dalits in Nepal, representing 13.33 percent of the total population.

Table 5: Dalit Population in Nepal (2001)[24]

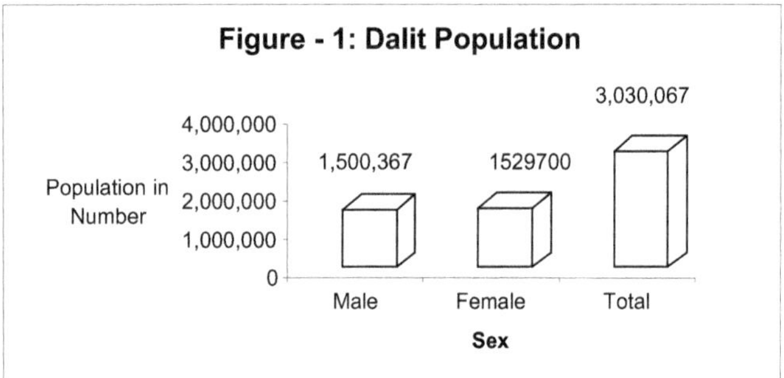

According to the NDC Field Survey of 2004, conducted in six Terai districts, almost 40 percent of the Dalits are involved in agricultural activity. Among them, one fifth work on their own farms and the rest work as wage labourers. Almost 10 percent are household assistants. About 14 percent are unemployed. Very few Dalits (less than one percent) work as blacksmiths and shoemakers; this shows that traditional occupation is declining. About 11 percent of the population work as housewives, drivers, social workers, sex workers, artisans, gardeners, etc. Two percent are involved in the public (school teachers) and private sectors.

The educational status of Dalits is very poor. The overall literacy rate of Dalits was 22.8 percent in the 1991 census compared to the national average of 39.6 percent. The male literacy rate was 33.9 percent compared to only 12.0 percent female literacy rate. The literacy rate of the Hill Dalits is much higher, 27 percent, compared to only 11 percent of the Terai Dalits. Only 4 percent of the females are literate among Terai Dalits compared to the 14.7 percent of female Hill Dalits. However, the male literacy rate, 40.2 percent, of the Hill Dalits is slightly above the national average. Of the total Dalits enumerated in 1991 census, Musahar have the lowest literacy rate of 4.2 percent whereas the highest is that of the Gaine at 31.1 percent. Likewise, the educational attainment of Dalits (Primary, Secondary, School Living Certificate (SLC), Intermediate and above) is only 14.6 percent compared to the 28.9 percent of the national average. According to the 2004 NDC survey, the literacy status of the

---

24 See Central Bureau of Statistics (CBS), "*Population census 2001 National Report*", *op. cit.* note 15.

Dalit lies at 35 percent – unfavourably low compared to the national average of 54 percent.[25]

Table 6 presents the Human Development Indicator (HDI) by caste/ethnic groups of Nepal. The table clearly shows the inferior situation of Dalit groups compared to other caste/ethnic groups. In 1998, the average life expectancy of the Dalits was just 42 years, which means 13 years (24 percent) less than the average national life expectancy. Similarly, per capita income of Dalits was 36 percent less than national average.[26]

Table 6: Selected Human Development Indicator by Caste / Ethnic Groups (1998)[27]

Caste / Ethnic Group	*Indicators*			
	Average Life Expectancy (in years)	Literacy rate in percent (aged 6 years & above)	Per Capita Income (in Rs.)	Per Capita Consumption (in Rs.)
Brahmin	60.8	58.0	9921	1533
Chhetri	56.3	42.0	7744	1197
Newar	62.2	54.8	11953	1848
Janajati	53.0	35.2	6607	6911
Dalit	42.0	23.8	4940	764
Nepal	*55.0*	*65.0*	*7673*	*11866*

Table 7 below presents the distribution of top level state representatives by caste/ethnic group. In 1999, there were no representatives of Dalits in the cabinet of the government. This finding clearly reflects the vulnerable situation of Dalits.

Table 7: Number of top level state representatives by Caste/Ethnic Group (1999)[28]

Sectors	*Caste / Ethnic Groups*						
	Brahmin / Chhetri	Madhesh	Newar	Janajati	Dalit	Others	Total
Constitutional Commission	14	3	6	2	0	0	25
Cabinet Minister	20	5	3	4	0	0	32
Judiciary	181	18	32	4	0	0	235
Legislative	159	46	20	36	4	0	265
Public Administrator	190	9	43	3	0	0	245

25 See "Percent Distribution of Population by Literacy Educational Attainment, 2004" in National Dalit Commission, *"Citizenship and Land Ownership Status of Dalit Community in Nepal"*, (NDC Kathmandu 2005), 11.

26 See Nepal South Asia Centre (NESAC), "*Nepal Human Development Report 1998", op. cit.* note 17.

27 *Ibid.*

28 See Govinda Neupane, *"Nepalko Jatiya Prasana (Question of Caste/Ethnicity in Nepal)"*, (Centre for Development Studies, Kathmandu 2000), 73. Please consider that there is an error in the data calculation done by the writer. The original table calculated a total of 1520; the author, however, added the figure which comes to a total of 1526.

Manager							
Political Leader (Central Level)	97	26	18	25	0	0	166
Local Governor	106	31	30	23	0	0	190
National Industry & Business	7	15	20	0	0	0	42
Education Professional	75	7	11	2	1	1	97
Cultural Institution	85	0	22	6	0	0	113
Science & Technology	36	6	18	2	0	0	62
Civil Society	41	4	8	1	0	0	54
Total	1011	170	231	108	5	1	1526

Overall, the involvement of Dalits in development activities is lower than that of other caste/ethnic groups. In other words, the status of Dalits is not as good as that of other caste/ethnic groups. The disadvantaged groups, particularly Dalits, have comparatively lower access to government institutions and organizations involved in development (e.g. agriculture and livestock development, forestry, health and education).[29] The excessive economic pressures and social exclusion prevent them from accessing resources equitably and living a normal human life. As a result, Dalits are the most marginalized caste group in Nepal.

IV. Regional disparities of Madhesh/Terai

People living in the southern plain area adjacent to India are called Madheshes.[30] Some people prefer to use the word Madhesh and some other the word Terai. The definition is contested. The Tharu, one of indigenous people of Terai (plain land) deny the existence of Madhesh and hence is preferable to use the name Terai. However, the regional party Madheshee People's Rights Forum (MPRF) is in favour of the name Madhesh; the forum also demands the so called "One Madhese one Pardhesh" (single federal unit) federal arrangements. In contrast to this demand, the Tharu, who are the indigenous people of the Terai, are demanding a Tharuhat autonomous region rather than granting single autonomous units, regions and federal state in the Terai region. The MPRF launched a Madhesh movement from 19 January to 7 February 2007. They demanded equal treatment and non-discrimination on the basis of regional arrangements, caste, religion, language, political views and economic conditions. It is estimated that a total of 27 people lost their lives during the Madhesh campaign. Moreover, there was no record kept of the destruction of the public and private properties during the movement.[31] The Madhesh movement brought to attention the

29 See Govinda Neupane, *op. cit.* note 27; Dilli R. Dahal, Yogendra B. Gurung, Kamala Hemchuri, Bidha Acharya & Dharma Swarnkar, *"National Dalit Strategy Report: A Situational Analysis and Strategy Report on Dalits"*, (Prepared for National Planning Commission, Action Aid Nepal, CARE Nepal and Save the Children US, Kathmandu 2002).

30 The total land area covers about 23 percent of the total area of Nepal (147181 sq. km).

31 See Support Nepal, *"Issues of Madhesh"*, Support Nepal 2007, available at:

regional issues of social disparities and discrimination.

A. Demographic and economic condition of Madhesh / Terai

According to the population census of 2001, 31.03 percent of the country's total population (23.15 million) lived in Madhesh /Terai districts. There are about 50 castes/ethnic groups in the Madhesh/Terai.[32]

Table 8: Demographic composition of Caste/Ethnic groups in Nepal (2001)[33]

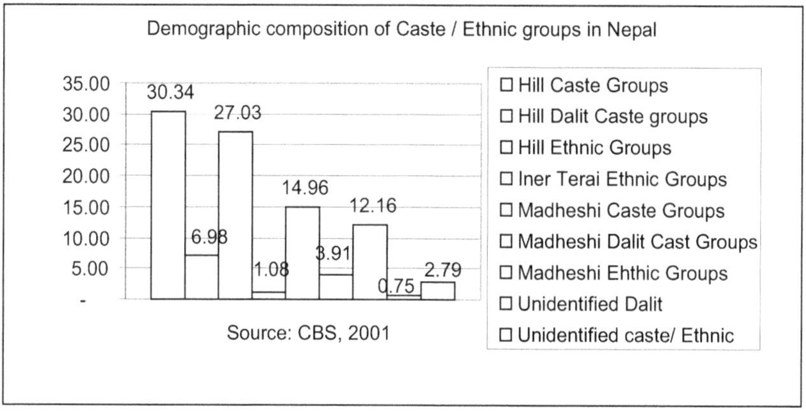

The human development indicator shows that there are regional disparities. The Madhesh/Terai is in the second position of the three geographical regions of Nepal. According to Human Development Report 2001 and 2009, the human development indicators for the mountain region are 0.386, 0.434, hill region 0.512, 0.543 and Terai region 0.478, 0.494 respectively. There are numerous minorities groups in the Mahdesh/Terai. The minorities and women have the lowest status in education, health and participation in government institutions. Moreover, Table 7 shows that the representation of the people from Madhesh is lower in the decision-making positions compared to Brahmin and Chetri and Newar; the participation, however, is better than the indigenous and Dalit population. Moreover, the participation of the Madheshi people in the security forces (Army and Police) is negligible.

---

http://www.supportnepal.org/publications.html

32 The Madhesh/ Terai ethnic groups are Kishan, Gangai, Jhangar, Tajpuria, Tharu, Danuwar, Dhanuk, Dhimal, and Meche, Koche, Satar etc. The higher caste groups are Yadav, Brahmin, Sharma, Rajput, Marwari, etc; there are also numbers of Dalit caste groups which are most marginalized in the Madhesh/Terai.

33 See Central Bureau of Statistics (CBS), *op. cit.* note 15.

Table 9: Incidence of poverty by geographical regions (1996)[34]

Ecological regions	*Percentage of population below poverty line*
Mountain	N/A
Hills	21.3
Madhesh	28.7
Nepal	24.9

The table above shows that people living below the poverty line is 21.3 percent. The Madhesh/Terai is a more prosperous region compared to the Hills, where the level of poverty is below the national level. The government tried to address the question of citizenship in Terai. The open border with the neighbouring country India and its' complex ethnic diversity also raised difficulties in addressing the question of citizenship for the indigenous people of Terai. The citizenship card[35] is a precondition to own property as well as to participate in politics. The state policy is discriminatory towards indigenous people living in Terai. In this context, the Madhises (residents of the Terai region) have struggled to get the citizenship card.

V. Religious Minorities in Nepal

Nepal is a multi-religious country. According to the 2001 population census, there are 11 religious groups. Nepal was a Hindu Kingdom till 2006. The House of Representatives (HoR) declared Nepal a secular nation-state on 18 May 2006. Some Hindu religious organizations objected to the declaration. Moreover, the World Hindu Federation[36] continues to raise the issue of religion. They demand a Hindu nation-state on a traditional basis.

Table 10: Population by Religion[37]

Religions	*Total Number*	*Percentage*
Hindu	18,330,868	80.62
Buddhism	2,442,526	10.74
Islam	954,024	4.20
Kirat	818,106	3.60
Jain	4,109	0.02
Christian	101,977	0.45
Sikha	5,890	0.03
Garute	1,480	0.01
Tapjura	2,817	0.01
Bahai	1,211	0.01
Others	78,994	0.35
Total	*22,736,934*	*100.00*

34 See Madheshee People's Right Forum (MPRF), *"Conspiracy Against Madhesh: Subversion of Democracy, Racial Discrimination, Internal Colonization, Aggression"*, (MPRF Kathmandu 2005).
35 The government provides a National Identity Card at 16 years of age to every citizen. It is an essential document to get jobs or driving license and enable the purchase of land etc.
36 The World Hindu Federation promotes the values of the Hindu religion (Biswa Hindu Parishad).
37 See Central Bureau of Statistics (CBS), *op. cit.* note 15.

Article 23 of the 2007 Interim Constitution (IC) guarantees religious freedom. However, in Article 23 (1) the Constitution clearly mentions that religious conversion is prohibited. According to Article 23 (2) of the IC, religious institutions can own properties. In addition, the government used to declare official holidays on Hindu festivals such as Falgun Purnima, Krishna Asthami, Dasain and Tihar etc. After the declaration of the secular state, the government declares holidays on other religious festivals too, for instance on Lhosar (a Buddhist new year), Christmas, Eid (Muslim festival), Maghi (Tharu festival), Chat (Madheshi community) and Ubhauli (Rai/Kirat festival).

The Hindu religion is in a dominant position compared to other religious beliefs/groups in Nepal. Hindu institutions such as temples, schools and universities used to receive grants from the government. The government did not provide financial or material support to other religious institutions such as madrasas or churches. In this context, Muslim and Christian communities have been demanding burial sites in Kathmandu. The two communities are purchasing their own burial sites as the government did not allocated space for them. In addition, the Dalits, as part of the Hindu religion, have not been allowed to enter the temples for prayer. To redress this situation, the government should treat all the religious groups on the basis of equality and non-discrimination principles as mentioned in the 2007 Interim Constitution.

VI. Linguistic Minorities in Nepal

The 2001 population census categorized 96 languages. A total of 48.61 percent of the population speaks the Nepali language. The second language spoken by number of speakers is Maithili with 12.3 percent. The speakers of Bhojpuri, Tharu, Tamang, Newar and Magar are spoken by 7.53, 5.86, 5.19, 3.63, 3.39 and 2.47 percent of the population, respectively. The groups make up less than 1 percent s. Some of the languages, such as Kusunda and Raute, are in a process of extinction: these minority communities do not have written scripts and the language is based on oral practices. The Nepali language became the lingua franca of the region west of Kathmandu in the 14th century and through the entire country since the 18th century. The adoption of Nepali as the national language of Nepal indeed favoured its native speakers to the detriment of non-Nepali speaking peoples, including the Newari-speakers of the Kathmandu valley.[38] The high caste Brahmin and Chettri have largely benefited by the declaration of Nepali as the official language of Nepal.

Table 11: Languages spoken by the population of Nepal (2001)[39]

Language	*Population*	*Percentage*
Nepali	11.053.255	48.61
Maithili	2.797.582	12.30
Bhojpuri	1.712.536	7.53

38 See Balkrishna Mabuhang *"Situation of Rights of Minorities in Nepal: Indigenous Peoples Perspectives"*, workshop paper presented at First South Asian Workshop on Combating Racism, Xenophobia and Discrimination against Ethnic Minorities and Indigenous People, Hotel Himalaya, Lalitpur 15-25 May 2004.

39 See Central Bureau of Statistics (CBS), *op. cit.* note 15.

Tharu	1.331.546	5.86
Tamang	1.179.145	5.19
Newar	825.458	3.63
Magar	770.116	3.39
Awadi	560.744	2.47
Bantawa	371.056	1.63
Gurung	338.925	1.49
Limbu	333.633	1.47
Bajjika	237.947	1.05
Urdu	174.840	0.77
Rajbansi	129.829	0.57
Sherpa	129.771	0.57
Hindi	105.765	0.47
Others	684.786	3.01
Total	*22.736.934*	*100.00*
Total languages classified : 93		

The Nepali language has played a pivotal role in the nationalization process. The constitution of 1990 recognized Nepali as the official language and all the other languages spoken in Nepal as national languages.[40] Similarly, Article 5(2) Interim Constitution of 2007 mentioned that Nepali will be the official language of Nepal. However, Article 5(1) recognizes all languages spoken in Nepal as national languages of the country. Similarly, Article 5(3) sanctions the use of mother tongues as official languages in local bodies and offices; the government is instructed to translate them into Nepali and keep the record for official purposes.

The medium of instruction in all school levels is Nepali. Children of minority communities are thereby particularly affected by the language policy of the government. In this context, the Ministry of Education has stated that almost all children who have dropped out of school are of indigenous nationality and other marginalized groups.[41] The major causes for the dropping out are related to the use of Nepali as the language of instruction. Similarly, children face problems due to the use of text books written in the Nepali language.

VII. Access to and Control over Resources

The access to resources is one of the key issues in the current political debate. Here too, Indigenous/Janajati and Dalit groups are marginalized.

A. Indigenous / Janajati

The Indigenous/Janajati faced difficulties after the state imposed the land distribution policy. The traditionally communally owned and utilized land of these peoples, especially of the Tamang, Dunuwar, Sunuwar, Majhi, Chepang, Hayu, Sherpa,

40 See Article 6 of the 1990 Constitution of Nepal.
41 See Education for All 2004-2009: Core Document, prepared by Ministry of Education (MOE), November 2003.

Kumal, Lepcha, and Rai was known as Kipat. The Kipat means that the land is communally owned and the natural resources within it, too. This is indicative of the territorial rights of a group of peoples or community. However, the Kipat land was confiscated during the unification of the country, particularly after the Land Reform Act of 1964.[42] The Indigenous people have been displaced due to the manipulation of land-ownership and resources. The major source of sustenance for Indigenous people is the agricultural system, but because of migration and land fragmentation the land holding of Indigenous people has decreased.

Furthermore, traditional professions have stopped being economically viable and alternative options are too few. Traditional knowledge, skills and techniques of Adivasis/Janajatis are vanishing, and there has been no effort made for their protection and support.

B. Dalits

Due to the continued practice of being Untouchable, most of the Dalits are deprived from access to and control over economic and other resources. Displacement from traditional occupations and a lack of employment opportunities in both agricultural and non-agricultural sectors are common problems of Dalits. Jha has estimated that about 68 percent of Dalits live below the absolute poverty line; among the total Nepalese population who live below the absolute poverty line most of them are Dalits.[43] Dalits suffer from the high rates of unemployment. There is no doubt whatsoever that Dalits are rich in skills related to their traditional occupations however, the processes of modernization or westernization, urbanization, globalization and liberalization that have been unfolding in the last five decades have further marginalized knowledge, skills and products based on the Dalits' traditional occupations. As early as 1998, Jha noted that the Hill Dalits such as Kami, Damai, Sarki and Gaine and Madhesi Dalits such as Tatma, Khatbe, Mushar and Dom lost the market for their traditional skills and products.[44] Such marginalization processes have pushed them to rely on agricultural and non-agricultural work, but there too they have few chances of finding employment. In such a situation Dalits become the hardest hit victims of poverty.

For the middle and lower class people, ownership of land means self-employment and non-ownership means unemployment. Data on Dalits' land ownership in Table 12 below reveals that 23 percent are landless, 48.7 percent own less than five ropanies (1 ropani is equal to 508.7 square metres), 15.6 percent own six to 10 ropanies, 9.6 percent own 10 to 20 ropanies and 3.1 percent own more than 20 ropanies of land. Furthermore, the lack of land ownership and the caste-imposed ban of purchasing milk produced by Dalits have made it impossible for the Dalits to engage in animal husbandry.[45]

---

42 See Lionel Caplan, *"Land and Social Change in East Nepal. A Study of Hindu Indigenous Relations"*, (Himal Books, Kathmandu 1970).

43 See Haribansha Jha, *"A Case Study of Selected VDCs of Saptari Districts of Nepal"*, (Action-Aid, Kathmandu 1998).

44 *Ibid.*, 4.

45 See Feminist Dalit Organization (FEDO), *"Dalits of Nepal - Issues and Challenges"*, (FEDO Lalitpur 2002), 84.

Table 12: Land ownership of the Dalits (2002)[46]

Dalit Caste	*Land ownership Status (%)*					
	Landless	Less than 5 Ropanies	6-10 Ropanies	11-20 Ropanies	More than 20 Ropanies	Total Cases
Kami	11.2	46.5	18.8	17.1	6.5	170
Damai	28.8	55.1	11.5	3.2	1.3	156
Sarki	7.6	47.8	24.2	16.7	3.8	157
Badi	39.1	39.1	13.0	4.3	4.3	46
Dhobi	33.3	66.7				3
Doom	88.2	11.8				17
Gaine	41.2	45.1	9.8	3.9		51
Hudke	100.0					8
Kasai	23.5	73.5	2.9			34
Musahar	33.3	55.6		11.1		9
Pode	21.7	56.5	21.7			23
Total	23.0	48.7	15.6	9.6	3.1	674

The finding of 2004 NDC Baseline Survey shows that more than half of the Terai based Dalits (53.03 percent) are landless.[47] Dalits, as a community, are the poorest: the average land owning per household among the Dalits is 2.46 ropani of khet (irrigated land) and 4.5 ropani of pakho (dry upland land). Landlessness is acute among all Dalit groups, and especially among the Terai Dalits.

VIII. Social Movements of Minorities in Nepal

The social movements of minorities started following the advent of democracy in 1990. The government allowed the registration of non-governmental organizations (NGOs). Minority groups and indigenous peoples then organized themselves under the umbrella of NGOs. Through this, the Indigenous/Janajatis movement has been able to force the government to recognize their demand for recognition. Similarly, the women's movement for equality gained pace and forced political parties to provide reservations quota for women. The government and NGOs encouraged girls to attend schools and universities. The government also brought a policy of inclusion toward women into the government services.

Nepal was a centralized state following unification. However, the decentralization programme launched by the government could not address the issues of inclusion of marginalized groups such as indigenous people, women and Dalits. The movement of different segments of people such as Indigenous people, Dalits and women forced to accept the proposal of state restructuring by political parties. As a result, Nepal's parliament agreed to restructure the country and declared Nepal a federal republic. The Constituent Assembly (CA) then formed the Committee on State Restructuring which proposed the creation of 14 provinces / states. The basis of such a reorganization of the state is still debated and some political parties are hesitant to restructure the country on the basis of ethnicity. Scholars and political parties

46 *Ibid.*, 83.
47 See National Dalit Commission (NDC), Baseline Survey Report, 2004.

discussed the possibility of restructuring the country on the basis of ethnicity, regional identity, language and territorial configuration.

In this context, minorities and indigenous peoples sought for the creation of inclusive democratic institutions to protect their fundamental rights. The major demand of the indigenous people are an independent commission for Janajati/Indigenous people, recognition of the mother tongue (linguistic rights), a policy review to guarantee the continuous process of inclusion of Janajati/Indigenous people into the government services and the preservation of traditional knowledge and skills,[48] as well as to abide by International Labour Organization (ILO) Convention 169 on Indigenous and Tribal Peoples. The Indigenous /Janajati sought a federal state with self-determination: organizations such as Limbuwan and Khambuwan (Eastern part of Nepal) demanded federal states with the right to self-determination.

In 2009 the Dalits raised their voices asking for the state authorities to respect the rights of the marginalized communities. Their demands were focused on minority representation in the government, equality, prohibition of the concept of being untouchable and racial discrimination, reservation quota in education, health and employment, the creation of social security for Dalits and the setting up of a Dalit Commission. Moreover, they have asked for the practice of being classed as untouchable to be banned completely.[49] In addition, Dalits have asked to be included into the upcoming Constitution of the Federal Republic of Nepal.

Meanwhile, the Madhesh/Terai group was neglected by the Kathmandu based rulers. Furthermore, due to the proximity to India, the Madheshi communities were discriminated on the basis of allegedly harbouring anti-nationalist feelings. Whilst the people from the Madhesh/Terai have struggled to gain citizenship certificates, their conditions have not been addressed since the birth of Nepali democracy in 1990. The grievances of the Madhesi people have increased. However, the voices of protest were not organized. The internal armed conflict (between the government of Nepal and Maoists) also did not provide ample opportunity to stage an organized protest. Only following the signature of the peace agreement between the Government and the Maoists were the Madhesh able to formulate their demands in an organized manner. Some of the groups, for instance the Janatantrik Terai Mukti Morcha (the Terai Peoples Liberation Front - JTMM), have turned to arms and are still fighting for the autonomy of the Terai region. However, the Madheshi Janadhikar Forum, the Nepal Sadvawana and Terai Loktantik Party have called for the recognition of the identity of Madheshi people; the creation of a single provinces of Madhesh, e.g. from the East Mechi river to the West Mahakali river; the right to self-determination; the provision of citizenship and the adherence to a three language policy; the cessation of the deforestation of the Terai region and the end of all racial discrimination against the people of Madhesh.[50] Except for some groups, the Madhesh movement has brought attention to the issues of the Madheshi by non-violent means.

---

48 The demand presented to the government of Nepal. Translated from the Daily News paper *The Kantipur* of 8 August 2007.

49 See Suvash Darnal, *op. cit.* note 18.

50 See Madheshee People's Right Forum (MPRF), *op. cit.* note 33.

IX. CONCLUSION

The Indigenous/Janajati, Dalits, and Madheshi have been dominated and discriminated against by the highly centralized state rulers (i.e. Chetri and Brahmins). As a result of direct and indirect discrimination, minorities were in a backward position. After the birth of democracy in 1990, minorities started to organize themselves and raised their voices for equal participation in governance. However, the political parties did not pay proper attention to their plight. In the meantime, the CPN-M also raised the issue of discrimination and the domination of certain groups, particularly Bhahunbadi and Chettri with the support from the Janajati/Indigenous people of Western Nepal. Furthermore, the Maoists are in favour of the creation of autonomous regions on the basis of ethnicity. Similarly, the issues were raised by NGOs as well. However, the voices of the Dalits and Madheshi were not listened to and were largely neglected during the time of the Maoist insurgency. The government initiatives were not effective to address these issues. The minorities initiated non-violent protests and pressurised the government to address their problems. The minority groups also joined hands with civil society, political parties and other actors to highlight minority issues. As a result of the continuous struggle, the government recognized the genuine problems, formulated a new policy and omitted discriminatory policies.

The upcoming constitution of the Federal Republic of Nepal should deal with the issues of a multicultural society. The new Constitution should address the issues of regional disparities and the discrimination on minorities. In addition, the government should discard discriminatory laws and policies, and process a real integration of minorities on the basis of respect and recognition.

CHAPTER 5

Human and Minority Rights in Bangladesh

Dr. Borhan Uddin Khan[*] & *Muhammad Mahbubur Rahman*[**]

I. INTRODUCTION

Human and minority rights situation of any country, these days, hardly misses the scrutiny of observers – from home and abroad. Bangladesh is no exception in this regard. The situation in Bangladesh is regularly portrayed in so many reports and studies originating from different states, NGOs, academics and activists.[1] As an addition to this huge collection of country study on Bangladesh's human and minority rights situation that mostly concentrate on cataloguing human and minority rights abuses committed and tolerated by state, the present paper rather attempts to view the situation from an overview perspective.

II. NORMATIVE FRAMEWORK OF HUMAN RIGHTS

Bangladesh is party to seven of the core nine international human rights treaties.[2] Bangladesh's participation to these international instruments began in 1979 when it

---

[*] Professor and Dean, Faculty of Law, University of Dhaka, Bangladesh.

[**] Assistant Professor, Department of Law, University of Dhaka, Bangladesh.

1 For some recent country study on human and minority rights situation in Bangladesh, see US Department of State, *"2009 Human Rights Report: Bangladesh"*, available at: http://www.state.gov/g/drl/rls/hrrpt/2009/sca/136085.htm (last accessed on 22 June 2010); Aio o Salish Kendra (ASK), *"Human Rights in Bangladesh 2008"*, (ASK, Dhaka 2009); Odhikar, *"Human Rights Report 2009: Odhikar Report on Bangladesh"*, (Odhikar, Dhaka 2010).

2 The core nine international human rights treaties comprise of: *International Covenant on Civil and Political Rights* [G.A. res. 2200A (XXI), 21 U.N. GAOR Supp. (No. 16) at 52, U.N. Doc. A/6316 (1966), 999 U.N.T.S. 171, entered into force March 23, 1976], hereinafter referred as 'CCPR'; *International Covenant on Economic, Social and Cultural Rights* [G.A. res. 2200A (XXI), 21 U.N.GAOR Supp. (No. 16) at 49, U.N. Doc. A/6316 (1966), 993 U.N.T.S. 3, entered into force January 3, 1976], hereinafter referred as 'CESCR'; *International Convention on the Elimination of All Forms of Racial Discrimination* [G.A. res. 2106 (XX), Annex, 20 U.N. GAOR Supp. (No. 14) at 47, U.N. Doc. A/6014 (1966), 660 U.N.T.S. 195, entered into force January 4, 1969], hereinafter referred as 'CERD'; *Convention on the Elimination of All Forms of Discrimination against Women* [G.A. res. 34/180, 34 U.N. GAOR Supp. (No. 46) at 193, U.N. Doc. A/34/46, entered into force September 3, 1981], hereinafter referred as 'CEDAW'; *Convention against Torture and Other Cruel, Inhuman or Degrading Treatment or* Punishment [G.A. res. 39/46, annex, 39 U.N. GAOR Supp. (No. 51) at 197, U.N. Doc. A/39/51 (1984), entered into force June 26, 1987], hereinafter referred as 'CAT'; Convention on the Rights of the Child [G.A. res. 44/25, annex, 44 U.N. GAOR Supp. (No. 49) at 167, U.N. Doc. A/44/49 (1989), entered into force September 2, 1990], hereinafter referred as 'CRC'; International Convention on the Protection of the Rights of All Migrant Workers and Members of Their Families [G.A. res. 45/158, annex, 45 U.N. GAOR Supp. (No. 49A) at 262, U.N. Doc. A/45/49 (1990), entered into force on July 1 2003], hereinafter referred as 'CRMW'; *Convention on the Protection and Promotion of the Rights and Dignity of Persons with Disabilities* [G.A. Res. 61/106, Annex I, U.N. GAOR, 61st Sess., Supp. No. 49, at 65, U.N. Doc. A/61/49 (2006), entered into force on May 2 2008], hereinafter referred as 'CRPD'; *International Convention for the Protection of All Persons from Enforced Disappearance* [G.A. res. 61/177, U.N. Doc. A/RES/61/177 (2006), yet to come into force], hereinafter referred as 'CPED'.

acceded to the CERD without any reservation or declaration. In 1984, Bangladesh acceded to the CEDAW but made reservation to Articles 2, 13(a), 16(1)(c) and 16(1)(f) on the ground of conflict with *Sharia* law based on Holy *Quran* and *Sunnah*.[3] However, on 23 July 1997, it withdrew its reservation on Articles 13(a) and 16(1)(f). While ratifying the CRC in 1990, Bangladesh made reservation to Article 14(1) and declared that Article 21 would apply subject to the existing laws and practices in Bangladesh.[4] Although Bangladesh offered no official reasoning as to such reservation and declaration, it is understandable that the concept of child's freedom of religion and the arrangement of child adoption – arguably not consistent with *Sharia*

---

3 Article 2 of the CEDAW reads: "States Parties condemn discrimination against women in all its forms, agree to pursue by all appropriate means and without delay a policy of eliminating discrimination against women and, to this end, undertake: (a) To embody the principle of the equality of men and women in their national constitutions or other appropriate legislation if not yet incorporated therein and to ensure, through law and other appropriate means, the practical realization of this principle; (b) To adopt appropriate legislative and other measures, including sanctions where appropriate, prohibiting all discrimination against women; (c) To establish legal protection of the rights of women on an equal basis with men and to ensure through competent national tribunals and other public institutions the effective protection of women against any act of discrimination; (d) To refrain from engaging in any act or practice of discrimination against women and to ensure that public authorities and institutions shall act in conformity with this obligation; (e) To take all appropriate measures to eliminate discrimination against women by any person, organization or enterprise; (f) To take all appropriate measures, including legislation, to modify or abolish existing laws, regulations, customs and practices which constitute discrimination against women; (g) To repeal all national penal provisions which constitute discrimination against women". Article 13(a) of the CEDAW reads: "States Parties shall take all appropriate measures to eliminate discrimination against women in other areas of economic and social life in order to ensure, on a basis of equality of men and women, the same rights, in particular: (a) The right to family benefits". Article 16(1)(c) of the CEDAW reads: "States Parties shall take all appropriate measures to eliminate discrimination against women in all matters relating to marriage and family relations and in particular shall ensure, on a basis of equality of men and women: [...] (c) The same rights and responsibilities during marriage and at its dissolution". Article 16(1)(f) of the CEDAW reads: "States Parties shall take all appropriate measures to eliminate discrimination against women in all matters relating to marriage and family relations and in particular shall ensure, on a basis of equality of men and women: [...] (f) The same rights and responsibilities with regard to guardianship, wardship, trusteeship and adoption of children, or similar institutions where these concepts exist in national legislation; in all cases the interests of the children shall be paramount".

4 Article 14(1) of the CRC says: "States Parties shall respect the right of the child to freedom of thought, conscience and religion". Article 21 reads: "States Parties that recognize and/or permit the system of adoption shall ensure that the best interests of the child shall be the paramount consideration and they shall: (a) Ensure that the adoption of a child is authorized only by competent authorities who determine, in accordance with applicable law and procedures and on the basis of all pertinent and reliable information, that the adoption is permissible in view of the child's status concerning parents, relatives and legal guardians and that, if required, the persons concerned have given their informed consent to the adoption on the basis of such counselling as may be necessary; (b) Recognize that inter-country adoption may be considered as an alternative means of child's care, if the child cannot be placed in a foster or an adoptive family or cannot in any suitable manner be cared for in the child's country of origin; (c) Ensure that the child concerned by inter-country adoption enjoys safeguards and standards equivalent to those existing in the case of national adoption; (d) Take all appropriate measures to ensure that, in inter-country adoption, the placement does not result in improper financial gain for those involved in it; (e) Promote, where appropriate, the objectives of the present article by concluding bilateral or multilateral arrangements or agreements, and endeavour, within this framework, to ensure that the placement of the child in another country is carried out by competent authorities or organs".

law – were the deciding factor behind such reservation and declaration. Bangladesh acceded to the CAT in 1998. However, as to Article 14(1) of the CAT that provides for guaranteed right of a torture victim to fair and adequate compensation,[5] Bangladesh made a declaration that undermines the essence of the provision.[6] This declaration having no official reasoning can be interpreted as a defensive strategy of Bangladesh, given its not-so-strong economic bases, not to accept an international norm at the cost of economic burden. In 1999, while acceding to the CESCR, Bangladesh made declaration with respect to Article 1 and thus qualified its recognition of self-determination right of peoples,[7] Articles 2 and 3 to qualify the covenant requirement relating to gender equality,[8] Articles 7 and 8 to limit its obligation regarding labour rights,[9] and Articles 10 and 13 to make application of

---

5 Article 14(1) reads: "Each State Party shall ensure in its legal system that the victim of an act of torture obtains redress and has an enforceable right to fair and adequate compensation, including the means for as full rehabilitation as possible. In the event of the death of the victim as a result of an act of torture, his dependants shall be entitled to compensation".

6 The Declaration reads: "The Government of the People's Republic of Bangladesh will apply article 14 para 1 in consonance with the existing laws and legislation in the country".

7 Article 1 reads: "(1) All peoples have the right of self-determination. By virtue of that right they freely determine their political status and freely pursue their economic, social and cultural development. (2) All peoples may, for their own ends, freely dispose of their natural wealth and resources without prejudice to any obligations arising out of international economic co-operation, based upon the principle of mutual benefit, and international law. In no case may a people be deprived of its own means of subsistence. (3) The States Parties to the present Covenant, including those having responsibility for the administration of Non-Self-Governing and Trust Territories, shall promote the realization of the right of self-determination, and shall respect that right, in conformity with the provisions of the Charter of the United Nations". The declaration made by Bangladesh reads: "It is the understanding of the Government of the People's Republic of Bangladesh that the words "the right of self-determination of Peoples" appearing in this article apply in the historical context of colonial rule, administration, foreign domination, occupation and similar situations".

8 Regarding gender equality, Article 2(2) reads: "The States Parties to the present Covenant undertake to guarantee that the rights enunciated in the present Covenant will be exercised without discrimination of any kind as to race, colour, sex, language, religion, political or other opinion, national or social origin, property, birth or other status". Article 3 runs: "The States Parties to the present Covenant undertake to ensure the equal right of men and women to the enjoyment of all economic, social and cultural rights set forth in the present Covenant". The declaration made by Bangladesh reads: "The Government of the People's Republic of Bangladesh will implement articles 2 and 3 in so far as they relate to equality between man and woman, in accordance with the relevant provisions of its Constitution and in particular, in respect to certain aspects of economic rights viz. law of inheritance".

9 Article 7 of the CESR reads: "The States Parties to the present Covenant recognize the right of everyone to the enjoyment of just and favourable conditions of work which ensure, in particular: (a) Remuneration which provides all workers, as a minimum, with: (i) Fair wages and equal remuneration for work of equal value without distinction of any kind, in particular women being guaranteed conditions of work not inferior to those enjoyed by men, with equal pay for equal work; (ii) A decent living for themselves and their families in accordance with the provisions of the present Covenant; (b) Safe and healthy working conditions; (c) Equal opportunity for everyone to be promoted in his employment to an appropriate higher level, subject to no considerations other than those of seniority and competence; (d) Rest, leisure and reasonable limitation of working hours and periodic holidays with pay, as well as remuneration for public holidays". Article 8 of the CESR reads: " (1) The States Parties to the present Covenant undertake to ensure: (a) The right of everyone to form trade unions and join the trade union of his choice, subject only to the rules of the organization concerned, for the promotion and protection of his economic and social interests. No restrictions may be placed on the

these provisions[10] conditioned by national resources and development plans.

---

exercise of this right other than those prescribed by law and which are necessary in a democratic society in the interests of national security or public order or for the protection of the rights and freedoms of others; (b) The right of trade unions to establish national federations or confederations and the right of the latter to form or join international trade-union organizations; (c) The right of trade unions to function freely subject to no limitations other than those prescribed by law and which are necessary in a democratic society in the interests of national security or public order or for the protection of the rights and freedoms of others; (d) The right to strike, provided that it is exercised in conformity with the laws of the particular country. (2) This article shall not prevent the imposition of lawful restrictions on the exercise of these rights by members of the armed forces or of the police or of the administration of the State. (3) Nothing in this article shall authorize States Parties to the International Labour Organisation Convention of 1948 concerning Freedom of Association and Protection of the Right to Organize to take legislative measures which would prejudice, or apply the law in such a manner as would prejudice, the guarantees provided for in that Convention". The declaration made by Bangladesh reads: "The Government of the People's Republic of Bangladesh will apply articles 7 and 8 under the conditions and in conformity with the procedures established in the Constitution and the relevant legislation of Bangladesh".

10 Article 10 of the CESR reads: "The States Parties to the present Covenant recognize that: (1) The widest possible protection and assistance should be accorded to the family, which is the natural and fundamental group unit of society, particularly for its establishment and while it is responsible for the care and education of dependent children. Marriage must be entered into with the free consent of the intending spouses. (2) Special protection should be accorded to mothers during a reasonable period before and after childbirth. During such period working mothers should be accorded paid leave or leave with adequate social security benefits. (3) Special measures of protection and assistance should be taken on behalf of all children and young persons without any discrimination for reasons of parentage or other conditions. Children and young persons should be protected from economic and social exploitation. Their employment in work harmful to their morals or health or dangerous to life or likely to hamper their normal development should be punishable by law. States should also set age limits below which the paid employment of child labour should be prohibited and punishable by law". Article 13 of the CESR reads: "(1) The States Parties to the present Covenant recognize the right of everyone to education. They agree that education shall be directed to the full development of the human personality and the sense of its dignity, and shall strengthen the respect for human rights and fundamental freedoms. They further agree that education shall enable all persons to participate effectively in a free society, promote understanding, tolerance and friendship among all nations and all racial, ethnic or religious groups, and further the activities of the United Nations for the maintenance of peace. (2) The States Parties to the present Covenant recognize that, with a view to achieving the full realization of this right: (a) Primary education shall be compulsory and available free to all; (b) Secondary education in its different forms, including technical and vocational secondary education, shall be made generally available and accessible to all by every appropriate means, and in particular by the progressive introduction of free education; (c) Higher education shall be made equally accessible to all, on the basis of capacity, by every appropriate means, and in particular by the progressive introduction of free education; (d) Fundamental education shall be encouraged or intensified as far as possible for those persons who have not received or completed the whole period of their primary education; (e) The development of a system of schools at all levels shall be actively pursued, an adequate fellowship system shall be established, and the material conditions of teaching staff shall be continuously improved. (3) The States Parties to the present Covenant undertake to have respect for the liberty of parents and, when applicable, legal guardians to choose for their children schools, other than those established by the public authorities, which conform to such minimum educational standards as may be laid down or approved by the State and to ensure the religious and moral education of their children in conformity with their own convictions. (4) No part of this article shall be construed so as to interfere with the liberty of individuals and bodies to establish and direct educational institutions, subject always to the observance of the principles set forth in paragraph I of this article and to the requirement that the education given in such institutions shall conform to such minimum standards as may be laid down by the State". The declaration made by Bangladesh reads:

Bangladesh acceded to the CCPR in 2000, but offered three declarations with respect to Articles 10(3),[11] 11,[12] and 14(3)(d).[13] Bangladesh also made reservation to 14(3)(d), so far it relates to an offender's right to be tried in his presence.[14] In 2007, Bangladesh ratified the CRPD without any reservation or declaration. Although signed in 1998, Bangladesh is yet to ratify the CRMW. The CPED, the only of the core nine international human rights instruments which is not in force, is neither signed nor ratified by Bangladesh.

It is thus evident that most of the treaties of international human rights law are either ratified or acceded to by Bangladesh. Regarding reservations and declarations that amount to qualification of Bangladesh's obligation, we can observe that these are mostly driven by economic and cultural considerations. Scarcity of resources is the main reason behind Bangladesh's declarations on Article 14(1) of the CAT providing

---

"While the Government of the People's Republic of Bangladesh accepts the provisions embodied in articles 10 and 13 of the Covenant in principle, it will implement the said provisions in a progressive manner, in keeping with the existing economic conditions and the development plans of the country".

11 Article 10(3) of the CCPR reads: "The penitentiary system shall comprise treatment of prisoners the essential aim of which shall be their reformation and social rehabilitation. Juvenile offenders shall be segregated from adults and be accorded treatment appropriate to their age and legal status". The declaration made by Bangladesh reads: "So far as the first part of paragraph 3 of Article 10 relating to reformation and social rehabilitation of prisoners is concerned, Bangladesh does not have any facility to this effect on account of financial constraints and for lack of proper logistics support. The last part of this paragraph relating to segregation of juvenile offenders from adults is a legal obligation under Bangladesh law and is followed accordingly".

12 Article 11 of the CCPR reads: "No one shall be imprisoned merely on the ground of inability to fulfil a contractual obligation". The declaration made by Bangladesh reads: "Article 11 providing that 'no one shall be imprisoned merely on the ground of inability to fulfil a contractual obligation,' is generally in conformity with the Constitutional and legal provisions in Bangladesh, except in some very exceptional circumstances, where the law provides for civil imprisonment in case of wilful default in complying with a decree. The Government of People's Republic of Bangladesh will apply this article in accordance with its existing municipal law".

13 Article 14(3)(d) of the CCPR reads: "In the determination of any criminal charge against him, everyone shall be entitled to the following minimum guarantees, in full equality: [...] to be tried in his presence, and to defend himself in person or through legal assistance of his own choosing; to be informed, if he does not have legal assistance, of this right; and to have legal assistance assigned to him, in any case where the interests of justice so require, and without payment by him in any such case if he does not have sufficient means to pay for it". The declaration made by Bangladesh reads: "So far as the provision of legal assistance in paragraph 3(d) of Article 14 is concerned, a person charged with criminal offences is statutorily entitled to legal assistance if he does not have the means to procure such assistance. The Government of the People's Republic of Bangladesh, notwithstanding its acceptance of the principle of compensation for miscarriage of justice, as stipulated in Article 14, paragraph 6, is not in a position to guarantee a comprehensive implementation of this provision for the time being. However, the aggrieved has the right to realise compensation for miscarriage of justice by separate proceedings and in some cases, the court suo moto grants compensation to victims of miscarriage of justice. Bangladesh, however, intends to ensure full implementation of this provision in the near future".

14 For text of Article 14(3)(d) of the CCPR, see, *ibid.* The reservation made by Bangladesh reads: "The Government of the People's Republic of Bangladesh reserves the right not to apply paragraph 3 (d) of Article 14 in view of the fact, that, while the existing laws of Bangladesh provide that, in the ordinary course a person, shall be entitled to be tried in his presence, it also provides for a trial to be held in his absence if he is a fugitive offender, or is a person, who being required to appear before a court, fails to present himself or to explain the reasons for non-appearance to the satisfaction of the court".

for guaranteed compensation for torture-victims, Articles 7 and 8 of the CESCR providing for some aspects of labour rights, Article 10(3) of the CCPR providing for reformative treatment and rehabilitation of prisoners, and Article 14(3)(d) of the CCPR requiring guaranteed right of an accused to legal representation. All these treaty provisions require such a huge burden on the governmental budget that the government of Bangladesh, arguably, cannot afford. Bangladesh's reservation to Articles 2 and 16(1)(c) of the CEDAW, Articles 14(1) and 21 of the CAT and declaration on Articles 2 and 3 of the CESCR are reflective of cultural considerations.[15] On the other hand, declaration on Article 11 and reservation on Article 14(3)(d) of the CCPR dealing with ban on imprisonment for civil liability and ban on trial in absentia respectively can be viewed as a strategy of convenience - not to disturb the long-standing legal procedures and practices of the courts. Once we look at the performance of Bangladesh in discharging the obligations arising out of international human rights instruments, it appears to be very poor. Bangladesh is yet to submit any country report under the CAT, the CCPR, and the CESCR. In case of

---

15 Compatibility of these provisions - dealing with gender equality, freedom of religion for children and legal arrangement of adoption – with *Sharia* law based on *Quran* and *Sunnah* is, in fact, a common concern in almost all the Muslim countries. However, the most voiced against concerns are related to the CEDAW. Since the dominant view of Islamic law scholars is against the gender-equality concept of the CEDAW, most of the Muslim states are very slow and cautious in ratifying the CEDAW. Moreover, among the Muslim states ratifying the CEDAW, reservation on gender-equality provisions appears to be a rule than an exception. Although most of the human rights scholars and activists are questioning the legitimacy of such reservation on the ground of inconsistency with the objects and spirits of the CEDAW, the Muslim states are consistently preferring, with very few exceptions, to avoid any international obligation that are alleged by them to be non-Islamic. On the other hand, a group of human rights scholars are trying either to demonstrate non-compatibility between gender equality and *Sharia* or to advocate reconstruction of *Sharia* in line with international standards. But, the extent to which their efforts have brought about changes in discourses on *Sharia* as applied in Muslim states is open to doubt. It is also relevant here to mention that the CEDAW is one of the most heavily reserved international human rights conventions. Because of its 'cultural and religious hegemonic character', there are some secular cultural objections raised against this instrument as well. Consequently, there are a good number of non-Muslim states putting reservation on the CEDAW provisions on gender equality. So far Bangladesh is concerned, it merits reference that Bangladesh is one of the very first Muslim states to ratify the CEDAW. Women rights activists are consistently arguing for withdrawal of reservation to the CEDAW and have succeeded to some extent as Bangladesh withdrew two reservations in 1997. See in general, Rebecca. J. Cook, "Reservations to the Convention on the Elimination of All Forms of Discrimination Against Women", 30 *Virginia Journal of International Law*, 1989-1990, 643-716; Bharathi Anandhi Venkatraman, "Islamic States and the United Nations Conventions on the Elimination of All Forms of Discrimination against Women: Are the Shari'a and the Convention Compatible?", 44 *American University Law Review*, 1994-1995, 1949-2028; Belinda Clark, "The Vienna Convention Reservations Regime and the Convention on Discrimination against Women", 85(2) *American Journal of International Law*, 1991, 281-321; William A. Schabas, "Reservations to the Convention on the Elimination of All Forms of Discrimination against Women and the Convention on the Rights of the Child", 3 *William & Mary Journal of Women and the Law*, 1997, 79-112; Christine Min Wotipka and Francisco C. Ramirez, "World Society and Human Rights: An Event History Analysis of the Convention on the Elimination of All Forms of Discrimination against Women", in Beth A. Simmons, Frank Dobbin and Geoffrey Garrett (eds.), "*The Global Diffusion of Markets and Democracy*", (Cambridge University Press, Cambridge 2008), 303-343; Nisrine Abiad, "*Sharia, Muslim States and International Human Rights Treaty Obligations: A Comparative Study*", (British Institute of International and Comparative Law, London 2008); Sigma Huda, "Women's Movement in Bangladesh", 5 *Asian Women* 1997, 133-143.

the CERD, the CRC and the CEDAW, although Bangladesh submitted several reports, most of them were long after due-date. Bangladesh has, so far, also largely neglected its legislative obligations under international human rights instruments.[16]

Now the question arises as to what extent such commitments of Bangladesh are to be interpreted in the framework of national constitution and domestic laws of Bangladesh. Human rights agenda had been in the forefront of its liberation struggle. The Proclamation of Independence dated 10 April 1971, which is also called the first interim provisional constitution of the land, indicated willingness of the nation to submit to the obligation of international law. After the emergence of Bangladesh as a sovereign nation, its Constitution was adopted on 4 November 1972 and came into force on 16 December 1972. In this Constitution, the Preamble provides that ". . . it shall be a fundamental aim of the state to realise . . . a society in which the rule of law, fundamental human rights and freedom, . . . will be secured for all citizens". Article 11 envisages that the Republic shall be a democracy in which fundamental human rights and freedoms and respect for the dignity and worth of the human person shall be guaranteed. In article 25 of the Constitution, 'respect for international law' has been figured as a mandatory guide for the state in its international relations. However, despite all these references to 'human rights' and 'respect for international law', the Constitution of Bangladesh, unlike many modern constitutions, maintains a classical 'dualist approach'[17] and accordingly does not acknowledge international human rights laws as a source of municipal law. Consequently, international treaties can become part of the domestic law in Bangladesh only if they are specifically incorporated in the law of the land. In other words, they are not self-operating in Bangladesh, i.e., treaty obligations concluded by Bangladesh cannot *ipso facto* be put into effect unless an enabling legislation is passed or enacted. Furthermore, the Constitution does not contain any specific provision, which obliges the state to implement international treaties.[18]

Because of this classical dualist approach to international standards, it is more profitable – in understanding the normative framework of Bangladesh - to look at the domestic standards of human rights. A humble look at the Constitution of Bangladesh reveals that core human rights norms are incorporated therein under two heads: "Fundamental Principles of State Policy"[19] and "Fundamental Rights".[20] The section

---

16 On legislative obligation under the CAT see, Muhammad Mahbubur Rahman and Sk. Samidul Islam, "Obligation of Bangladesh under Article 4 of the UN Convention Against Torture and Other Cruel, Inhuman or Degrading Treatment or Punishment, 1984: A Performance Audit", 10(1&2) *Bangladesh Journal of Law*, 2006, 119-148.

17 On dualist approach to international law, see Louis Henkin, *International Law: Politics and Values*, (Martinus Nijhoff Publishers, Dordrecht/Boston/London 1995), 64-71; J.G. Starke, "Monism and Dualism in the Theory of International Law", 17 *British Year Book of International Law*, 1936, 66-81; Edwin Borchard, "Relation between International Law and Municipal Law", 27(2) *Virginial Law Review*, 1940, 137-148.

18 For more details, see Mohammad Monirul Azam and Mostafa Mahmud Naser, "Status of International Human Rights Law within the Domestic Jurisdiction: The Context of Bangladesh", 1(2) *Asian Journal of International Law*, 2006, 277-305; Sheikh Hafizur Rahman Karzon and Abdullah Al Faruque, "Status of International Law under the Constitution of Bangladesh: An Appraisal", 3(1) *Bangladesh Journal of Law*, 1999, 23-47.

19 The Constitution of the People's Republic of Bangladesh, Part.II, Articles 8-25.

20 The Constitution of the People's Republic of Bangladesh, Part.III, Articles 26-47A.

on 'Fundamental Rights' includes articles on equality before law,[21] non-discrimination,[22] equality of opportunity in public employment,[23] right to protection of law,[24] right to life and personal liberty,[25] safeguards as to arrest and detention,[26] prohibition of forced labour,[27] protection in respect of trial and punishment,[28] freedom of movement,[29] freedom of assembly,[30] freedom of association,[31] freedom of thought and conscience, and of speech,[32] freedom of profession or occupation,[33] freedom of religion,[34] right to property,[35] protection of home and correspondence,[36] and right to enforce fundamental rights.[37] This catalogue of rights is broadly compatible with almost all the norms of civil and political rights recognized by the 1948 Universal Declaration of Human Rights,[38] and the CCPR. These rights are judicially enforceable.[39] On the other hand, the part II on 'Fundamental Principles of State Policy' includes almost all the norms of economic, social and cultural rights recognized by the CESCR. These rights, however, are not judicially enforceable.[40]

III. Institutional Framework of Human Rights

The Supreme Court of Bangladesh being the guardian of the Constitution is the most important institution in domestic human rights framework.[41] Since fundamental rights are judicially enforceable through constitutional litigation before the Supreme Court, this apex court is mandated to remedy any violation of civil and political rights - that are styled as 'fundamental rights' in the Constitution - of any aggrieved person.[42] There is hardly any doubt that if anyone tries to prove that higher judiciary in Bangladesh enjoys judicial independence, it is more convenient for him to speak more

21 Article 27.
22 Article 28.
23 Article 29.
24 Article 31.
25 Article 32.
26 Article 33.
27 Article 34.
28 Article 35.
29 Article 36.
30 Article 37.
31 Article 38.
32 Article 39.
33 Article 40.
34 Article 41.
35 Article 42.
36 Article 43.
37 Article 44.
38 See United Nations General Assembly Resolution 217A(III), UN Doc. A/810 at 71 (1948). [hereinafter referred as 'UDHR'].
39 See Article 44 read in conjunction with article 102.
40 Article 8(2).
41 The Supreme Court is the apex court of the country. It comprises of two Divisions namely, the Appellate Division and the High Court Division. See, The Constitution of the People's Republic of Bangladesh, Article 94(1).
42 The High Court Division of the Supreme Court of Bangladesh is constitutionally empowered to enforce fundamental rights of any person. See, The Constitution of the People's Republic of Bangladesh, Article 102.

of the stories of enforcement of aggrieved persons' fundamental rights through constitutional litigation. In fact, the Supreme Court of Bangladesh in this regard has a good track record which is broadly credible and frequently acclaimed of. Nevertheless, from a human rights perspective, there are other important criteria to evaluate the judicial performance, especially in the context of Bangladesh. Accordingly, a series of questions confronts the task of reviewing the judicial performance in enforcing human rights standards: "What is the jurisprudence of enforcing international human rights instruments, when the Constitution does not regard them as part of domestic law?", "How and to what extent economic, social and cultural rights are to be enforced, when the Constitution regards them as fundamental principles of state policy that are not judicially enforceable?", "How to extend the protection of fundamental rights to those aggrieved persons who do not have access to the Supreme Court?". In the paragraphs that follows an attempt is made to answer these critical questions.

Although international law is not constitutionally recognized as a part of domestic law, in the early years of the statehood of Bangladesh, the apex court of the country, in the case of *Kazi Mukhlesur Rahman v. Bangladesh*, creatively used relevant international law materials including authors of international repute to draw therefrom 'authoritative support' for its conclusion although its conclusion could reasonably be substantiated on the basis of constitutional interpretation.[43] In a famous personal liberty case - *State v. Deputy Commissioner, Satkhira* - the High Court Division of the Supreme Court of Bangladesh invoked, for the first time in its history, the UDHR and the CRC as an aid to inform its understanding of statutory and constitutional rights.[44] Similarly, in many other cases, particularly since 1990s, the higher courts have demonstrated their consciousness about the relevance of internationally agreed norms of human rights. However, not all these cases have clarified to what extent decisions of the courts were influenced by such references to international standards since most of the cases ultimately relied on domestic laws, and not on international standards, to substantiate the decisions. Critics may argue that use of such references is just a decorative fashion aimed at beautifying the judgments rather than to strengthen human rights jurisprudence. However, these references are positive instances at least for two reasons. Firstly, reference to international human rights law, even when reservoir of national laws is resourceful, shows compliance of municipal laws with international standards and thereby increases the legitimacy and quality of the judicial decision-making. Secondly, this tendency of referring international standards has potentials to gradually lead the courts to a better invocation of international human right laws. Since the late 1990s, the invocation of international human rights instruments including UN Declarations and resolutions or reports of international organizations has turned into a more positive trend. The Appellate Division in the case of *Bangladesh v. Prof. Golam Azam*, drew assistance from some principles of the 1961 Convention on Reduction of Statelessness[45], notwithstanding the fact that the Convention was not ratified by the state.[46] In *Dr. Mohiuddin Farooque v. Bangladesh*,

---

43 26 DLR (1974) (AD) 44.
44 45 DLR (1993) 643.
45 989 U.N.T.S. 175, entered into force on December 13, 1975.
46 46 DLR (1994) (AD) 194.

the Appellate Division invoked the provisions of the Rio Declaration on Environment and Development and refereed to *'Our Common Future'*, the report of the World Commission on Environment and Development, and the UDHR while progressively interpreting the constitutional standing provision in order to extend public interest standing to an environmental rights group.[47] In *Bangladesh Legal Aid and Services Trust (BLAST) v. Bangladesh*, the Court urged the government to frame a code of conduct for the law enforcing agencies on the basis of 'UN Code of Conduct for Law Enforcement Officials', a General Assembly Resolution of 1979, in order to reduce excesses and abuse of power by the law-enforcers.[48] In the case of *Prof. Nurul Islam v. Government of Bangladesh*, to substantiate its decisional logic, the Court not only made references to international instruments creating state responsibility, but also reminded the government of its constitutional obligations.[49] To quote from the judgment: "Article 25(1) of our Constitution casts an obligation upon the State to respect for International Law and the principles enunciated in the United Nations Charter and the WHO resolutions".[50] In *H.M. Ershad v. Bangladesh*, the Appellate Division paves the path for applying norms of international human rights instruments in Bangladesh.[51] In this case although the Appellate Division found a complete answer from the Constitution to support its decision, it clearly registered the possibility of applying international human rights norms to compensate statutory deficiencies or to remove ambiguities in statues.[52] Taking recourse to international human rights standards by the higher courts of Bangladesh is not exclusively limited to constitutional litigations. In *Abdul Jalil v. Sharon Laily Begum*, an ordinary civil claim concerning dispute as to parental custody rights, the Appellate Division referred to the 1959 UN Declaration on the Rights of the Child[53] to interpret the principle of welfare of the children.[54] In a recent case, *The State vs. Md. Roushan Mondal @ Hashem*,[55] the High Court Division while interpreting the 1974 Children Act,[56] a juvenile justice legislation, made an in-depth intellectual investigation into and clarified adequately the domestic relevance of international human rights law and accordingly heavily relied upon international human rights instruments. The judgment referred to the CRC, the CCPR, the United Nations Standard Minimum Rules on the

---

47 49 DLR (1997) (AD) 1.
48 4 BLC (1999) (HCD) 600.
49 52 DLR (2000) (HCD) 413.
50 *Ibid.*
51 21 BLD (2001) (AD) 69.
52 His Lordship B. B. Roy Chowdhury, J. added the following vibrant words: "The national courts should not, [...], straightway ignore the international obligations which a country undertakes. If the domestic laws are not clear enough or there is nothing therein the national courts should draw upon the principle incorporated in the international instruments. But in the cases where the domestic laws are clear and inconsistent with the international obligations of the state concerned, the national courts will be obliged to respect the national laws, but shall draw attention of the law-makers to such inconsistencies."
53 See United Nations General Assembly Resolution 1386 (XIV) of 20 November 1959. 14 U.N. GAOR Supp. (No. 16) at 19, U.N. Doc. A/4354 (1959).
54 18 BLD (1998) (AD) 21.
55 59 DLR (2007) 72.
56 Act No. XXXIX of 1974.

Administration of Juvenile Delinquency (the Beijing Rules)[57] and the United Nations Guidelines for the Prevention of Juvenile Delinquency (the Riyadh Guidelines)[58]. In particular, this case shows an approach of 'harmonious interpretation' between domestic laws and international human rights laws. In a more recent judgment of 2009, the High Court Division observed that: "It is now an accepted rule of judicial construction to interpret municipal law in conformity with international law and conventions when there is no inconsistency between them or there is a void in the domestic law".[59] Thus it appears that the Court is gradually moving forward to enforce international human rights standards in domestic jurisdiction although critics argue for more robust activism on this issue.[60]

Although economic, social and cultural rights are not judicially enforceable according to the domestic constitution, day by day, the judiciary is demonstrating more activism when asked to enforce some basic necessities of life. Creative interpretation of enforceable fundamental rights is paving this way of enforcement, *albeit* limited, of economic, social and cultural rights.[61] Accordingly, in many instances, the Court has enforced the right to accommodation,[62] right to livelihood[63] and protection of environment,[64] although none of them fall under the category of enforceable fundamental rights as articulated in the constitution.

Since a vast majority of people in Bangladesh are either ignorant of their fundamental rights or too poor to enforce their rights, the question of constitutional enforcement of their rights remained in the forefront of legal debates for many years. While the judiciary was traditionally committed to the rigid interpretation on the *locus standi* of a litigant, constitutional litigation for the protection of public interest by a person, who is not aggrieved in the strict sense of term, remained for many years a concept foreign to the constitutional jurisprudence of the Court. In 1996, the case of *Dr. Mohiuddin Farooque v. Bangladesh*, opened up a new frontier - public interest litigation (PIL).[65] Since then, PIL is largely being used to enforce human rights of common people who

---

57 See United Nations General Assembly Resolution 40/33, annex, 40 U.N. GAOR Supp. (No. 53) at 207, U.N. Doc. A/40/53 (1985).

58 See United Nations General Assembly Resolution 45/112, annex, 45 U.N. GAOR Supp. (No. 49A) at 201, U.N. Doc. A/45/49 (1990).

59 See *Bangladesh National Women Lawyers Association (BNWLA) v. Government of Bangladesh and Others*, Writ Petition No. 5916 of 2008 (unreported).

60 See Ridwanul Hoque and Mostafa Mahmud Naser, "The Judicial Invocation of International Human Rights Law in Bangladesh: Questing a Better Approach", 46(2) *Indian Journal of International Law*, 2006, 151-186.

61 On how the Court has used the constitutional provision on fundamental right to life as a site for the creation of new rights and entitlements including economic, social and cultural rights, see Muhammad Mahbubur Rahman, "Right to Life as a Fundamental Right in the Constitutional Framework of India, Bangladesh and Pakistan: An Appraisal", 17(1) *Dhaka University Studies*, Part – F, Journal of the Faculty of Law, 2006, 143-178.

62 See *Ain-O-Salish Kendra (ASK) and others v. Government of Bangladesh and others*, 19 HCD (HCD) (1999) 488; *Modhumala v. Government of Bangladesh*, Writ Petition No. 59 of 1994 (unreported).

63 See *Bangladesh Society for the Enforcement of Human Rights (BSEHR) and others v. Government of Bangladesh and others*, 53 DLR (2001) 1.

64 See *Rajdhani Unnayan Kortripokkho (RAJUK) and another v. Mohshinul Islam and another*, 53 DLR (AD) (2001) 79.

65 49 DLR (1997) (AD) 1.

could not otherwise activate judicial protection of their rights.[66] Moreover, in some instances, the courts are, on their own initiatives, taking responsibility to enforce human rights of vulnerable people.[67]

What is most worrying is that Bangladesh does not have any other strong institutional mechanism, apart from the Supreme Court, to countercheck human rights abuses. Although the Constitution provides for the establishment of an office of ombudsman[68] and a law to set up the office was enacted back in 1980, the people of Bangladesh are consistently being fed by the political parties with their pledges to establish an office of ombudsman. After a decade of long civil society movements for the establishment of a human rights commission and donor groups' pressures to that end, the government finally set up, in 2008, a commission that is hardly visible or active in responding to human rights violations.

IV. Minority Rights Situation

This section attempts to present an overview of the minority rights situation in Bangladesh. Although Bangladesh has a considerable number of religious and ethnic minorities,[69] the Constitution, unlike many other domestic constitutions, does not recognize any minority and therefore allows no special protection or promotion for them. Starting with the conviction that this absence of normative framework is conducive to the violation of minority rights, the following paragraphs concentrate on highlighting the overall situation of religious and ethnic minorities.

According to the latest census report, there are 10.3 percent religious minorities in Bangladesh. They are mainly from Hinduism (9.2 percent), Buddhism (0.7 percent), and Christianity (0.3 percent). There are some other people of different beliefs also, though in a very negligible quantity (0.2 percent).[70] Low intensity violence causing a sense of insecurity is the major problem faced by religious minorities in Bangladesh.[71] In most of the(se) cases, Hindu communities are the primary victims of violence. In particular, during the communal unrest in the neighbouring India and during national election and post-election period, the incidents of violence against Hindu communities

---

66 See generally, Naim Ahmed, "*Public Interest Litigation in Bangladesh: Constitutional Issues and Remedies*", (Bangladesh Legal Aid and Services Trust, Dhaka 1999); Asia Foundation, "*Protecting the Common Good: Successes in Public Interest Litigation*", (The Asia Foundation, Dhaka 2002); Jona Razzaque, "*Public Interest Environmental Litigation in India, Pakistan and Bangladesh*", (Kluwer Publications, The Hague 2004).

67 See Ridwanul Hoque, "*Suo Motu* Jurisdiction as a Tool of Activist Judging: A Survey of Relevant Issues and Constructing a Sensible Defence", 8 *Chittagong University Journal of Law*, 2003, 1-31.

68 Article 77.

69 In Bangladesh perspective, almost all the linguistic minorities are identical with ethnic minorities.

70 See Gobinda Chandra Mandal, "Treatment of Law to the Minorities in Bangladesh: Rhetoric and Reality", in Mizanur Rahman (ed.), "*Human Rights & Corruption*", (Empowerment through Law of the Common People, Dhaka 2007), 219-228, at 220.

71 For a credible account on the situation of religious minorities in Bangladesh see, *Situation in Bangladesh* (Interim report of the Special Rapporteur of the Commission on Human Rights on the elimination of all forms of intolerance and of discrimination based on religion or belief), A/55/280/Add.2, 9 August 2000.

escalate.[72] Occasionally, there are also reported incidents of violence against Christian minorities. Legislation of vested property is another concern for religious minorities, particularly for the Hindu community. After the independence of Bangladesh, all alleged enemy properties and assets were vested in the government of Bangladesh by the 1972 Bangladesh (Vesting of Property and Assets) Order.[73] In many instances, the political and social elites have used this law to dispossess the Hindu minorities from their properties. The disadvantages faced by religious minorities in Bangladesh are manifested in the gradual demographic change in the number of minorities. The proportion of the largest religious minority, the Hindus, has consistently been going down.[74]

In Bangladesh 27 different indigenous or tribal ethnic groups accounting for 1.13 percent of the population are officially recognized, though different organizations claim the number as up to 45.[75] Most of them are concentrated in the Chittagong Hill Tracts (CHT).[76] The history of the indigenous people of CHT during the last century is a history of gradual erosion of autonomy leading to ethnic armed conflict.[77] This erosion of autonomy reached its peak during the drafting of the Constitution of Bangladesh in 1972. To the utmost disappointment of the indigenous people of CHT, the Constitution declared Bangladesh as a unitary state,[78] ruling out the possibility of having a complete autonomy for CHT.[79] Consequently, they started full-fledged armed struggle along Maoist lines.[80] In response to this armed struggle for autonomy, the government of Bangladesh not only resorted to military action to overpower the indigenous community but also adopted an aggressive settlement policy in CHT to

---

72 On the violence against Hindu minority following the national election of 2001 see, Amnesty International, "*Bangladesh: Attacks on Members of the Hindu Minority*", (Amnesty International Doc. ASA 13/006/2001).

73 See Article 2 of the President's Order No.29 of 1972.

74 The head count shows that while the population of Muslims rose by 219.5 percent during 1941-91 that of Hindus increased only by 4.5 percent. According to the 2001 census report, religious minorities in Bangladesh are only 10.3 percent, while they were 12.7 percent and 13.3 percent in census reports of 1991 and 1981 respectively.

75 See Gobinda Chandra Mandal, "Treatment of Law to the Minorities in Bangladesh: Rhetoric and Reality", in Mizanur Rahman (ed.), "*Human Rights & Corruption*", (Empowerment through Law of the Common People, Dhaka 2007), 219-228, at 220.

76 Over the centuries, CHT has been the home of thirteen indigenous ethnic groups - Chakma, Marma, Tripura, Tanchangya, Mro, Murung, Lushai, Khumi, Chak, Khyang, Bawm, Pankhua, and Reang. Of them, Chakmas - accounting for one-half of the ethnic population of CHT - form the largest group followed by Marma and Tripura.

77 See Muhammad Mahbubur Rahman, "Autonomy for Indigenous People of CHT: Aftermath of the 1997 Peace Accord", in Thomas Benedikter (ed.), "*Solving Ethnic Conflict through Self-Governance: A Short Guide to Autonomy in Europe and South Asia*", (EURAC Research, Bozen/Bolzano 2009), 100-103.

78 See Article 1 of the Constitution of the People's Republic of Bangladesh.

79 See Selina Haq and Ehsanul Haque, "*Disintegration Process in Action: The Case of South Asia*", (Bangladesh Institute of Law and International Affairs, Dhaka 1990); Amena Mohsin, "*The Politics of Nationalism: The Case of the Chittagong Hill Tracts Bangladesh*", (University Press Limited, Dhaka 2002).

80 See for details, Asish Nandy, "*The Intimate Enemy: Loss and Recovery of Self Under Colonialism*", (Oxford University Press, Delhi 1983), xv.

outnumber the indigenous people.[81] The successive governments actively resettled non-indigenous Bengalis from plain lands to CHT in exchange for land, cash and other incentives.[82] Accordingly, the demographical composition of the area drastically changed – the Bengali settlers became almost 50 percent of the total population in 1991 from less than 10 percent in 1947.[83] This triggered an ethnic character to the conflict. To pacify this conflict, the successive governments initiated numerous efforts which ultimately succeeded in 1997 when the government of Bangladesh signed a peace accord - Chittagong Hill Tracts Peace Accord (CHT Peace Accord) - with the representative of the indigenous people.[84] In order to strengthen local governance and ensure autonomy for CHT, the peace accord designed a three-tier framework of administration wherein Chittagong Hill Tracts Regional Council would have the central role. However, an assessment on the extent to which various aspects of autonomy for indigenous people of CHT, as was promised in the accord, has been fulfilled to date presenting a frustrating picture.[85] More importantly, the prospect of the accord in ensuring autonomy in the days to come is also challenged by various complicated issues and factors. There is no denying the fact that the 1997 peace accord has ensured a pause on long-standing self-determination armed conflict. However, unless the question of autonomy of CHT, which was the root cause of conflict, is resolved by implementing the peace accord and addressing the issues and challenges concerned with such implementation, it would be unrealistic to expect sustainable peace in CHT. The sooner the provisions of the accord are implemented, the quicker will be the mitigation of many of the existing problems and the elimination of the causes of potential conflict.

Bihari people constitute another important ethnic group in terms of human rights violation. In Bangladeshi parlance, the Urdu-speaking Muslim people who had migrated to the then East Pakistan from Uttar Pradesh, Madhya Pradesh and Rajasthan

---

81 See Raja Devasish Roy, "The Population Transfer Programme of 1980s and the Land Rights of the Indigenous Peoples of the Chittagong Hill Tracts", in Subir Bhaumik, Meghna Guhathakurta and Sabyasachi Basu Ray Chaudhury (eds.), "*Living on the Edge: Essays on the Chittagong Hill Tracts*", (South Asia Forum for Human Rights and Calcutta Research Group, Calcutta 1997), 167-208.

82 See Raja Devasish Roy, "The Discordant Accord: Challenges towards the Implementation of the Chittagong Hill Tracts Accord of 1997", *Journal of Social Studies*, 2003, April–June, 6.

83 According to the 1991 census, the total population of the CHT is 974,465. Of them 501,145 (i.e. 51 percent) are Jumma people and the rest 473,300 (i.e. 49 percent) are Bangladeshi people.

84 For full text of the accord, visit: http://www.chtcommission.org/?page_id=94 (last accessed on 23 June 2010).

85 For an analysis on the implementation of the agreement, see generally, Faustina Pereira, "The Chittagong Hill Tracts Peace Accord and the Long Road to Peace: A Case Study", in Joshua Castellino and Niamh Walsh (eds.), "*International Law and Indigenous Peoples*", (Martinus Nijhoff Publishers, Leiden 2005), 293-302; Amena Mohsin, "*The Chittagong Hill Tracts, Bangladesh: On the Difficult Road to Peace*", (Lynne Rienner Publishers, London 2003); Ishtiaq Jamil and Pranab Kumar Panday, "The Elusive Peace Accord in the Chittagong Hill Tracts of Bangladesh and the Plight of the Indigenous People", 48(4) *Commonwealth & Comparative Politics*, 2008, 464-489; Muhammad Mahbubur Rahman, "Autonomy for Indigenous People of CHT: Aftermath of the 1997 Peace Accord", in Thomas Benedikter (ed.), "*Solving Ethnic Conflict through Self-Governance: A Short Guide to Autonomy in Europe and South Asia*", (EURAC Research, Bozen/Bolzano 2009), 100-103.

are categorized as 'Biharis'.[86] The communal riot of Bihar during 1946-47 led this ethnic community to take refuge in the territory of Bangladesh, a province of the then Pakistan.[87] In the early days of Pakistan, there was confusion as to the legal identity of these people, for instance whether they would be regarded as refugees or voluntary migrants or political asylees or stateless persons. To resolve the confusion, they were granted the citizenship of Pakistan in 1951. Subsequently, because of their active anti-liberation role, the Biharis became subject to widespread political persecution preceding and during the 1971 liberation war of Bangladesh as well as in the aftermath of liberation. Since then, the Biharis are suffering from a crisis of their legal identity and status. When the government of Bangladesh offered them the citizenship of Bangladesh, some 600,000 Biharis accepted the offer while 539,669 registered with the International Committee of the Red Cross (ICRC) opting to return to Pakistan.[88] Thereafter, from 1973 to 1993, some 178,069 Biharis were repatriated to Pakistan.[89] At present, it is generally estimated that there are more than 300,000 Biharis in Bangladesh, half of whom lives in 116 camps all over the country. For several decades the successive governments of Bangladesh have been treating the Biharis who opted for repatriation to Pakistan but are left in Bangladesh as 'refugees', not as 'citizens'. Ultimately, the Supreme Court of Bangladesh had to confirm that Biharis are citizens of Bangladesh and the mere fact that a person opts to migrate to another country cannot takeaway his citizenship.[90] Despite this recognition of identity, Biharis in Bangladesh, particularly those living in camps, are facing social exclusion and severe discrimination in every aspect of life – education, employment, health services, business, access to justice, development, etc. Their living conditions in the camps is not only sub-standards but also inhuman.[91]

V. Violation of Rights: Beyond Denial and Condemnation

Human rights reports on Bangladesh – be it published by US Department of State, international human rights NGOs such as Amnesty International, Human Rights Watch, or local NGOs such as Ain O Salish Kendra (ASK), Odhikar, etc. – highlight several common patters of human rights violations. These include, *inter alia*, extra judicial killing, torture, arbitrary arrest and detention, infringement of freedom of

---

86 See Sultana Nahar, "Biharis in Bangladesh: Present Status, Legal Impediments and Solutions", in Chowdhury R. Abrar (ed.), "*On the Margin: Refugees, Migrants and Minorities*", (Refugee and Migratory Movement Research Unit, Dhaka 2000), 173-183, at 173.

87 See for details, Lord Ennals, "Biharis in Bangladesh: The Third Great Migration?", 8(2) *Journal of Muslim Minority Affairs*, 1987, 238-245.

88 See Iftekharul Bashar, "Unresolved Statelessness: The Case of Biharis in Bangladesh", 10 *Journal of International Affairs*, 2006, 87-116, at 94.

89 See Sumit Sen, "Stateless Refugees and Right to Return: The Bihari Refugees of South Asia", 12(1) *International Journal of Refugee Law*, 2000, 41-70, at 55.

90 See *Mukhter Ahmed v. Government of Bangladesh and others*, 34 DLR (1982) 29; *Abdul Khaleque v. The Court of Settlement and others*, 44 DLR (1992) 273; *Abid Khan and others v. Government of Bangladesh and others*, 55 DLR (2003) 322.

91 For an exclusive account on the socio-economic condition of the Biharis in Bangladesh, see Mizanur Rahman (ed.), "*A Community in Transition: The Biharis in Bangladesh*", (Empowerment through Law of the Common People, Dhaka 2003); B. Whitaker *et al.*, "*The Biharis in Bangladesh*", (Minority Rights Group (MRG), London 1977).

press and freedom of assembly, domestic violence and violation of women's and indigenous people's rights. With very few exceptions, these reports demonstrate a common tendency to target the state and end up in criticizing and blaming the state. This type of unidirectional and predictable conclusion processed through an asocial, acultural and ahistorical investigation very often sweeps the complexities of reality under carpet. On the contrary, the government of Bangladesh always seems ready with its own version of human and minority rights situation that is hardly anything but straightforward denial of the violation incurred. The successive governments are resorting to manipulation of facts and legal processes to hide out many acts that are alleged by civil society and international community as violation of international human rights standards. They hardly take any pro-active actions to minimize or handle rights violation incidents or attempt to rationalize and justify its actions, wherever necessary, by any culture specific or contextualized interpretation of international standards, even when such interpretation is possible within the discourse of international human rights law. This tendency of false denial and cunning engineering on part of a government brings for it a crisis of credibility in the eye of its people and at the same time transmit a sense of human rights concept that is purely absolutist and overtly universal calling for no cultural contextualization. Where's then the way-out? Does this discourse of condemnation and denial contribute anything substantial for the common people who are the ultimate victims of most of the incidents of human rights violation? Probably, not.

The authors contend that most of human and minority rights abuses are consistent in Bangladesh. No clear pattern is evident in terms of the political complexion of the party in power; rather, if any pattern exists, it is in terms of identity and status of victims of such abuse. In most of the cases, the unfortunate victims are from the marginalized sections of the society, persons having notorious criminal records, activists engaged in political opposition. This trend definitely calls for digging deeper into the problem. The design of the present paper does not allow any comprehensive investigation into the root cause of human and minority rights violations in Bangladesh. However, the paper contends that neither the mere denial by the government nor the mere condemnation of the government for human rights violation does unveil the true disease, it just overemphasizes the symptoms. Human rights violation in Bangladesh should not only be seen as a problem of deviation by its state functionaries from their commitment to rights standards, but also have potentials to be interrogated as a consequence of problems in identifying and employing pragmatic and effective norms and strategies for the management of human rights issues. To substantiate this argument, the present section concentrates on the most voiced human rights violation in Bangladesh - extra judicial killing, torture, arbitrary arrest and detention – as a point of reference.[92]

Extra judicial killing, torture, arbitrary arrest and detention - all these are concerned with the management of criminal justice system. Why the government deliberately

---

92 On the extent and intensity of these human rights abuses, see M Rafiqul and S.M. Solaiman, "Torture under Police Remand in Bangladesh: A Culture of Impunity for Gross Violations of Human Rights", 4(2) *Asia-Pacific Journal on Human Rights and the Law*, 2003, 1-27; Human Rights Watch (HRW), *"Ignoring Executions and Torture: Impunity for Bangladesh's Security Forces"*, (HRW, New York 2009).

allow, if not actively encourage, the extra-judicial killing of criminals? Why are law-enforcing authorities not sympathetic to human rights standards while arresting or detaining a person? Why is torture a common strategy employed by police officials? It would be a too simplistic idea to explain these maladies in terms of government's individual or group interests, or law enforcing agencies, or to regard them just as a violation of norms. The historiography of human and minority rights situation in Bangladesh can substantiate the point. We have to look at the late eighteen century, when the British colonial rulers usurped the political power of Bengal and laid the foundation of present-day legal and administrative systems.[93] Before the 1757 Battle of Polashi,[94] the province of Bengal – comprising among others the area of present day Bangladesh – was ruled by local Nowab under the Mughal Empire based in Delhi.[95] The sources at our hands do not permit us to infer, with a reasonable degree of accuracy, the overall human and minority rights situation in pre-colonial Bengal, but definitely enable us to depict the situation, at least partially. During this time, Bengal was the richest province in the Mughal Empire and its people in general had standard socio-economic life.[96] The most common criticism against the legal system of pre-colonial era[97] is that its criminal justice practices varied between two extremes of excessive leniency and intolerable severity.[98] Strict adherence to rigorous law of evidence followed during that time enabled many offenders to escape punishments. On the other hand, once the guilt of an accused was proved, he was subject to severe

---

93 In fact, the political culture derived from the colonial experiences may be a useful starting point for understanding variations in respect for human rights [Neil J. Mitchell and James M. McCormick, "Economic and Political Explanations of Human Rights Violations", 40(4) *World Politics*, 1998, 476-498, at 480].

94 On this historic battle, see Michael Edwards, *"The Battle of Plassey and the Conquest of Bengal"*, (BT Batsford, London 1963); Michael Edwards, *"Plassey: The Foundation of an Empire"*, (Hainish Hamilton, London 1969); Penderal Moon, *"The British Conquest and Dominion of India"*, (Duckworth, London 1989).

95 On Mughal Empire see generally, John F. Richards, *"The Mughal Empire"*, (Cambridge University Press, Cambridge 1995); Jadunath Sarkar, *"Mughal Administration"*, (Sarkar, Calcutta 1963).

96 See generally, S.G. Panandikar, *"The Wealth and Welfare of the Bengal Delta"*, (Calcutta University Press, Calcutta 1926); Sunil Kumar Datta, *"The Raj & the Bengali People"*, (Firma KLM, Kolkata 2002); Sushil Mondal, *"History of Bengal"*, (Prakash Mandir, Vol. I, Calcutta 1970); Luke Scrafton, *"A History of Bengal Before and After the Plassey, 1739-1758"*, (Firma KLM, Calcutta 1975); Atul Chandra Roy, *"History of Bengal: Mughal Period, 1526-1765 AD"*, (Nababharat Publishers, Calcutta 1968); Muhammad Abdur Rahim, *"Social and Cultural History of Bengal"*, (Pakistan Historical Society, Vol. I, Karachi 1963); Tapan Raychaudhuri, *"Bengal under Akbar and Jahangir: An Introductory Study in Social History"*, (A. Mukherjee, Calcutta 1953); Anisuzzaman Chowdhury, "Bangladesh: A Semi-Feudal, Semi-Colonial Society", in Chowdhury E. Haque (ed.), *"Bangladesh: Politics, Economy and Society"*, (University of Manitoba, Winnipeg 1987), 33-48; Susil Chaudhuri, *"Trade and Commercial Organisation in Bengal, 1650-1720"*, (Firina KL Mukhopadhyay, Calcutta 1975).

97 For a general overview on this legal system, see Wahed Husain, *"Administration of Justice during the Muslim Rule in India"*, (Calcutta University Press, Calcutta 1934); Sajida S. Alvi, "Religion and State during the Reign of Mughal Emperor Jahangir (1605-27): Nonjuristical Perspectives", 69 *Studia Islamica*, 1989, 95-119.

98 See Sir Edmund C. Cox, *"Police and Crime in India"*, (Manu Publications, New Delhi 1976), 53.

punishments like crucifixion, mutilation, stoning, and the like.[99] Moreover, in the absence of any statutory code, "what was the exact law on a particular crime or what was the punishment for it, could never be known before the pronouncement of sentence by the *Qadi* or Magistrate".[100] In the absence of any catalogue of human rights abuses within the criminal justice system, one can infer such violations from all these potential factors – loopholes in criminal law, cruel punishments, uncertainty of laws, etc. However, because of the low level of crime rates[101] and a general reluctance of the people to resort to official courts of law,[102] such inference cannot be stretched too far. After thc battle of Polashi, the penetration of colonial rule into the indigenous society and economy[103] brought about various new dimensions in public life. British India in general and Bengal in particular witnessed a sharp rise in violence and an unprecedented decline in the law and order situation.[104] Lord Minto wrote in 1810 that robbery, accompanied by murder, was prevailing in every part of Bengal.[105] Simultaneous operation of two factors – "expropriation of available social surplus characteristic of the predatory phase of the colonial rule in Bengal"[106] and "disappearance of the Mughal system or rural control, which had by and large successfully maintained the social equilibrium" – contributed to this anarchic

---

99 See Tapas Kumar Banerjee, "The Substantive Criminal Law Prior to the Indian Penal Code", in K.N. Chandrasekharan Pillai and Shabistan Aquil (eds.), "*Essays on the Indian Penal Code*", (Indian Law Institute, New Delhi 2005), 3-32, at 16.

100 See Tapas Kumar Banerjee, "*Background to Indian Criminal Law*", (Oriental Longmans, Calcutta 1963), 62. Also see Sri Ram Sharma, "*Mughal Government and Administration*", (Popular Prokashan, Bombay 1951), 200-201.

101 Warren Hastings, the first Governor General of India, wrote in 1772: "Let the justice of this distinction of punishment be examined by its effects. There are not many instances of robbery in India, where these principles prevail, scarce any of murder. A traveller may pass through a whole province unarmed and sleep in security in the open plain. He will have no enemies to dread but the wild beasts." See M.E. Monckton Jones, "*Warren Hastings in Bengal 1772-1774*", (Clarendon Press, Oxford 1918), 157-158.

102 See generally, Werner F. Menski, "Crime and Punishment in Hindu Law and under Modern Indian Law", 58(4) *R'ecueils de la Soci'et'e Jean Bodin*, 1991, 295–334; J.D.M. Derrett, "*Religion, Law and the State in India*", (Faber and Faber, London 1968); Werner F. Menski, "*Indian Legal System Past and Present*" (SOAS Law Department Occasional Paper No. 3, London 1997).

103 For an analysis of this penetration process, see David Washbrook, "Law, State and Agrarian Society in Colonial India", 15(3) *Modern Asian Studies*, 1981, 649-672.

104 See Arun Mukherjee, "*Crime and Public Disorder in Colonial Bengal 1861-1912*", (KP Bagchi, Calcutta 1995); Ranjan Chakrabarti, "*Authority and Violence in Colonial Bengal*", (Bookland Pvt. Ltd., Calcutta 1997); Anand A. Yang (ed.), "*Crime and Criminality in British India*", (University of Arizona Press, Arizona 1985); David Arnold, "Police Power and the Demise of British Rule in India, 1930-47", in David M. Anderson and David Killingray (eds.), "*Policing and Decolonisation: Politics, Nationalism and the Police, 1917-65*", (Manchester University Press, Manchester 1992), 42-61.

105 See Romesh Chunder Dutt, "*The Economic History of India under Early British Rule: From the Rise of the British Power in 1757 to the Accession of Queen Victoria in 1837*", (Routledge, London 2000), 14.

106 See Teresa Hayter, "*The Creation of World Poverty: An Alternative View to the Brandt Report*", (Pluto Press, London 1981), 45; Peter Fryer, "*Black People in the British Empire: An Introduction*", (Pluto Press, London 1993), 18-20; Nicholas B. Dirks, "*The Scandal of Empire: India and the Creation of Imperial Britain*", (Harvard University Press, Cambridge 2006); Nick Robins, "*The Corporation that Changed the World: How the East India Company Shaped the Modern Multinational*", (Pluto Press, London 2006).

situation.[107] In response, the British rulers started the colonial transformation of indigenous criminal law system. This gradual process finally ended up with codification of the Penal Code of 1860[108] and the 1898 Code of Criminal Procedure[109] – the two most basic criminal law still to-date. Grounded in Benthamittee philosophy, these two laws are still now followed in Bangladesh. These laws were claimed by the British rulers as legislation pregnant with 'rule of law' and 'due process of justice'. Now the question arises as to whether the fathers of these laws succeeded to stick to the high principles of 'rule of law' and 'due process of justice' while managing criminal administration of justice in Bengal. While inquiring this issue, one should not be surprised to find that the 1871 Criminal Tribes Act[110] enacted for the registration of nomadic, indigent or troublesome tribes as criminal tribes, prescribed a range of penal measures against such tribes without the requirement of criminal acts actually being proven against them or their members.[111] This Act was initially applied only in the Punjab, North-West Provinces and Oudh. Over time it was gradually extended to other parts of India and by 1947, no less than three million adult males were registered under the Act.[112] In Bengal, this law came into operation in 1876 and targeted two specific tribes – the Bediyas and the Maghiya Doms.[113] When confronted with the problems of thugs[114] and the 1857 Sepoy mutiny,[115] the British

---

107 See Basudeb Chattopadhyay, "*Crime and Control in Early Colonial Bengal 1770-1860*", (KP Bagchi & Company, Calcutta 2000), 22.

108 Act. No. XLV of 1860.

109 Act. No. V of 1898.

110 Act. No. XXVII of 1871.

111 See for details, Preeti Nijhar, "*Law and Imperialism: Criminality and Constitution in Colonial India and Victorian England*", (Pickering & Chatto, London 2009); Mark Brown, "The Politics of Penal Excess and the Echo of Colonial Penality", 4(4) *Punishment & Society*, 2002, 403-423; Mark Brown, "Race, Science and the Construction of Native Criminality in Colonial India", 5(3) *Theoretical Criminology*, 2001, 345-368; Nicholas B. Dirks, "*Castes of Mind: Colonialism and the Making of Modern India*", (Princeton University Press, New Jersey 2001).

112 See for details, A.J. Major, "State and Criminal Tribes in Colonial Punjab: Surveillance, Control and Reclamation of the 'Dangerous Classes'", 33 *Modern Asian Studies*, 1999, 657-688; S. Nigam, "Disciplining and Policing the 'Criminals by Birth', Part 1: The Making of a Colonial Stereotype – The Criminal Tribes and Castes of North India", 27 *Indian Economic and Social History Review*, 1990, 131-164; S. Nigam, "Disciplining and Policing the 'Criminals by Birth', Part 2: The Development of a Disciplinary System, 1871-1900", 27 *Indian Economic and Social History Review*, 1990, 257-287.

113 See Anindita Mukhopadhyay, "*Behind the Mask: The Cultural Definition of the Legal Subject in Colonial Bengal (1715-1911)*", (Oxford University Press, New Delhi 2006), 156.

114 According to the traditional account, the thugs were a fraternity of ritual stranglers who preyed on travellers along the highways of nineteenth-century India [George Bruce, "*The Stranglers – The Cult of Thuggee and Its Overthrow in British India*", (Longmans, London 1968); John R. McLane, "Bengali Bandits, Police and Landlords after the Permanent Settlement", in Anand A. Yang (ed.), "*Crime and Criminality in British India*", (University of Arizona Press, Arizona 1985), 26-47]. Although some post-colonial scholars dismiss the traditional historicity of thugs [Parama Roy, "Discovering India, Imagining Thuggee", 9(1) *Yale Journal of Criticism*, 1996, 121–45; Amal Chatterjee, "*Representations of India, 1740–1840: The Creation of India in the Colonial Imagination*", (Mcmillan, Basingstoke 1998)], the presence of groups who were called – arguably in derogatory connotation and with coloured misrepresentation creating myths - 'thugs' is not historically unfounded [Kim A. Wagner, "Thuggee and Social Banditry Reconsidered", 50(2) *The Historical Journal*, 2007, 353-376; Kim A. Wagner, "The Deconstructed Stranglers – A Reassessment of

administration of justice readily responded with disproportionately deterrent sentencing strategies, arguably sidelining the principles of due process of justice. In particular, during the trials of 1857 mutiny, the British authorities developed several methods to execute mutineers and suspected mutineers. One of such methods was to blow away the offender from the mouth of artillery cannon.[116] Similarly, the 1915 Defence of India Act empowered the authorities to enforce extraordinary emergency powers without any regard to the 'due process' requirement. Under this law, some 800 orders were made in Bengal.[117] In the subsequent years, a good number of other laws were passed that authorized the executive to place individuals under personal restraint or executive detention, in spite of the absence of sufficient grounds to institute any judicial proceeding, whenever justified to maintain British alliances with foreign governments, preserve tranquillity in the princely states, or preserve the security of the state from foreign hostility or internal commotion.[118] Faced with all these facts, one may argue that the colonial rulers deviated from the 'rule of law' and 'due process of law' models just for furthering their colonial interests. This thesis merits consideration. At the same time, the hypothesis that these laws were not adequate to respond to the growing problem of crimes and hence administrators had to resort to inhuman management of criminal justice administration also requires investigation. It must be clarified here that this hypothesis does not justify inhuman management of criminal justice system rather it points at the possible lacunae of the basic criminal laws and their non-adjustability with local social fabrics. The authors contend that to unveil the real picture behind extra judicial killing, torture, arbitrary arrest and detention, we must find an answer to the question: "Do these practices constitute a frustrated governmental or police responses to the crisis of 'due process' management of law and order situations?". There is also a need to identify the factors that contributed to the variation in crime situation of 1772 as narrated by Warren Hastings and the situation of 1810 as narrated by Lord Minto.[119] Is it due to their variation in perception or variation in fact? If this is a variation in fact, is it due to legal factors, *i.e.*, variation in criminal law under Mughal administration and that under British

---

Thuggee", 38(4) *Modern Asian Studies*, 2004, 931–963; Kim A. Wagner, "*Thuggee: Banditry and the British in Early Nineteenth-Century India"*, (Macmillan, Basingstoke 2007)].

115 See generally, Lord Roberts, "*Forty One Years in India: From Subaltern to Commander in Chief"*, (Richard Bentley & Son, London 1898); W.G. Broehl, "*Crisis of the Raj: The Revolt of 1857 through British Lieutenants' Eyes"*, (University Press of New England, Hanover 1986); Col. G.B. Malleson, "*Kaye's and Malleson's History of the Indian Mutiny of 1857-8"*, (Longmans, London 1897).

116 See Mark Brown, "The Politics of Penal Excess and the Echo of Colonial Penality", 4(4) *Punishment & Society*, 2002, 403-423.

117 See Ramesh Chandra Majumder, "*History of Modern Bengal, Part 2 (1905-1947): Freedom Movement"*, (G. Bharadwaj and Company, Calcutta 1978), 141.

118 See for more details, A.W.B. Simpson, "Round Up The Usual Suspects: The Legacy of British Colonialism and the European Convention on Human Rights", 41 *Loyola Law Review*, 1996, 629-712, at 646-648; Anil Kalhan et al., "Colonial Continuities: Human Rights, Terrorism and Security Laws in India", 20(1) *Columbia Journal of Asian Law*, 2006, 93-234, at 126-132; Charles Townshend, "*Britain's Civil Wars: Counter Insurgency in the Twentieth Century"*, (Faber and Faber, London 1986), 145-149; Nasser Hussain, "*The Jurisprudence of Emergency: Colonialism and the Rule of Law"*, (University of Michigan Press, Michigan 2003).

119 See footnotes 100, 104 and the accompanying texts.

administration? Is there a causal relation, in contexts of Bangladesh, between economic situation of the state and its crime rate, and between crime rates and human rights violation by law enforcing agencies? To what extent the present regime on criminal justice system is responsive to the societal need of penal justice? Is it enough to reserve all the blames for the poor functioning of criminal law on the police or the courts, as if the body of criminal law itself is beyond any question? If the authorities suffer from crisis with the management policies, will the international standards serve as magic bullets or will be given a culturally variant interpretation? All these questions are relevant to understand any systematic and consistent practices within the criminal justice system. By putting these questions, we do not however claim conclusively that the norms and strategies that Bangladesh applies for management of criminal justice is the root cause of extra judicial killing, torture, arbitrary arrest and detention; rather, we claim that it is a potential hypothesis requiring a more detailed investigation that is always missing in the human rights discourses on Bangladesh.
Accordingly, government, civil society and international community should re-examine the efficacy of and accordingly rethink their efforts for promoting human and minority rights protection. The government should consider the protection of its peoples' rights as a sacred duty that is ultimately beneficial for the government in the long-run; government should also understand that false pretence to maintain international standards which are beyond its capacity, given the socio-cultural contexts of the state, once such standards are violated belittles its credibility as well as legitimacy. Contrarily, if the government becomes proactive to offer culture specific interpretation of international standards to sphere exemption from adhering to human rights obligation not consistent with socio-cultural realities, the legitimacy that the government extracts from its people in a faithful manner is far more than the legitimacy it presumes to gain from the international community through deceitful means - fabrication and manipulation of facts. Civil society and international community should understand that "antiseptic analysis" of rights situation in any given jurisdiction ending up with "hysterical condemnation" of its government and excluding the potential socio-economic and historical factors that can be interrogated as origins of the rights violation, can be counterproductive in the sense that it might serve as "normalization and rountinization of the very harms it seeks to condemn".[120]

VI. In lieu of conclusion

In the end, the paper argues that country studies on human and/or minority rights performances as against international standards should not only be meant to produce branding or rating of countries, as often done in human rights literature. Over the last few decades, voluminous studies and reports on human and minority rights situation of different countries have ultimately succeeded, with or without deliberate attempt, to create a new identity for states – a so called "human rights image". Whatever may be the consequence – good or bad – of such image-branding at the international level, ground level realities belie the utility of such studies and reports. It is therefore no

120 The quoted phrases, although originally used in a different context, are borrowed from: David Kennedy, "The International Human Rights Movement: Part of the Problem?", 15 *Harvard Human Rights Journal*, 2002, 101-126, at 124-125.

wonder that countries branded as human and minority rights violators or scoring low grades in its human and minority rights performance, according to these reports and studies, are consistently continuing its same level of records. Change of governments, restructuring of political structure of authority, institutional changes: nothing is being proved to create any significant change in the fate of common people – the ultimate victims of human rights violation. When it appears that international human rights norms are observed more in violation than in compliance in a particular state or in a number of states – causally or incidentally, most of which are non-western and/or post-colonial states, it is a too simplistic approach, unless we outright reject the relevance and essence of enquiring into a long-lasting common tradition, to blame the delinquent state(s) and expect a reversal driven by good-will. This tells us that human and/or minority rights country studies are not to be seen as a tool only to interrogate states from viewpoints of international standards but also to interrogate international standards from the viewpoints of states.

CHAPTER 6

Territorial autonomy in India

Thomas Benedikter[*]

I. Introduction

Before giving an overview on territorial autonomy in the Indian Union, it is useful to recall a suitable definition of territorial (in Europe also "regional") autonomy as used in the present essay: "Autonomy can be defined as a means of internal power-sharing aimed to preserve the cultural and ethnic variety, while respecting the unity of a state. It consists in permanently transferring a certain amount of powers suitable for those purposes to a certain territory, giving its population the possibility of self-government, and leaving only residual responsibilities to the central state."[1] As a general rule, autonomous territories possess no international character, and are not treated as states for the purposes of international law. Thus, autonomy can be defined as a means of internal power-sharing aimed at preserving cultural and ethnic variety, while respecting the unity of a state. According to another scholar, who has been a consultant for autonomy issues around the world including Nepal, autonomy is "[...] a device to allow ethnic or other groups that claim a distinct identity to exercise direct control over affairs of special concern to them while allowing the larger entity to exercise those powers that cover common interest".[2]

Autonomy is a special device designed to accommodate a particular part of a state if its population differs from the majority population of that state. It should be remarked that territorial autonomy, as today operating in about 60 regions in 20 states in all

---

* Thomas Benedikter, economist and social researcher in Bozen (South Tyrol, Italy), committed to journalistic and humanitarian purposes, spent about two years with research and project activities in Latin America, the Balkans and South Asia (especially in Nepal, Kashmir, Sri Lanka and India's Northeast) and is writing for several news-magazines and reviews on ethnic minorities and ethnic conflicts. He collaborated with the European Academy of Bozen EURAC (Department of Minority Rights) for a Europe-South Asia Exchange on Supranational (Regional) Policies and Instruments for the Promotion of Human Rights and the Management of Minority Issues (EURASIA-Net) with South Asian partners. Apart from other books on ethnic conflicts and minority protection systems recently he published *"The World's Modern Autonomy Systems"* (EURAC Bozen), *"Language Policy and Linguistic Minorities in India"* (LIT Berlin/Münster, 2009*), "A Short Guide to Autonomy in South Asia and Europe*" (EURAC Bozen 2009), at:
http://www.eurac/edu/eurasia-net/PROJECT+DELIVERABLES.htm

1 See Thomas Benedikter, *The World's Modern Autonomy Systems,* EURAC Bozen 2009, p. 19, available at: http://www.eurac.edu/Org/Minorities/IMR/Projects/asia.htm

2 See Yash Ghai, Autonomy and ethnicity: negotiating competing claims in multiethnic states, Hongkong 2000, p. 484, and Joachim Heintze defines territorial autonomy as follows: "In international law autonomy means that a part or territorial unit of a state is authorised to govern itself in certain matters by enacting laws and statutes, but without constituting a State of their own."; furthermore: H.J. Heintze, "On the legal understanding of autonomy" in Markku Suksi (ed), *Autonomy: Implications and Applications* (Kluwer Law International, 1998) p.7

continents, has been established also in federal states in two forms: on sub-state-level (as a unit of a federated subject of that state as in India and Belgium) or as a special category of territorial power sharing along the ordinary federated units of that federation (as in Canada). Ethnic-linguistic or national minorities are the classic population to demand autonomy, especially when settling homogeneously in their original homeland, but autonomy has been accorded also due to geographical ("islandness") and historical reasons.[3]

This above given definition focuses on the fundamental purposes of autonomy of a legally defined scheme of territorial power sharing, mostly established to protect minority groups, in which legislative and executive – and sometimes jurisdictional - powers are attributed to a territorial community (region, province, district) endowed with a freely elected regional assembly. A clear distinction has to be drawn with regard to other concepts and forms of power-sharing and self-rule such as reservations for indigenous peoples, asymmetrical federalism and associated statehood. Moreover, the criteria by which a regional autonomy can be considered to be a "genuine autonomy" must be clarified from the very outset, as they clearly distinguish this particular democratic and ethnically non-exclusive form of self-government under the full sovereignty of a central state, from some hybrid or non-perfect arrangements that can also be found under the label of "autonomy" in some states. Under this approach both non-democratic autonomous areas or autonomies operating in a non-democratic state cannot be regarded as "genuine working autonomies" (e.g. the F.A.T.A. and the Northern Areas of Pakistan, Uzbekistan's, Tajikistan's or China's autonomous entities). Furthermore a minimum standard of legislative and executive powers is required in order to be qualified as a genuine autonomy. Sub-state entities not vested with legislative and executive powers cannot be branded as autonomies (e.g. the Union Territories in India and the Chittagong Hill Tracts in Bangladesh, Corsica in France, Rodriguez in Mauritius). To put it bluntly, there is a minimum standard of powers and democratic procedures of self-government of a regional polity, without which talking about "autonomy" becomes meaningless.

II. Jammu and Kashmir's Lost Autonomy

The first territorial autonomy established in the Indian Union has been the one of the formerly princely state of Jammu and Kashmir. The instrument of accession of Jammu and Kashmir's last Maharaja and India's government of 1947 agreed to grant this Muslim dominated State special, far reaching autonomy. This occurred apart from the territory's quest to obtain a self-determination referendum under the aegis of the UN, which was ultimately never held. This form of autonomy, originally in 1950 enshrined in Article 370 of the Constitution[4], left the Centre with only powers of

3 For the complete list of working territorial autonomies and further definitions see: Thomas Benedikter, *The World's Modern Autonomy Systems*, p. 16-20

4 Constitution of India - Part XXI - *Temporary, transitional and special provisions.* Article 370. Temporary provisions with respect to the State of Jammu and Kashmir:

(1) Notwithstanding anything in this Constitution,-

(a) the provisions of article 238 shall not apply in relation to the State of Jammu and Kashmir;

(b) the power of Parliament to make laws for the said State shall be limited to- (i) those matters in the Union List and the Concurrent List which, in consultation with the Government of the State, are

defence, foreign affairs and communication on the territory of Jammu and Kashmir. But beginning in 1953 these provisions were eroded step by step. Finally Jammu and Kashmir was transformed in a normal member state of the Indian federal state without abolishing Article 370 of the constitution, which was *de facto* outdated. Curtailing Kashmir's special autonomy and interfering heavily and constantly in its internal affairs later brought about an escalation of the political crisis, popular unrest and protest, and the President's rule. Eventually full-fledged civil war and armed militancy broke out in 1990. To date Jammu and Kashmir has not found a stable solution and a peace that does justice to the claims of the Muslim population. The issue of self-government lies unresolved, and after the traumatic experiences of repression by India's security forces over the last 18 years, a majority of the valley no longer favours Kashmir's membership in the Union at all. Abolishing the special autonomy, originally granted to Kashmir by Delhi, as in similar cases elsewhere, caused long lasting political contention, military conflict and alienated the Muslim population from the rest of India.[5] Apart from Jammu and Kashmir India's constitution embraces some more special provisions with limited scope for certain states Nagaland (371A), Sikkim (371F), Assam (371B), Manipur (371C), Arunachal Pradesh (Art. 371H) etc., without neither *de jure* nor *de facto* configuring its federal system as an "asymmetrical federal system".

---

declared by the President to correspond to matters specified in the Instrument of Accession governing the accession of the State to the Dominion of India as the matters with respect to which the Dominion Legislature may make laws for that State; and (ii) such other matters in the said Lists as, with the concurrence of the Government of the State, the President may by order specify. *Explanation.* For the purposes of this article, the Government of the State means the person for the time being recognized by the President as the Maharaja of Jammu and Kashmir acting on the advice of the Council of Ministers for the time being in office under the Maharaja's Proclamation dated the fifth day of March, 1948;

(c) the provisions of article 1 and of this article shall apply in relation to that State;

(d) such of the other provisions of this Constitution shall apply in relation to that State subject to such exceptions and modifications as the President may by order specify: Provided that no such order which relates to the matters specified in the Instrument of Accession of the State referred to in paragraph (i) of sub-clause (b) shall be issued except in consultation with the Government of the State: Provided further that no such order which relates to matters other than those referred to in the last preceding proviso shall be issued except with the concurrence of that Government.

(2) If the concurrence of the Government of the State referred to in paragraph (ii) of sub-clause (b) of clause (1) or in the second proviso to sub-clause (d) of that clause be given before the Constituent Assembly for the purpose of framing the Constitution of the State is convened, it shall be placed before such Assembly for such decision as it may take thereon.

(3) Notwithstanding anything in the foregoing provisions of this article, the President may, by public notification, declare that this article shall cease to be operative or shall be operative only with such exceptions and modifications and from such date as he may specify: Provided that the recommendation of the Constituent Assembly of the State referred to in clause (2) shall be necessary before the President issues such a notification.

5 See Sumantra Bose, "*Kashmir – Roots of Conflict, Paths to Peace*", (Harvard University Press Cambridge, Mass. and London 2003); and Thomas Benedikter, "*Il groviglio del Kashmir*", (Editori FRILLI, Genova 2005).

III. Territorial (Sub-State) Autonomy in India

India is the only South Asian state that has enshrined some forms of regional territorial autonomy in its Constitution for some few districts and regions at the sub-state-level (5th and 6th schedule).[6] Some of these provisions of speciality are no longer applied, as it is the case with article 370 with respect to Jammu and Kashmir; others are an expression of India's "asymmetrical federalism." This concept, beyond the Union and the centre, provides for some additional rights to single states, based on their special character and interests. In India, apart from the federated states with special features, there are also Union territories and autonomous districts on a sub-state-level known as "entities with a limited autonomy." Moreover, the 73rd and 74th Amendments to the Constitution ensured the devolution of some limited powers at the village and town level defined *Panchayati Raj*.

Under the special protection clause in Art. 371 Constitution, tribal customary laws, procedures, and land rights are protected. Part XVI of the Constitution ensures special provisions for scheduled castes, scheduled tribes and other under-developed classes, which are usually not linked to territories, but to specific social groups.[7] Some of them can be compared to concepts of "cultural autonomy" applied in Europe, while some are established on a territorial basis. Under the 5th Schedule some provisions for "local autonomy" are provided in order to protect the interests of smaller tribal groups who are placed within larger units of a state.[8] This annex to the Constitution provides a limited platform by way of formation of "Tribes Advisory Councils", which can articulate the aspirations of the indigenous communities. Yet, neither the Council has any executive power nor does it enjoy any legislative or judicial powers in administering the justice within the scheduled areas. The legislative power is vested with the Governor and the Council has the duty to advice him on his desire. The Governor is empowered to apply his discretion regarding the applicability of any law passed by the parliament or the State legislature in the scheduled areas. In consultation with the "Advisory Council" he can make laws for the scheduled areas

- prohibiting or restricting transfer of land;
- regulating the allotment of land;
- regulating money lending business.

The Union President should assent to all these regulations. Thus, the 5th schedule, although envisaging to protect tribal interests, does not assign any concrete right of territorial autonomy to the tribal peoples.[9]

---

6 The 5th and 6th schedule of India's constitution is to be found at: http://www.constitution.org/cons/india/shed05.html and http://www.constitution.org/cons/india/shed06.html

7 See the full text at: http://www.constitution.org/cons/india/p16.html

8 See Article 244A on the scheduled and tribal areas at: http://www.constitution.org/cons/india/p10244a.html as well as the 5th schedule of India's Constitution, available at: http://www.constitution.org/cons/india/shed05.html

9 The denial of substantial autonomy to India's Adivasi peoples is described by Bosu Mullick, *"The Jharkhand movement – Indigenous peoples' struggle for autonomy in India"*, (International Work Group for Indigenous Affairs (IWGIA) document, Copenhagen 2003).

Territorial autonomy as defined in the introduction has been established in India since 1951 under the 6th schedule of her Constitution. The 6th schedule contains detailed provisions for "Autonomous District Councils" (ADC) in districts dominated by so-called tribal peoples. The main purposes of these provisions are to preserve the distinct cultures of tribal peoples, to prevent economic exploitation of such peoples by non-tribal peoples, and to allow them to develop and administer themselves. This scheme, although termed "Provisions as to the Administration of Tzribal Areas in the States of Assam, Meghalaya, Tripura and Mizoram",[10] departed from a mere concept of "ethnic reservations" as provided by the 5th schedule, establishing autonomous territories with mixed populations and fully democratic institutions based on general suffrage. Although limited in its scope, the legislative councils of the autonomous districts established by the 6th schedule are based on very elaborate legislation and safeguarded by the Union government. They were tasked with granting sufficient autonomy to prevent radical secessionist claims and movements and thus the further splitting up of the States, especially in the Northwest and the Northeast of the country.

10 out of 13 ADCs have been established in the four North-eastern States of Meghalaya, Assam, Mizoram and Tripura, one in West-Bengal and two in Jammu and Kashmir (Leh and Kargil). The latter three have been established under State law, not under the 6th schedule. In the rest of the country, however, no such district autonomies have been created, although India has 330 districts, many of which host ethno-linguistic or tribal minorities. About 50 of these districts have an ethno-linguistic majority different from the majority population of their respective State and thus would be eligible to a certain degree of cultural or territorial autonomy in order to preserve the particular cultural character of the concerned area.[11]. As far as genuine territorial autonomy is concerned, the 6th schedule of the Constitution is India's present standard. On the other hand, the regional councils constituted by the North-eastern States by State Act do not enjoy all the powers available under the 6th schedule. Even within this schedule, certain autonomous councils, like Bodoland, Karbi Anglong and North Cachar managed to obtain greater powers granted by specific constitutional amendments made to this schedule. Hence, there is certain flexibility in the application of the Constitution's provisions concerning district autonomy.

---

10 For the full text of the 6th schedule of India's constitution see: http://www.constitution.org/cons/india/shed06.html

11 The author has elaborated such issues in his recent research: T.B., *"Language Policy and Linguistic Minorities in India"* (LIT Berlin/Münster, 2009).

A. India's Autonomous Districts and Autonomous Hill Districts[12]

Autonomous District	*area (in km²)*	*population (2001)*	*capital*	*ethnic composition**	*year of constitution*
1. Bodoland	8.970	2.631.289	Kokrajhar	ST: 1.354.627 SC 137.594	07.12.2003
2. Karbi Anglong	10.434	813.311	Diphu	ST: 452.963 SC: 29.200	17.11.1951 14.10.1976
3. North Cachar	4.890	186.189	Haflong	Dimasa, Kuki, Hmar, Zemei, Hrangkhawls	17.11.1951 2.2.1970
4. Garo Hills	8.167	865.045	Tura	Garo, smaller groups	22.02.1972 (1979 division)
5. Jaintia Hills	3.819	295.692	Jowai	Pnar, Jaintia, Khasi	22.02.1972
6. Khasi Hills	7.995	1.060.923	Shillong	Khasi, smaller groups	22.02.1972
7. Tripura Tribal Area	7.132	679.720**	Khumwng	ST: 679.720	
8. Chakma ADC	k.a.	k.a.	Chawngte	Chakma	1987
9. Lai ADC	k.a.	k.a.	Lawngtlai	Lai	1987
10. Mara ADC	k.a.	55.000	Siaha	Mara	1987
11. Darjeeling Gorkha Hill Council	3.144	1.609.172	Darjeeling	ST: 179.153 SC: 209.856	22.08.1988
12. Aut. Hill Devel. Council Leh	45.110	117.232	Leh	ST: 92.200 (Ladakhi)	28.08.1995
13. Aut. Hill Devel. Council Kargil	14.086	119.307	Kargil	ST: 105.377 (Purigba, Balti, Brokpa)	01.07.2003

* SC= scheduled caste; ST= scheduled tribe

** This figure accounts for the tribal population of the district only, which accounts for at least 90 percent of the total population, which is more than 700.000. Ethnic groups in the Tripura Tribal District: Bhil, Bhutia, Chainel, Chakma, Garo, Holan, Kuki, Lepcha, Lushai, Mog, Munda, Moatia, Orang, Riang, Santal, Tripura, Uchai.

*** The Darjeeling Gorkha Hill Council, and the Autonomous Hill Councils of Leh and Kargil have been established by state laws of West Bengal and Jammu and Kashmir respectively, and are not enshrined in the 6th schedule of the Constitution.

12 Source: official websites of the Autonomous District Councils.

The legislative powers of these autonomous districts include:[13]

- land transfer;
- forest (other than reserved forest);
- water bodies (for the purpose of agriculture);
- regulation of shifting cultivation;
- village or town committees and administration;
- appointment or succession of chiefs or headmen;
- inheritance or property;
- marriage and divorce;
- social customs;
- money lending and trading activities of non-residents or non-tribal people living in the area;
- primary education;
- dispensaries, markets, cattle pounds, fisheries;
- roads, road transport, ferries and waterways.

The District Council is allowed to levy and collect taxes on land and buildings as well as tolls on persons. Moreover it can collect taxes on professions, trades, callings and employment, animals, vehicles, boats, entry of goods into the local markets, goods carried on ferries, the maintenance of schools, dispensaries and roads. The ADCs are also entitled to get a share of royalties accruing to the State annually on account of extraction of minerals. The management of these revenues is guided by rules and regulation set by the Governor.

B. The Autonomous Districts in Northeast India

All the matters on which district council is empowered to legislate are also enumerated in the so-called "State List". In order to ensure the legislative autonomy of the district council, the 6th Schedule provides that no act of the State legislature shall apply to any autonomous district unless the respective district council adopts and approves the same.[14]

---

13 See Article 3 of the 6th schedule of the constitution at http://www.constitution.org/cons/india/p21371 a.html.

14 As an example of such provision p. 12 of the 6th schedule may be quoted:
[Application of Acts of Parliament and of the Legislature of the State of Assam to autonomous districts and autonomous regions in the State of Assam].- (1) Notwithstanding anything in this Constitution- (a) no Act of the 2[Legislature of the State of Assam] in respect of any of the matters specified in paragraph 3 of this Schedule as matters with respect to which a District Council or a Regional Council may make laws, and no Act of the 2 [Legislature of the State of Assam] prohibiting or restricting the consumption of any non-distilled alcoholic liquor shall apply to any autonomous district or autonomous region 3[in the State] unless in either case the District Council for such district or having jurisdiction over such region by public notification so directs, and the District Council in giving such direction with respect to any Act may direct that the Act shall in its application to such district or region or any part thereof have effect subject to such exceptions or modifications as it thinks fit; (b) the Governor may, by public notification, direct that any Act of Parliament or of the [Legislature of the State of Assam] to which the provisions of clause (a) of this sub-paragraph do not apply shall not apply to an autonomous district or an autonomous region [in that State], or shall apply to such district or region or any part thereof subject to such exceptions or modifications as he may

Regarding the judiciary the 6th schedule provides for a two-tier-system at the district and village level.[15] At the village level, the village council is empowered to trial suits and cases between the parties belonging to scheduled tribes. At the district level the district courts are empowered to act as a court of appeal in respect of all suits and cases triable by a village court. This differentiation in the judiciary mirrors the original "tribal character" of the 6th schedule autonomy. Originally, it has created a legal framework specifically for tribal communities, allowing self-administration on social and economic fields deemed most relevant for tribal communities, as agriculture, forests, fishery and local markets. But it is highly questionable whether this form of autonomy really covers all relevant powers required by such peoples for the preservation of their ethnic and cultural identity and for acting as comprehensive agency for the economic and social development of their homeland.

For their financial funding the ADCs are mostly depending from grants-in-aid, coming from the central government in New Delhi, but mainly routed through the State government. This mechanism provides a leverage which is being often used to bring the ADC in line with State policies. The resulting financial dependence and the instrumental use of dependency of State decision-makers remain a major bone of contention in the relation between the district council and the state governments.

Under the autonomous councils, constituted under the 6th Schedule, there is no adequate devolution of powers to the village level and most power is concentrated at the district level itself. Instead, if there are different scheduled tribes in an autonomous district, the Governor may, by public notification, divide the area or areas inhabited by them into autonomous regions.[16] Whereas in other States of India a certain amount of administrative power has been attributed to the institution of *Panchayati Raj* under the new 11th Schedule of the Constitution, the areas covered by the 6th schedule are not encompassed in this form of decentralization.[17] In these mostly tribal areas there are traditional systems of governance at the village level, ranging from autocracy or semi-autocracy to full participative democratic procedures and institutions. Thus, there is a certain discrepancy between autonomy at district level and the denial of municipal or local administrative autonomy of the village bodies. The village development boards in Nagaland offer one example of the models that can be adopted. Even in Arunachal Pradesh and in the plain areas of Assam, Manipur and Tripura, where Panchayati Raj have been established, more powers need to be devolved to these institutions.

The role of the Governor, appointed by the Union's president for each federated State of India, is considerable also *vis-á-vis* the 6th schedule-autonomies. Apart from the matters on which the district council has legislative powers, the Governor has the discretionary power in deciding whether the laws, made by the State legislature on

---

specify in the notification. Similar articles are in force for Meghalaya (p. 12A), Tripura (p. 12AA) and Mizoram (p.12B of the 6th schedule).

15 The administration of justice in the autonomous districts and autonomous regions is regulated by p. 4 of the 6th schedule. See http://www.constitution.org/cons/india/shed06.html

16 Article 1 (2) of the 6th schedule. Article 2 (2) reads: "There shall be a separate Regional Council for each area constituted an autonomous region under subparagraph (2) of par (1)."
See http://www.constitution.org/cons/india/shed06.html

17 See: http://www.constitution.org/cons/india/shed11.html; The Bodoland Memorandum in point 4.8 abolishes the Panchayati regime on the autonomous territory. See http://www.bodolandcouncil.org

matters not covered by autonomous legislation of the district, will be directly applicable to the autonomous district or not.[18] The applicability of the laws made by the parliament in these areas is also put under the discretion of the Governor, in case of Assam, and the President, in case of other North-eastern States. The Governor is also entitled to nominate a certain number of the members of the Autonomous Councils and to suspend the legislation if he deems them no longer effective. Thus the district councils have been provided with a certain legal shield against encroachment by the respective State, but they are fully exposed to the discretionary power of the Governor.
The limited form of autonomy provided by the 6th Schedule of the Constitution could not quell the quest for self-determination of the Naga peoples, who in 1963 achieved "statehood" in India without giving up military resistance for full independence. Nor could such a form of autonomy granted in the form of ADC meet the widespread demand of some smaller peoples of India to have their own federated state, especially in the Northeast; full "statehood" was eventually accorded to Meghalaya, Mizoram, Arunachal Pradesh and Tripura. Later, and with the creation of the Bodoland Territorial Council in 2003,[19] a range of further clauses were added to the 6th schedule, extending the scope of their autonomy. Nevertheless some of the Autonomous Districts went on claiming for full statehood in India could not be accommodated. In 2010 the territory of Telangana, hitherto a part of Andhra Pradesh, is about to achieve the status of a federated state of the Indian Union, without having before experienced any form of territorial autonomy.
Hence, in India the pattern of combining ethnicity – regarding small peoples or national minorities - with exceptional autonomies remains quite contradictory. The Indian Constitution emphasises republican values and fundamental human and civil rights standards throughout the whole territory, and in principle does not allow "ethnic autonomy". In practise, in order to solve local and regional conflicts, forms of limited territorial autonomy had to be created, admitting implicitly that on a state level the majority rule of a liberal democracy generates a permanent threat to every minority representation and participation in politics and power. On the other hand, new indigenous elites dominating autonomous districts have been tempted to transform such autonomous region in "ethnic spaces", as some Indian scholars assert.[20]

IV. India's Sub-State Autonomies: New "Ethnic Spaces"?

Such scholars warn of the risk that the concept of autonomy might lead to new ethnically biased states and sub-state entities by vesting their indigenous peoples with

---

18 The Governor's powers to annul, suspend acts and resolutions of District and Regional Councils is provided by Article 15 of the 6th schedule, his power to dissolution of ADCs in Article 16 of the 6th schedule. See: http://www.constitution.org/cons/india/shed06.html
19 See the Bodoland Accord at: http://www.bodolandcouncil.org
20 See Sanjay Barbora, "Experiences of Autonomy in the East and North East – A report on Third Civil Society Dialogue on Human Rights and Peace", (Calcutta Research Group (CRG), Kolkata 2003); and Chaudhury/Das/Ranabir Samaddar (eds.), "Indian Autonomies – Keywords and Keytextes", (Kolkata 2005).

special privileges but leaving out other "denizens," in other words, recent immigrants not members of the titular ethnic groups or not members of "scheduled tribes."[21] They warn against the creation of autonomies with two or three classes of citizens:

a) Citizens members of the titular ethnic group;
b) Indian general citizens;
c) Foreign immigrants.

Similar scenarios are sometimes envisaged in some European autonomous regions, leading to legal action by EU-citizens, not belonging to the "indigenous population" against alleged violations of the principle of equality and discrimination on the grounds of residency and language. In India's Northeast, a large share of the population is registered under Scheduled Tribes (STs)-status, and some groups and individuals not belonging to such STs appear to be excluded from some benefits of the territorial autonomy provided by either the States listed under Article 371 of the constitution or by the 6th schedule-to autonomous districts. Non members of Sts, for example, may be excluded from exercising some trades and business,[22] and they are partly excluded from political representation as both in the States of Assam, Meghalaya, Tripura and Mizoram seats are reserved for SCs and STs in the Legislative Assemblies of the states and of the ADCs.[23]
New social injustices are brought about that carry the potential for social and ethnic conflict. At this point, the very rationale of territorial autonomy has to be recalled: autonomy is a modern democratic sense cannot allow for new discrimination (reverse, e.g. against the members of the national majority population living in the area), privileging just one group at the expense of smaller groups. Modern autonomies are incompatible with the idea of indigenous reservations as existing in the Americas.[24]
Autonomy exists to give ethno-linguistic communities the chance to preserve their identity in their traditional homeland, but within a democratic setting inclusive of all legally resident people, with and without citizenship. In a region where these communities are compactly settled, it exists to redress the structural disadvantages of ethnic minorities in states with a different titular majority. In India this also refers to federated states' linguistic majorities. The national majority's implicit power in all domains of life, from culture to media, from economy to politics, from public jobs to military careers, remains largely unquestioned. Territorial autonomy should not create a similar "ethnic space" that allows reverse discrimination, but a legal space wherein

---

21 See Sanjib Baruah, "Durable Disorder – Understanding the Politics of Northeast India", (Oxford India, 2005), Section V on "Citizens and Denizens," 183-210; and Sanjay Barbora, "Experiences of Autonomy in the East and North East – A report on Third Civil Society Dialogue on Human Rights and Peace", (Calcutta Research Group (CRG), Kolkata 2003).
22 According to Article. 10 of the 6th schedule the ADCs have the power to make regulations on money lending and trading by non-tribals. See http://www.constitution.org/cons/india/shed06.html
23 See Part XVI, article .332 of the Constitution, on "Reservation of Seats for SC and ST in the Legislative Assemblies of the States, on See http://www.constitution.org/cons/india/p16.html. Such reservation of seats, however, will cease after 60 years from the commencement of the constitution (Article 334).
24 For the distinction of ethnic reservation to territorial autonomies see Thomas Benedikter, "*The World's Modern Autonomy Systems*", (EURAC Bolzano/Bozen 2009), section on "America's reservations for indigenous peoples", 202-211, available at:
http://www.eurac.edu/Org/Minorities/IMR/Projects/asia.htm

substantial equality of opportunity is ensured for all groups sharing the same region.[25] If conceived as a common democratic space with consociational power sharing, territorial autonomy is not exclusive, but inclusive by nature, as long as the necessary institutional safeguards are provided. Regional democracy, however, must not mirror the structural ethnic dominance of a group on national level, if necessary precautions are taken.

This is a normative statement against which working autonomies must be measured. Neither in Europe nor on other continents do autonomies always coherently act in accordance with such principles. Several autonomous regions have been brought before the European Court of Justice for violating fundamental rights enshrined in EU-treaties. Why should it be different in India? Thus, the challenge lies in making arrangements to ensure that full civil rights are granted to all legally resident citizens irrespective of ethnic affiliation as well as arrangements for protecting internal minorities. Thus, the concept and the scope of powers of the 6th Schedule autonomy obviously is too narrow for both enhancing and stabilizing the position of the "titular" tribal or indigenous or minority peoples of a given area and ensuring the consociational participation of all ethnic groups sharing the same territory. The titular majority itself is called upon to strike a balance between the interests of indigenous peoples and non-tribal resident citizens who contribute to regional welfare. Or in other terms: internal minority protection has to be reconciled with democracy.

If the 6th Schedule no longer offers such a scheme of regional autonomy, and, in the absence of other constitutional options (e.g. Union territory with legislation), it is little wonder that some regional communities seek full statehood (in India: Telengana, which achieved this goal in 2009, and Gorkhaland). Discrimination on ethnic grounds is detrimental to autonomous communities in an additional sense. If persons living in such regions, belonging to the majority population in the rest of the country are victimised by autonomous institutions or just perceived and presented as victims by national media to the general electorate, this will prevent central states from both enlarging the existing autonomy and establishing new autonomies. On the other hand, India's constitution ensures to every citizen the same right of free movement and mobility, and - unlike European states – has no clear regulations concerning internal migration and the right of settlement. Against the background of huge internal social and economic divides between various areas, the absence of efficient means of control on internal migration becomes a factor undermining the substantial autonomy of autonomous regional communities.

V. A Burning issue of Territorial Autonomy in India: Immigration

Smaller regional communities and areas that are home to indigenous peoples are vulnerable to demographic change. Several examples around the world show drastically how state-sponsored migration or even systematic population transfer (*transmigrasi* in Indonesia) has undermined the ethnic-social equilibrium of a region

25 Substantial equality means not only the absence of individual discrimination, but equal opportunities: a regime of full public bilingualism, official recognition of minority languages and religions, provision of equal means for cultural services and institutions for all groups, an education system in mother tongue, no discrimination on ethnic grounds in recruitment for public jobs, same opportunities in achieving political charges, affirmative action for historically discriminated groups.

and threatened the very existence of minority peoples (other cases: Bangladesh and the Chittagong Hill Tracts, Indonesia and Borneo, Philippines and Mindanao, China and Xinjiang, Nicaragua and its Atlantic Coast Autonomous Region, Sri Lanka and its Northeast etc). Such smaller regional communities need some control over migration flows if they are to avoid being outnumbered by non-indigenous or non-autochthonous populations. Political stability in the region, social equilibrium between groups, the control of regional resources, and ultimately peace and cultural identity cannot be achieved if demographic development is completely left to external dynamics. This issue must again be sharply distinguished from alleged "internal discrimination," which excludes resident citizens who are not members of regional majorities (or scheduled tribes in India) from certain rights and resources. In Bodoland it makes a difference whether one speaks about a non-scheduled Santal immigrant from West Bengal arrived yesterday, or a Rajbongshi settling there since many generations. The phenomenon of uncontrolled migration is perceived as a threat not only by ethnic minorities in the Northeast (the Bodos in the BTC, the Karbi in Karbi Anglong, the Kokborok in Tripura etc.), but also by State majority peoples (the Assamese of Assam, the Manipuri of Manipur, Garo and Khasi of Meghalaya). Uncontrolled migration, by reversing ethnic majorities, undermines the social position of resident peoples, the general cultural framework, and in the long run, the very legitimacy of autonomy. Incidentally, no sovereign state tolerates free migration under similar arguments: why should autonomous communities not refer to the same arguments?

Hence, devices must be established to enable autonomous regions to control migration to a certain extent, setting provisions consistent with general rules on citizenship and fundamental freedoms of their country. Regions in Europe and South Asia are adopting various means for the same purpose. The Aland Islands have established an "Island citizenship," preventing non-Swedish speaking Finnish citizens to run a business on Aland. South Tyrol has a strict regime of bilingualism requiring each public servant to be fluent in both official languages; furthermore some social benefits and political rights are granted only to persons with legal residency in the region.[26]

Karbi Anglong and Bodoland, as aforementioned referring the regulations of seat reservation in four states' assemblies of India's Northeast, have a regime of seat reservations in the political bodies for STs, which ensures a certain control of the indigenous peoples on legislation and administration. Furthermore some ADCs apply restrictions on land property and land transfer to non-tribal and non-resident people.[27] This has also been a traditional right of the State of Jammu and Kashmir. The Tripura Tribal Area District as well as Arunachal Pradesh move a step further: the "inner line

---

26 The active voting right is regulated by Article 25 of the Autonomy Statute of South Tyrol. See: http://www.provinz.bz.it/lpa/autonomy/autonomy_statute_eng.pdf

27 See point 4.2 of the Memorandum of Settlement on Bodoland Territorial Council, which reads: "A provision will be made in para 2(1) of the Sixth Schedule for increasing the number of members for BTC up to 46 out of which 30 will be reserved for Scheduled Tribes, 5 for non-tribal communities, 5 open for all communities and 6 to be nominated by Governor of Assam from the unrepresented communities for BTC area of which at least two should be women. Nominated members will have the same rights and privileges as other members, including voting rights. Election from the 40 constituencies of BTC shall be on the basis of adult franchise. The term of the elected members of BTC shall be for 5 years." For the full text of the memorandum see: http://www.bodolandcouncil.org

permit" regulation is a kind of internal border to prevent the free influx of settlers into indigenous areas. The means may vary, but the request of autonomous communities is a common one: although a territorial unit of a major state, covered by its legal constitutional order, they do not accept being fully exposed to arbitrary migration movements.

Autonomy in a normative perspective must empower regional communities, not create local fiefdoms with indigenous leadership just replacing foreign dominance. Moreover, autonomy must be meaningful in its scope and material basis. If the number and kind of powers devolved to autonomous bodies is scarce and the powers of control and interference of both superior levels (State and Governor) is too large, real autonomy cannot unfold. If the financial means are too scarce and come too late, and no sources of revenue are assigned to the autonomous governments, they cannot really act as major agents of local development. The division of powers has to be as clear as possible and neutral institution – the Supreme or Constitutional Court – must be the place of negotiation and settlement for any kind of dispute under the rule of law. Finally, in ethnically mixed regions a consociational form of regional government is a must, if stability, the inclusion of all major groups, and interethnic peace is to be achieved. This is the real key to long-term sustainability of regional autonomy established mainly to accommodate an ethnic minority or a smaller tribal people: if the titular ethnic group of an autonomy is not able to include both the members of the state's majority people and other smaller indigenous minority groups in a common project of regional welfare and development, the whole construction is at risk. New violence will trigger counter-violence by victimised groups. Arbitrary discrimination of weaker groups by autonomous legislation and administration will provoke a backlash by the Centre and the groups concerned; violence will eventually bring about new constraints on real autonomy.

Hence, autonomy does not exist to create new discrimination and ethnic cleavages, but to redress the structural imbalance present in nation states or in federated states with a single dominant culture and ethnicity. It is there to create a legal-political space for efficient minority protection, for substantial equality of opportunity, and for consociational self-government of a common home. Ultimately, it is an issue of justice and of quality of democracy, bringing the political power closer to the people.

VI. Conclusion: Transcending the "6th Schedule-Autonomy"

India's federal system in its 62 years of history was repeatedly reshaped: it was first reorganized along linguistic lines, and later further states were carved out from existing ones. In addition India adopted forms of sub-state autonomy or special autonomy, in which smaller ethnic groups were to be accommodated or "minor conflicts" to be settled, but without a coherent scheme. Whereas all major linguistic groups during the linguistic reorganisation of the Indian Union in the 1950s and 1960s were granted their own state, the smaller peoples in the Northeast were not, or at least, only much later (Manipur, Meghalaya, Arunachal Pradesh) or only after protected military violence (Mizoram, Nagaland); while the 6th schedule autonomy was applied to some areas in the Northeast, in order to avoid the further division of Assam, other States in central India including West Bengal refrained from granting such autonomy even to numerically very sizeable regional or tribal communities (Gorkhaland, Santals, Bhili, Gondi, Ho, Kurukh/Oraon and others).

Thus both the basic constitutional principles of territorial power sharing in India appear far from being coherently applied: on the one hand there is federalism for equal or symmetric power sharing between the centre and all federated units, and on the other territorial autonomy to meet requirements for territorial power sharing at the sub-state level has been established only exceptionally. This is a serious problem as India's federalism is marked by strong centralism: the federal government is vested with unusual powers for a federation, while at State level most powers are concentrated in the hands of the State administration. Local democracy is provided only by the institution of the *panchayat*s – the democratic councils in villages and municipalities. We have to keep in mind that European federations and regional states are not bigger than West Bengal (Germany, the most populous European state after Russia, has 82 million citizens), but are articulated in federal units or autonomous communities with the size of Indian districts. Therefore there is still a great need and potential for further decentralization to the lower units that make up the single federated states. This can occur in a symmetric form, including all sub-state entities, or in an asymmetric form, reserved for some districts with special needs and interests, such as those inhabited by ethnic minorities and tribal peoples. Territorial autonomies can be established even outside the federal units, as claimed by concerned political organizations from Ladakh and Gorkhaland. But if regional autonomy on a sub-state level does not match the people's expectations, demands for a full-fledged federated state will reappear on India's political agenda.

The institution of India's "Autonomous District Councils," under the 6th Schedule of the Constitution, was originally conceived as a solution for tribal peoples and ethnic conflicts in the Northeast during the initial period of nation building. Established by the fathers of the Constitution to avoid splitting up the multiethnic Northeast, which was faced with a variety of self-determination claims by tribal peoples, the ADCs in their current form cannot meet the political requirements on the ground. It worked as a temporary painkiller, but the pain was to remain.[28] Assam was split up, and four resulting states (Assam, Meghalaya, Manipur and Tripura) adopted the 6th Schedule autonomy to accommodate sub-state self-government demands by smaller ethnic communities and peoples. The very ethnically homogeneous Northeast remained conflict ridden. After many uprisings, violent rebellions, and years of low intensity warfare and military resistance by guerrilla groups and "national liberation fronts", some ethnic groups and peoples managed to obtain their own federated states, including Mizoram, Nagaland and Meghalaya. Other states, such as West Bengal, Jammu and Kashmir, and Assam, had to accord territorial district autonomy to their own minorities (Leh and Kargil, Karbi Anglong and North Cachar Bodoland). The smaller Northeastern States, such as Tripura and Mizoram, had to come to terms with their internal ethnic heterogeneity. Nevertheless, the existing legal setting and scope as given by the 6th Schedule does not offer sufficient political space for a fully autonomous cultural and language policy or for the comprehensive range of powers needed to allow the ADC to be the most important agent for social and economic development in the area. The State government and the Union governor of the

---

28 See Ranabir Samaddar, "Minority Rights and Forms of Autonomy in South Asia", in: Zelim A. Skurbaty (ed.), *Beyond a one-dimensional state: an emerging right to autonomy?*, (Martinus Nijhoff Publishers: Leiden/Boston, 2005), 551.

respective State exert major hierarchical control, while neither has a sufficient or autonomously controlled financial base.
In addition to the limited scope of the 6th Schedule-autonomy, there is a need to focus on the quality of democracy and governance allowed by these territorial autonomies. The population of some ADCs in the Northeast sees autonomy as just an institutional process, and do not feel sufficiently involved. The participation of the people and civil society of some ADCs remained very low. This is due to both the weak institutional design and the particular form of the elite-determined political setting at the sub-state level in India. The mere decentralization of power to local elites – as was the case in Darjeeling - is not enough. There must be provisions to ensure good governance, accountability of the politicians, minority protection and consociational mechanisms of power sharing.
Some other features of the 6th Schedule autonomy, however, no longer appear appropriate for genuine autonomous legislation and decision making: relying on the Governor's strong role in surveillance rather than giving the judiciary the main responsibility for dissolving disputes, financial dependency on the respective state, the ADCs' lack of power to create their own revenues, gaps in the application of official language policies, the need for fair regulations for recruitment on territorial basis, and the need of forms of immigration control to the autonomous area that are compatible with fundamental rights of all citizens.
The 6th Schedule has implicit limitations, as unrest in several autonomies such as Karbi Anglong, North Cachar and Mizoram's ADCs demonstrates. Some features of this autonomy were extended in 2003, when the 6th Schedule was amended to accord greater autonomy to Bodoland. But the Gorkhaland issue can no longer be met with the means of limited self-governance offered by the 6th Schedule. The political evolution of India's Northeast clearly shows that continuous pressure from the ground, political organization and popular pressure led first to serious negotiations between the regional communities and the Centre, then to the establishment of autonomies, and eventually to an increase in territorial autonomy. The complex power sharing settlement in the Northeastern states has not yet come to an end, nor has the Kashmir issue been resolved. The majority of tribal peoples still live in States like Madhya Pradesh, Orissa and Jharkhand, while several peoples, such as the Santhali, Gonda, Munda, and Ho are mostly scattered across several states, but often form a majority on the district level. Lacking political organization and influence they could generate movements for territorial or cultural autonomy, although it is high time they do so, if they want more attention and a real commitment for the protection of their minority rights. The 6th schedule autonomy might not be enough to meet this demand of autonomy, let alone reservations and tribal councils under the 5th Schedule.

CHAPTER 7

Autonomy, Kashmir and International Law

Kaiyan Homi Kaikobad*

I. Introduction

This paper seeks to reflect on the notion of and issues attendant with autonomy followed by an application of these matters to the Kashmir dispute. It is important to note that this paper seeks to focus on the topic from the point of view of law, and in particular international law; it eschews looking at the question of the politics and sociology of autonomy although these perspectives also have a major role to play.

II. Preliminary Comments on Autonomy

It will be appropriate to look at certain essential preliminary aspects of autonomy with a view to providing perspective. Hence, in the first instance, attention will focus on certain essential terminology and provenance, followed up in the second section on the general meaning and description of autonomy. Thereafter in the third section reference will be made to the legal issues surrounding the notion of autonomy from the point of view of international law.

A. General Meaning and Description

While the notion of autonomy itself is fairly straight-forward, it is important to note that there is no fixed definition of this kind of territorial regime. Nor is there any fixed terminology and in view of that it will suffice to provide a short descriptive account, an account which starts by observing that autonomy is primarily a legal state of affairs wherein a territorial unit within a State exercises a degree of governmental control which is characterised by a variable measure of independence from either the central authorities or from other territorial units therein or both. In other words, the power exercised by the territorial unit is greater and/or more extensive than either the rest of that State or other territorial units therein; or where all territorial units exercise similar degrees of separateness from the centre within that State, provided always that sovereignty continues to vest in the mother State or centre thereof. In short, the control over government and administration which an autonomous unit exercises is usually separate from the general administrative structure of the State. It may exercise powers by virtue of the different and higher levels of authority it is allowed to exercise from the rest of that State.

Nor, as remarked earlier, is there any uniformity in usage. Hence, different autonomous units may well have different names. Thus an autonomous unit may be described as a Special Region or Special Administrative Region or Zone, the nomenclature used for Hong Kong, a republic an independent republic, a dependency

* Professor of International Law, Brunel Law School, Brunel University.

or Dependent Territory, or an autonomous region, or Associate State, as in Palau in Micronesia; or even State, as used in the official description of the State of Azad Jammu and Kashmir. The essential point is that international law is blind to varied terminology for such autonomous units and autonomy as long as the essential characteristics are met.

B. Essential Features and Provenance

In terms of features, and as an aid to furthering an understanding the notion of autonomy described above, it is not difficult to identify two kinds of features which attend this concept, namely positive and negative. As far as the positive aspect is concerned, autonomy is generally speaking a territorial regime which, while in principle separated from the main administrative structure of the territorial State, is nonetheless so closely linked or attached in law and/or fact that the two are in fact inseparable. As far as the negative aspect is concerned, an autonomous region, while linked closely to the main territorial State, enjoys a degree of self government independent from the State which claims and exercises sovereignty over the region; thus it lacks the essence of Statehood. Hong Kong and Macau are good examples of these two features. Thus while these two entities enjoy a large degree of independence from the sovereign authority in Beijing, they are undeniably Chinese in historical, geographical ethnic and cultural terms.

It is also useful to identify the features and factors which are not necessary for an autonomous relation between the mother State and the unit. First, geographical separation is neither synonymous nor vital to autonomy, although it may be factor in allowing autonomous status. Thus Hong Kong and Macau have a degree of geographical separation from China in that they consist mainly of islands and insular features and hence are not part of the mainland. Yet that is not a reason why they are autonomous units within China. Indeed, as the High Court of Australia held in the context of Hong Kong special administrative region or HKSAR, "It is not to the point that this region or area is not geographically divorced from what might be called the metropolitan area of that country [namely the people's republic of china]."[1]

Secondly, there ought not to be any confusion between an enclave and an autonomous unit. An enclave is a parcel of territory belonging to a State which is separated from that State but is either completely or partially surrounded by another State, that is, a State with which it has no links of sovereignty. Thus while Cabinda is surrounded by the Democratic Republic of Congo and the sea to the west, it appertains to Angola south of the border; and Ocussi, an enclave belonging to Timor-Leste, is geographically separate therefrom and is partially surrounded by West Timor, Indonesia and by the sea to the north. However, it is the case that Alaska, while wholly separated from the United States geographically, is not an enclave of the latter not only because it is geographically rather extensive, but also because it has an extremely large coastline on four sides of its territory and only two land sectors adjoin Canada. Of course there is nothing in law which precludes an enclave from enjoying autonomy, but that is not an essential element in the status of an enclave.

---

1 *Attorney General (Commonwealth of Australia) vs. Tse Chu-Fai and Another* 114 *ILR* 384, 398.

Thirdly, a clear distinction needs to be drawn between territories which are separated from the host, territorial or mother State[2] and which consequently enjoy a degree of autonomy as a result of armed hostilities between the host or mother State and an occupying power. In such circumstances, the position of the territory will be determined by reference to the fact that it is in belligerent occupation of that autonomous unit. Entities separated by occupying forces after belligerency will not be *de jure* autonomous units although they may well be *de facto* autonomous entities. The difficulty is that this can be a very complex situation. States have indeed been known to argue that the forces occupying the territory are in fact liberators and that in fact any continuation of integration would be contrary to law. In view of the complexities of such a situation, it is perhaps safer to exclude rather than include units of this kind from this study.

C. *Autonomy as a Creature of Law and Fact*

It is the last point made above which informs this category of observations. The creation or termination of an autonomous unit is governed by law, the point being that any unit, which claims autonomy from the mother entity, must claim that autonomy on the basis of law. By way of example then because the separation of the province of Manchuria by the Japanese armed forces in 1931was an unlawful act then all attempts to create either an independent State/Kingdom, as an autonomous entity known as Manchukuo, would also be unlawful, and subject to the doctrine of non recognition.[3] Acts of this kind, of course, also engage the international responsibility of the State acting unlawfully, namely Japan.

Thus two kinds of law are applicable here, namely international and domestic law. Where the existence of the autonomous unit is owed to treaties or international participation and guarantees and the like; or where the entity's existence is unlawful by way of international law, then acknowledgment of that illegality will preclude that unit from becoming autonomous in international law. The same applies where the above case of autonomy is primarily of internal, domestic law and politics as seen in the context of the constitutional laws of the territorial or mother State.

II. THE CREATION OF AUTONOMOUS UNITS

It is tempting to present a brief account of some of the different and varied ways in which autonomous entities have come into existence. The reason for this temptation is easy to fathom. The process of the creation provides substantial insight into the heart of the matter: it shows why it was that an autonomous entity was created in the first place and its justification thereof. Important to note is that while they have been listed below as discrete processes there is a degree of overlap and congruence between them and that fact ought to be kept in mind. Nonetheless they have been itemised below.

2 These terms will be used interchangeably to refer to the State which hosts the autonomous unit or units.

3 See on this James Crawford, "*The Creation of States in International Law*", (Clarendon Press, Oxford 1979), 59-60.

A. *By way of historical and/or feudal processes*

This is perhaps the foremost way in which an autonomous entity can come into existence, that is, by way of historical and feudal consolidation and processes. Inner Mongolia Autonomous Region is perhaps a foremost example of this insofar as the Mongolian princes, as George W. Keeton notes, enjoyed a large measure of autonomy even in the days of the Chinese Empire.[4] The Chinese Manchu emperors extended their authority into Mongolia in the 18th century[5] and gradually consolidated their control. While Outer Mongolia became a Soviet dependency following the Russian Revolution, Inner Mongolia remained with China although separatist tendencies remained strong when Japan invaded Manchuria in 1931.[6] Hence, it was a logical step which the Communist regime took when, even before it had assumed power in 1949, to grant Inner Mongolia autonomous status in 1947.

B. *By way of realignment of empire or disintegration*

Entities enjoying varying degrees of autonomy may also come about by way of re-alignment following the disintegration of empire or realignment thereof. Here Kosovo provides an example. Claimed as the very heartland of the Serb nation,[7] Kosovo was detached by the Balkan League from the waning Ottoman Empire as a result of the First Balkan War in 1912 and large parts thereof were consequentially absorbed by Serbia and Montenegro,[8] but then Albania, which had gained a degree of autonomy from the Ottomans[9], fought over it and incorporated it into its territories in 1915.[10] However, soon afterwards Serbia took it back in 1918 where it remained until 1941 when Nazi Germany and Italy invaded and took control of Yugoslavia. Kosovo was occupied by Italy and was then allocated to Albania.[11] In 1945 it was re-absorbed by Tito's Yugoslavia amid conflicting claims from different Albanian political groups, that is, those claiming Kosovo for Albania and those for integration with Yugoslavia.[12] Nonetheless, in July 1946, Kosovo, or Kosmet,[13] was declared an

---

4 See George W Keeton, China, "*The Far East and the Future*", (Stevens, London 1949), 187.
5 Ibid, 117.
6 Ibid, 187.
7 See Peter Radan, "*The Break-up of Yugoslavia and International Law*", (Routledge, London 2002), 154; and Bruce McFarlane, *Yugoslavia Politics, Economics and Society*, (Printer Publishers, London and New York 1988), 30; and Duska Anastasijevic, "The Closing of the Kosovo Cycle: Victimisation versus Responsibility", in Albrecht Schnabel and Ramesh Thakur (eds.), "*Kosovo and the Challenge of Humanitarian Intervention, Selective Indignation, Collective Action and International Citizenship*", (United Nations University Press, Tokyo 2000), 44, at 59, note 4.
8 See J. R. Marriott, "*The Eastern Question An Historical Study in European Diplomacy*" (Fourth edition, Clarendon Press, Oxford 1940), 465; Tim Judah, "*Kosovo War and Revenge*", (Yale University Press, USA 2002), 17; and Marie-Janine Calic, "Kosovo in the Twentieth Century: A Historical Account" in Albrecht Schnabel and Ramesh Thakur (eds.), *op. cit.* note 7, 19-20.
9 See Marie-Janine Calic, *op. cit.* note 8, 20.
10 See Tim Judah, *op. cit.* note 8, 19-20.
11 *Ibid.*, 26-27; and Marie-Janine Calic, *op. cit.* note 8, 20. Further, see William H. Seton-Watson, "Albania", in Arnold Toynbee, and Veronica Toynbee (eds.), "*The Realignment of Europe*", (Oxford University Press, Oxford 1955), 371 at 374.
12 See Marie-Janine Calic, *op. cit.* note 8, 20-21.
13 A portmanteau word for Kosovo and Metohija. It reverted back to Kosovo in 1963.

autonomous entity within the Republic of Serbia and Montenegro, a federal unit of the Federal Republic of Yugoslavia.[14]

C. *By way of imperialism*

There are a good many examples of the creation of autonomous entities by way of protectorates by the metropolitan powers. As far as imperialism is concerned, reference may be made to the group of sheikhdoms on the Arabian littoral of the Persian Gulf. Previously known light-heartedly as the Pirate Coast, this region was the scene of great European competition, particularly Portugal, France and Great Britain. Eventually and starting from the early years of the nineteenth century, the latter prevailed, motivated no doubt by a policy consideration consistent with the elimination of piracy which posed a constant threat to maritime traffic in the Persian Gulf, Arabian sea and in turn the Empire in India.[15] Kuwait, Muscat, Oman, Bahrain and the sheikhdoms of Abu Dhabi, Dubai, Sharjah and Ras al Khaimah were brought under individual protectorates. The Trucial States as they became known enjoyed a good range of powers by way of internal autonomy, having left by way of treaty, the responsibility of foreign affairs and defence to Britain. These classic examples of protectorates were terminated, again by way of treaty with the United Kingdom, and assumed full sovereignty in 1971.

D. *By way of colonialism*

As far as colonialism is concerned, a plethora of examples exist, and again the British Empire does duty. Just one of these examples is the group of about three hundred princely States which were dotted across the entire sub-continent. These States, including the extremely large Kashmir and Hyderabad states, and the extremely small Hunza, were principalities enjoying various degrees of autonomy, and although legally not part of British India were administratively linked to the latter in terms of officials and appointments and accountability and to that extent these were in fact a variety of colonial control.

E. *By way of decolonisation*

Autonomous units may be created at the time of decolonisation by the newly independent State or by the relevant source of power or authority. This could either be by way of a new arrangement following a failure to agree a disposition thereof; or it may be a perpetuation of the old colonial regime. The Eritrean experience is an example of the former. While Eritrea was absorbed fully by Italy as a colony in 1890, Ethiopia remained independent of Italy but came briefly under Italian control between 1935 and 1947.[16] However after the end of the 1939-1945 War, there was no

---

14 See Marie-Janine Calic, *op. cit.* note 8, 20-21.

15 See Husain M. Al-Bahrana, "*The Gulf Arabian States Their Legal and Political Status and Their International Problems*" (Second revised edition), (Librairie du Liban, Beirut 1975), Chapter 2, Part One, 25 *et seq*.

16 See Kaiyan H. Kaikobad, "The Eritrea-Ethiopia Boundary Commission: A Legal Analysis of the Boundary Delimitation Decision of 13th April 2002 and Relevant Decisions", in Andrea de Guttry,

agreement between the Allied Powers, the United Nations and Ethiopia as to its final disposition, and thus finally in 1952, the United Nations General Assembly resolved to merge Eritrea with Ethiopia but as an autonomous federated unit.[17] It was the abrogation of this autonomous status in November 1952 which gave birth to the independence movement, a movement which culminated in 1991 when Ethiopia's military junta finally caved in and when a peace conference in Addis Ababa agreed to grant Eritrea its independence.[18]

F. By way of perpetuation of colonialism

As far as the perpetuation of the colonial system is concerned, the Federally Administered Tribal Areas of Pakistan furnish an example. The British Empire, as it gradually crept through north-westwards in India in the eighteenth and nineteenth centuries began to face resistance greater than it had in the south-east; and after annexing the Punjab and the Pathan homelands in the plains, the so-called North West Frontier Province, in the middle of the nineteenth century, the British administration and its forces found themselves hugely stretched. It was therefore politic for the British to allow the Pathans living in the narrow highlands strip bordering Afghanistan to the west to maintain their own tribal systems and accordingly entered into treaty relations with them which guaranteed informal autonomy and minimal interference with loose control by the Political Agent. These Tribal Areas, as they began to be called, were ancestral homelands of the Afridis, the Waziris, the Mohammands, and other Pathan tribal nations, and they decided in 1947 to align themselves with Pakistan as the British departed and the Government of Pakistan, anxious not to generate any centrifugal tendencies, perpetuated the British system of control and administration.[19]

G. By way of perpetuation of imperialism

Although colonialism is today primarily of historic interest, its reverberations and after-effects are still to be felt in the international community of States and while there is absolutely no prospect or question of any return to colonialism, some acts of former colonies and newly independent States fall in the category which could easily be described as a perpetuation of colonialism or imperialism. India's latter day absorption of Bhutan and its relations with Sikkim provide an example of this category of State conduct. Bhutan and Sikkim are both small Himalayan historical entities. Both were at one stage in their history, vassal kingdoms of Tibet, and hence indirectly acknowledged China as overlord. Sikkim lies between Nepal to the west and Bhutan to the east. British expansion into Sikkim was conspicuous by the middle

---

Harry Post and Gabriella Venturini (eds.), "*The 1998-2000 War between Eritrea and Ethiopia An International Legal Perspective*", (T M C Asser Press, The Hague 2009), 171-172.

17 See Resolution 390A of 1950: Kaiyan H. Kaikobad, *op. cit. supra* note 16, 173.

18 See Kaiyan H. Kaikobad, *op. cit.* note 16, 173.

19 Generally, see James W. Spain, "*The Way of the Pathans*" (Second edition, Oxford University Press, Karachi 1972), Chapter 3; and L. F. Rushbrook Williams, *The State of Pakistan* (Revised edition, Faber and Faber, London 1966), 64 *et seq*.

of the nineteenth century,[20] and by 1860, the kingdom had begun to agree concessions and control to this European power via the Treaty of Tumlong.[21]

China recognised Sikkim's effective protectorate status in the Sikkim-Tibet Convention of 1890, but Britain agreed to leave part of Sikkim to Tibet. Accordingly, it became necessary to divide it by way of a boundary line along the Chumbi Valley on the southern or Indian side of the Himalayan watershed leaving the northern part to Tibet.[22] The southern part of Sikkim continued as a protectorate under the British Government.[23] The motivation informing British policy was to use the Tibetan plateau as a buffer against China[24] and it therefore suited the British Indian Government to use Sikkim as a protectorate which obviated the prospect of merging it with British India, that is, the territory ruled directly by Britain in all manifestations of sovereign authority in India. On this view then after the independence of India in 1947, the standard strategic policy considerations of the British Raj did not apply and yet, India was motivated to perpetuate this colonial state of affairs, at least for the time being.

Thus, in 1950, Sikkim and India agreed to continue the protectorate status, according it a degree of autonomy.[25] This, however, was not enough for India, and so following internal turmoil, the Government of India took the opportunity which presented itself, and annexed Sikkim in 1974. There was, to be sure, a referendum in 1975 on the future status of the kingdom, that is, whether it should be an absolute monarchy, or become a "constituent unit" of the Indian Union.[26] It was reported that the vote went in favour of the latter. Thus, after over one hundred years of being a quasi-independent Himalayan kingdom, Sikkim had to succumb to the status of a being a "constituent unit" of the Indian Union,[27] and, importantly, it did not even attain the position of an Associate State.

Bhutan poses more problems. It has had close links with Tibet by virtue of natural affiliations and commercial ties,[28] and it enjoyed the status of a vassal to it, but began to succumb to British control in the seventeenth century when it concluded a treaty in 1774 with Great Britain, a treaty wherein it agreed to give tribute to the latter and cede territory to British India.[29] Control over Bhutan was tightened by way of the treaty of 1865, and then in 1910, the foreign relations of Bhutan were vested in British India

---

20 See Premen Addy, "*Tibet on the Imperial Chessboard the Making of British Policy towards Lhasa, 1899-1925*", (Sangam Books, London 1984), 16.

21 See Peter Macalister-Smith, "Sikkim" in Rudolf Bernhardt (ed.), *Encyclopedia of Public International Law* (First edition), Max Planck Institute for Comparative Public Law and International Law, vol. xii, 1981, 345-346; and Barry Turner (ed.), *"The Statesman's Yearbook 2001"*, (Macmillan, London, 2000), 831.

22 See Alastair Lamb, "*Kashmir A Disputed Legacy*", (Oxford University Press, Karachi 1992), 50, note 47; and Premen Addy, *op. cit. supra* note 20, 17.

23 See Alastair Lamb, *op. cit. supra* note 22, 50, note 47.

24 See Premen Addy, *op. cit. supra* note 20, 17.

25 See Peter Macalister-Smith, *op. cit. supra* note 21, 347.

26 *Ibid.*, 347.

27 *Ibid.*, 347.

28 See Peter Macalister-Smith, "Bhutan", in Rudolf Bernhardt (ed.), *op. cit.* note 21, 63. Further see Joanne Maher (ed.) "*Europa World Yearbook 2009*", (Routledge, London 2009), vol. ii, 888; where the entry makes reference to giving greater autonomy to Bhutan in the fields of external and military affairs.

29 See Peter Macalister-Smith, *op. cit. supra* note 28, 65.

via another agreement. Bhutan accepted that while it would be guided by the British Indian Government in foreign affairs, internal self government was assured.[30] Dependency was strengthened when British India agreed to and did enhance levels of assistance. The same subservient status as a client State or protectorate was continued in 1949 when Bhutan agreed to maintain Britain's arrangements with India and be guided by it in matters of foreign affairs.[31] Importantly all military weapons were subject to Indian approval and assistance, thus allowing it to control Bhutan's defence capabilities.[32] However, in 2007, the two entities concluded an updated version of their 1949 Friendship Treaty,[33] Article 4 of which provides:

"The Government of India agrees that the Government of Bhutan shall be free to import, from or through India into Bhutan, whatever arms, ammunition, machinery, warlike material or stores as may be required or desired for the strength and welfare of Bhutan, and that this arrangement shall hold good for all time as long as the Government of India is satisfied that the intentions of the Government of Bhutan are friendly and that there is no danger to India from such importations. "

The Government of Bhutan agrees that there shall be no export of such arms, ammunition and materials outside Bhutan either by the Government of Bhutan or by private individuals

It appears therefore that India seems to be softening its position towards the Himalayan kingdom. In fact, however, this provision does not appear to mark a major shift of policy and Indian defence control over Bhutan will continue in more subtle ways. The facts as stated above could be seen as tending to show that Bhutan is in fact a vassal State to India as opposed to having autonomy, but that would constitute ignoring the fact that its links with India have the constituent hallmarks of a protectorate, namely where defence lies with the dominant territorial unit. The best that can be said then is that Bhutan is an example of a semi-sovereign entity, or of possessing autonomy *sui generis*.

H. By way of treaty and internationalisation

The autonomy of a territorial unit may also come about by way of treaty, that is, autonomy may be grounded and guaranteed by way of an international agreement between the dominant State and the ceding State. The difference between this category and the categories of colonialism and imperialism outlined above is in fact minimal, perhaps even non-existent, but for purposes of this study, there is one difference. Here the ceding State and the dominant State agree to an arrangement whereby part of the territory of the ceding State is administered as an autonomous entity as opposed to an integrated unit thereof. This arrangement may in fact be a way forward as a compromise settlement in a disputed situation. It may be useful here to make reference to the arrangement made by the British and Chinese Governments in 1984 with respect to Hong Kong.

---

30 *Ibid.*, 65-66.
31 *Ibid.*, 69.
32 *Ibid.*, 67.
33 Text on the Bhutannica web-site.

By way of the treaties of 1842 and 1843, China had given Hong Kong in perpetuity to Great Britain, and then in 1860, China ceded more territory in perpetuity to the latter State. However, in 1898, China concluded a treaty with Great Britain which gave the latter the New Territories in lease for 99 years.[34]

Thus, when the United Kingdom began its negotiations with China over the future of Hong Kong, it was conscious that it had mixed status over that parcel of territory. While part of it could in principle be given complete freedom because it had sovereignty over those territories, the latter would not have been viable without the New Territories;[35] but more importantly, the United Kingdom had no sovereignty to transfer as far as the New Territories were concerned. Nor would China have tolerated independent entities on its south eastern coastline. Any independent units would probably have been absorbed by Beijing almost immediately. This state of affairs, its realism, persuaded the British Government to pursue the best possible regime for Hong Kong, whilst excluding complete independence. Thus in 1984, a treaty, referred to as the Joint Declaration, was concluded by the Parties.[36] The United Kingdom agreed that from 1 July 1997, it would not exercise sovereignty over Hong Kong and that the territory would become an [autonomous] administrative region within China for a period of fifty years. In short the autonomy of Hong Kong is in fact an obligation imposed upon China by way a binding treaty provision, although one which is limited by time as opposed to being permanent. The autonomous status of Hong Kong is also of course regulated by Chinese domestic law, but the decision to make Hong Kong into a "Special Administrative Region" is based in the treaty between the United Kingdom and China in 1984.

I. By way of domestic arrangements

A State may embark on a policy of granting certain entities and territorial minority nations a degree of autonomy as an acknowledgment of their distinct personality within the territorial sovereignty of the host national State. Reference to this can be made to the Azores. Lying in the middle of the Atlantic, the nine islands of Azores came under Portuguese influence and expansionism in the fourteenth century onwards[37] and subsequently became a place of refuge for political exiles[38] escaping the two dozen revolutions between 1910 and 1926.[39] The year 1976 marks the beginning of the period when some political stability began to emerge in Portugal, one

---

34 See A. D. Hughes, "Hong Kong", in Rudolf Bernhardt (ed.), "*Encyclopedia of Public International Law*" (Second edition), Max Planck Institute for Comparative Public Law and International Law, vol. ii, 1990, 870. For an official UK account of the history, see Misc. No. 28 (1984), Cmd. 9352, 252-253.

35 See A. D. Hughes, *op. cit.* note 34, 871. The "inability to assume long-term possession of the New Territories" was already agitating the colonial authorities by the third decade of the twentieth century: see Peter Wesley-Smith, *Unequal Treaty 1898-1997 China, Great Britain and Hong Kong's New Territories*, (Oxford University Press, Hong Kong 1983), 156 *et seq*.

36 For the Draft Text, see 23 (1984) *ILM* 1366; and for the definitive text, see *Cumulative Digest of United States Practice of International Law 1981-88*, vol. i, Washington, DC, 1993, 240.

37 See Thomas Benedikter, "*The World's Working Autonomous Regional Autonomies An Introduction and Comparative Analysis*", (Anthem Press, London 2007), 204.

38 *Ibid.*

39 See Florence Elliott and Michael Summerskill, "*A Dictionary of Politics*" (Revised edition), (Penguin, London 1961), 279.

reflection of which was that the Constitution granted Azores and Madeira the status of "Autonomous Regions" of Portugal with the caveat that the sovereignty of Portugal over the Azores remained unaffected.[40]

Similarly, the Kurdish nation of Iraq has enjoyed a good degree of autonomy both *de facto* and *de jure*. As long ago as 1970, Iraq had agreed to grant autonomy to the Kurds but the there were difficulties on the question of the allocation of Kirkuk,[41] a city peopled by Kurds, Arab Iraqis and Turkmen. However, autonomy laws were promulgated in 1974 but the Kurdish Democratic Party clamoured for postponement until a fresh census was held.[42] Matters were further complicated by the fact that the KDP was unable to cooperate with and warred with the Patriotic Union of Kurdistan. Greater autonomy was demanded by these factions from the centre throughout the 1980s and the Kurdish Autonomous Region was established in May 1988[43] but Baghdad began a forced withdrawal of Kurds from the Region in order to create a buffer zone along the Turkish-Iraqi frontier, a policy which caused major problems for the Iraqi Government in terms of Kurdish resistance.[44] In 1991, the Kurds agitated for the implementation of the 1970 Peace Plan but there was a period in the early 1990s when the two main parties had a rift and matters deteriorated.[45] In 1992, elections were organised by the Kurdish Iraqi Front to the Iraqi Kurdish National Assembly, and by 1996 Kurdish autonomy was re-established by Baghdad. After the defeat of the Iraqi army in March-April 2003, the Kurds began to continue to press for their autonomy and in the 2005 Constitution the Kurdish Autonomous Region was once established.[46] The Kurdish Regional Government is the manifestation of this autonomy.

J. By way of post armed conflict settlement and management

Finally, for current purposes, some account must be made of territorial units which have acquired autonomy as a way forward in a dispute settlement process following the end of internal civil strife or military conflict. Autonomy in this kind of situation represents a compromise between two conflicting demands, that is, secession on one side and continued unity with the host State on the other. The Aceh conflict in Indonesia is a good example.

Fiercely independent minded, the Acehnese were late in being subdued by the Dutch[47] and have been motivated to defend their distinct sense of identity as forcefully as ever, and importantly even against the newly independent successor State of Indonesia. An orthodox version of Islam and Islamic traditions has been a veritable source of their collective identity and secessionist movements since the early 1950s. The Movement

---

40 See Thomas Benedikter, *op. cit.* note 37, 204.

41 See Joanne Maher (ed.), "Iraq" in *Europa World Yearbook 2009* note 28, 2344-2345. See also Kjell-Åke Nordquist, "Autonomy as a conflict solving mechanism—an overview", in Markku Suksi (ed.), "*Autonomy: Applications and Implications*", (Kluwer Law, The Hague 1998), 60 at 75.

42 See Dilip Hiro, "*Desert Shield to Desert Storm*", (Paladin, London 1992), 51.

43 See Joanne Maher, *op. cit.* note 41, 2345.

44 *Ibid.*; and Dilip Hiro, *op. cit.* note 42, 52-53.

45 See Joanne Maher, *op. cit.* note 41, 2344-46.

46 *Ibid.*, 2345.

47 This account based largely on Thomas Benedikter's masterful study, *op. cit.* note 37, 291-99.

for an Independent Aceh, or GAM, began to clash with Indonesian armed forces in the early part of the seventh decade of the twentieth century; but this protracted conflict is one which is characterised by ceasefires and resumption of hostilities.[48] Accordingly, an agreement between the Indonesian military and the Aceh separatists was indeed concluded in 2001, but it collapsed soon thereafter and there was a resumption of hostilities. It was, ironically, the tragedy of the tsunami of 2004 which actually brought the two sides to the negotiating table in Helsinki, the reason for which is the fact that Aceh lost nearly a quarter of million inhabitants as a direct effect of the giant tidal wave. A new peace agreement was concluded in 2005 wherein the autonomy of Aceh was affirmed. It was an autonomy which left defence, foreign affairs, national security, monetary and fiscal policies, justice and religious freedoms in the hands of the central Indonesian Government. The *quid pro quo* for Indonesia of course is that Aceh's GAM has foresworn independence.

III. Essential Characteristic Features of Autonomous Units and Autonomy

Autonomy may be described and explained by reference to some salient characteristics, all of which are discussed below.

A. Self Government

This is in fact central to the notion of autonomy;[49] it is the existence of a substantial degree of self government which actually defines a territorial unit claiming to be an autonomous entity. Indeed, the term autonomy means self government. There are various points to be made under this heading. First, self government in an autonomous unit may either be *de facto* or *de jure*. This means that while the powers of government exercised by an entity claiming to be an autonomous unit may be a lawful and constitutional exercise of power, they may also be some cases where this exercise of power is unconstitutional and to that extent unlawful, and hence in principle only a *de facto* situation on the ground. It is the case that many situations of this kind do exist ranging from territorial entities which have broken free from central control by way of revolutionary means on the one side and, on the other, entities which have or sought to and have amassed various degrees of power but not formally vested in them. This kind of *de facto* autonomy existed in the Kurdish region in the northern parts of Iraq after the central Iraqi Government began gradually to lose its firm grip on the region after 1991 and finally lost all control after the US-UK invasion in 2003. In terms of domestic and constitutional law the exercise of such power is clearly unlawful, but *international* law will not be concerned with that aspect unless and until that entity begins to claim that it is a State, and when it does so, issues of statehood, international personality and recognition will come into play; but, importantly, if and when that happens, it will cease to be an autonomous unit and become an unrecognised State. For international law the point of interest lies in the fact that that the autonomous unit is not a sovereign entity or nor can it exercise sovereignty or sovereign rights; and that that entity is importantly part of another territorial unit,

48 *Ibid.*, 291-94.
49 Generally see James Crawford, *op. cit.* note 3, 211-14.

namely the host or mother territorial State and which is, to that extent, devoid of full international legal personality.

Secondly, every case of self government does not necessarily mean autonomy. It is a fact that every unit, big or small, in a State will have some measure of power and control independent of the central government. Thus a village district may well have the power to decide upon matters of local administration with respect to schools and colleges, medicine, health and hospitals the like. Yet it would be idle to regard that village as being an autonomous territorial unit of the State. The essential criterion then is the nature, scope and effect of the powers exercised; and the closer they get to or are consistent with higher State functions of a public kind, then the closer that entity is to being described as an autonomous unit. In other words, for autonomy, there must in the first place, be a set of powers which approximate to high government as opposed simply to local administration, and secondly the power actually exercised ought necessarily to be substantial in degree and scale.

Thirdly, an autonomous unit within a territorial State will typically be a regime different or separate or special from the "stock" government and administration of the State. Another way of expressing this point is to observe that it is normal to expect that the powers associated with self government vested in an entity will be different from those provided to other territories and units within that State under the constitution. Example here can be derived from the different kinds of autonomous regimes prevalent within China and the Russian Federation.[50] Both have their standard systems of government with several autonomous units in each State as a separate or special legal system of government. Importantly, of course, this element is not crucial or vital to the concept under study. There are at least two reasons.

First, some States are comprised throughout with autonomous units, with no other standard or stock regime other than a system of autonomous units of various kinds. Both Spain and the United States fall in this category. Spain has seventeen autonomous communities and two autonomous cities.[51] It is true of course that the three small islands off the coast of Morocco, although regarded as autonomous islands are in fact administered directly by the central government in Madrid, and that this hardly a "stock regime". The United States has fifty highly autonomous states and one Federal district; and a number of dependent areas. Thus, both States have a form of government where largely autonomous entities are associated with each other through one over-arching government, which, as far as the United States is concerned, is the Federal Government, and which for Spain is the central government whose nominal head is the King. In this kind of a legal order, there are no standard or stock systems which have no autonomous units therein as an exception.

The second reason is that there may well be different categories of special regimes with varying degrees of powers but which do not have autonomy in the sense of self

---

50 See Hans-Joachim Heintze, "On the Legal Understanding of Autonomy", in Markku Suksi (ed.), *op. cit.* note 41, 7-15. It is important to remember that Russia's autonomous regions and districts have degrees of autonomy. Under Article 66 of the 1993 Russian Constitution, autonomy is regulated by federal law and an agreement between bodies of state power of the territory or the regions. Also see Article 77.

51 See Sergio Bartole, "Regionalism and Federalism in the Italian Constitutional Experience", in Markku Suksi, *op. cit.* note 41, 173-199. The autonomy however is limited in scope and varied in legal character: see 199 and 210-12.

government. This then in a sense dilutes the notion of different or special kind of regime, and here the United States can be cited as an example. Apart from the fifty federating units or "states" and one Federal District of the United States, there are some "dependent areas" which are administered by the Federal Government of the United States in Washington, DC. Examples of this are Baker and Howland Islands, Jarvis Island, Johnston Atoll, Kingman Reef, Midway Islands, Palmyra Atoll, Navassa Island and Wake Island. Thus although these Pacific Island Wildlife Refuges are special dependent regimes, they lack any self government, and are hence not autonomous.[52] The seven Union Territories of the Indian Republic, including the Andaman and Nicobar Islands, Lakshadweep, Dadra and Nagar Haveli and Daman and Diu are in a similar situation.[53] These territories are special and different regimes controlled by the Federal Government but are not characterised by self government. Similarly, Spain's External Territories include Chafarinas and Penon de Alhucemas, two groups of islets, and Penon de Velez Gomera, a fort on tidal peninsula, are designated autonomous islands but are in fact centrally administered by the Government in Madrid.[54]

B. *Measure of Self Government: Variable and Dynamic Degrees of Autonomy*

This flows from the above. Powers of self government are not quite obviously uniform for different autonomous units. Hence every autonomous unit will have its own degree of autonomy, ranging from a minimal scale and extent of power to a high degree of self government and then to such a high degree of autonomy that the unit is for all intents and purposes a separate State.

The first noteworthy point is that the phenomenon of varying degrees of power and autonomy are both intra-national and inter-national. Accordingly, different autonomous units in different countries will have varying degrees of power as compared to their own units as well as other units in different States. Thus, to the extent that the *lander* are autonomous units within the Federal Republic of Germany, they are relatively less autonomous than the cantons of Switzerland[55] but more so than the federating states of the Indian Union.[56] As far as internal domestic comparisons are concerned, it is a fact that both Macau and Hong Kong enjoy a higher degree of autonomy than Tibet Autonomous Region. Similarly, the entity known as Azad Kashmir in Pakistan enjoys much greater autonomy than the powers of self government enjoyed by the several Pakistan Pathan tribal and territorial units along its border with Afghanistan.

Secondly, these variations, or rather stark variations in autonomous powers, are a combination of historical, legal and political factors. Thus the power differential with respect Hong Kong and Macau is a direct result of China's bilateral agreements with

---

52 These islands are administered by the US Department of the Interior, US Fish and Wildlife Service, Hawaii; Palmyra and Wake are part of Pacific Remote Islands Marine National Monument: see Joanne Maher (ed.), *op. cit.* note 28, vol. ii, 4925-26.

53 See D.K. Singh, "*The Constitution of India*" (Sixth edition), (Eastern Book Co., Lucknow 1975), Section 1(3); and the First Schedule, 605; and Barry Turner (ed.), *op. cit.* note 21, 841-49.

54 See "Spanish External Territories" in Joanne Maher (ed.), *op. cit.* note 21, 4203.

55 Technically, while Switzerland is a confederation it is in all respects a federation.

56 See Thomas Benedikter, *op. cit.* note 37, 307.

the United Kingdom and Macau concluded in 1985 and 1987 respectively affirming a high degree of autonomy but excluding the powers of defence and foreign affairs for the next fifty years. Importantly, China agreed to this arrangement as a direct result of the fact that Macau and Hong Kong were administered as entities separate from China and because they had very successful national economies. Similarly, the reason why there is a difference in the autonomy enjoyed by Azad Kashmir and the Pathan tribal areas is because a weak form of self government in Azad Kashmir would almost certainly prejudice or compromise Pakistan's legal position in its long-running dispute with India. A central plank of Islamabad's policy in the dispute is that the Kashmiri nation has an inalienable right of self determination and that India must afford that nation an opportunity freely to exercise that right. The fact that Azad ("Free") Kashmir already exercises a high degree of autonomy constitutes evidence that Pakistan's policy in Kashmir is consistent with its demands of India on the matter.
It is dynamic in the sense that peoples can change modify enhance or reduce their powers provided where the law, domestic, constitutional and international, allows such procedures. This applies to subsequent changes regarding degrees of self government. Thus following civil unrest in the Azores/Madeira in the 1980s, especially with respect to the vexed question of the introduction of a special flag and anthem for the islands of the Azores, the Spanish President Mr Soares decided to abandon the flag and anthem proposal and to extend Azorean autonomy.[57]

C. *The Role of Sovereignty*

One essential fact in autonomous territorial units is that they lack the element of sovereignty; and that the latter is vested in the mother or host territorial unit.[58] The essence of the point here is that while the status of the unit may be that of autonomy, which allows the former to exercise various degrees of power over its allotted territory as opposed to the central government, that separation from the territorial State does not mean that the latter has no sovereignty over the unit. For purposes of both the unit and the international community of States, the link between the two is that of sovereignty. In *Interpretation of the Memel Statute* (*Merits*) advisory opinion,[59] the Permanent Court of International Justice observed that when Lithuania acquired rights and title to Memel Territory under the Convention of Paris of 1924, it undertook to secure autonomy to the latter within the limits fixed by the Statute of Memel, but that: "[I]t certainly was not the intention of the Parties to the Convention that the sovereignty should be divided between two bodies which were to exist side by side in the same territory. Their intention was simply to ensure to the transferred territory a wide measure of legislative, judicial, administrative and financial decentralisation, which should not disturb the unity of the Lithuanian State and should operate within the framework of Lithuanian sovereignty."[60]

---

57 *Ibid.*, 205-06.

58 Generally, see Joshua Castellino, "*International Law and Self Determination*", (Martinus Nijhoff Publishers, The Hague 2000), Chapter 1.

59 *PCIJ Reports*, *Series A/B*, No. 49 (1932), 294.

60 *Ibid.*, 313. *Cf.* the Joint Dissenting Opinion of Judges de Bustamante, Altamira, Schucking, and Eysinga: 346-48; and also see 343.

In more recent times, this issue was raised in *Eritrea vs. Yemen Phase One: Territorial Sovereignty and Scope of the Dispute* [61] where the Arbitration Tribunal, in response to the claim made by Yemen that it had title to the disputed Red Sea Islands by virtue of its status under the Ottoman Empire, had this to say regarding this assertion:

"The so-called Treaty of Da'an of 1911 was in fact an internal instrument by which the Imam of Yemen obtained for himself greater internal powers of autonomy within the Ottoman Empire. However, sovereignty over all the possessions, including the islands in dispute, remained vested in the Empire itself until it was legally divested of its Arabian possessions after the First World War."[62]

The term sovereignty is used in various ways, not least because it is a term which is regularly employed by political scientists, historians and legal experts to describe various situations. For lawyers, sovereignty is absolute power, but importantly, it is power based in law. Legal scholars try to impart a degree of sophistication by identifying a variety of aspects thereof, only two of which are relevant here, namely external and internal sovereignty. For their purposes, external sovereignty is supreme power which knows no external competition, external, that is, to the State.

Accordingly, a sovereign power to be truly sovereign must not face serious debilitating competition for power and control from another State. In the context of autonomy, the point is that the authority being wielded by the State sovereign over the autonomous unit must not be subject to any real and substantial interference by any other power. Of course, and very importantly, any kind of collaboration by the mother or host State with another State which is based in law, as for example, a bilateral agreement, then collaboration that does not constitute an erosion of absolute sovereignty over that unit. The Good Friday Agreement of 1998 between the United Kingdom and the Republic of Ireland is an example of this, for the latter is allowed a measure of participation, albeit limited, by way of cross-border governmental institutions, as for example, the North-South Ministerial Council.[63]

The problem of Gibraltar is another example. Here, the United Kingdom and Spain both claim sovereignty over Gibraltar, but it is the former which has possession and control over it as an Overseas Dependency which gives the latter a high degree of autonomy. As a foreign power Spain seeks to assert and maintain its claim over the Rock,[64] but its attempts to do so are in no way threatening to the United Kingdom. As such there is no real competition, and accordingly no real challenge to its sovereignty. The United Kingdom is not inclined to yield to Spanish claims, not least because its inhabitants have no desire to merge with the Spanish Kingdom.

In terms of the Kashmir dispute, while there is very limited autonomy in the Indian part of Kashmir, New Delhi is always conscious of an external power attempting to exert influence and control over its part of Kashmir, namely Pakistan. The on-going

---

61 114 *ILR* 1.

62 *Ibid.*, 46.

63 For the text of the agreement, see 37 (1998) *ILM* 751, and in particular Strand Two, paragraphs 1, 2, 5 and 13. The latter provision stipulates that the Northern Ireland Assembly and the North-South Ministerial Council are interdependent and that one cannot function successfully without the other. The Republic of Ireland is a member of the said Council.

64 See Government Printer, *The Spanish Red Book on Gibraltar*, Madrid, 1965.

dispute between the latter and India over Kashmir has been the cause of three wars, and this is because India, faced with a weak revolt in Kashmir, is anxious that it not been seen as succumbing to Pakistan.[65]

The second aspect is internal sovereignty, where the source of absolute power is not subject to any serious challenge by any other source of power internal to the State. In other words, an absolute sovereign in a State is one which knows no internal competition for superiority in power and control. Where an autonomous unit begins to give and succeeds in giving serious competition to the sovereign, it is then that the latter will be seen as having no, little or waning internal sovereignty as the case may be. In the *Interpretation of Memel Statute* (*Merits*) case, the Permanent Court held that the interpretation of the scope and extent of executive power of the Memel Territory had to be guided by the general scheme of the Paris Convention of 1924 and the Statute of Memel Territory annexed thereto. Accordingly, the right of the President of the Directorate to continue to exercise such powers was not absolute and that to argue otherwise "would result in a President being able to violate the Statute and flout the authorities of the Lithuanian Government so long as he carried the Chamber with him. Such an interpretation would destroy the general scheme of the Convention [...]."[66] It went on to hold:

"The dismissal of the President of the Directorate by the Governor would constitute a legitimate and appropriate measure of protection of the interests of the State only in cases in which the acts complained of were serious acts calculated to prejudice the sovereign rights of Lithuania and violating the provisions of the Memel Statute, and when no other means are available."[67]

Thus if and when, for example the Kurdish Autonomous Region asserts itself against the supreme power-wielders in Baghdad, it will then be arguable that the latter has no internal sovereignty over the State, or part thereof. The same is true for the Tibetan separatists but more importantly this is the kind of situation which the Indian Government is keen to avoid in Kashmir. The autochthonous movement for a free and sovereign and independent Kashmir has rejected the limited autonomy which India has allowed it; and the violent struggle and terrorism which breaks out from time to time is indicative of the competition for supreme control which is going on, although it is the case that perfect ascendancy for which the Kashmiri independence struggle is continuing is nowhere in sight as yet.

D. *The Location of Sovereignty and the Suppression and Violation of Autonomy*

A territorial unit which is autonomous will lack the crucial element of sovereignty, and then this raises its very own legal problems. If the autonomous territorial unit is distinguished by the fact that it does not exercise sovereignty but autonomy, then in the light of the above discussion, the question arises whether it could be argued that the territorial State has no real sovereignty over that autonomous unit. This limitation

---

65 See generally, M. J. Akbar, "*India: The Siege Within Challenges to a Nation's Unity*", (Penguin, New Delhi 1985), Part III.

66 *See supra* note 59, 317.

67 *Ibid.*, 319.

was prominent in the wake of the *Angelo Breard* and the *La Grand* cases.[68] In the latter case, Germany argued:

"[T]hat the United States is under an international obligation to carry out in conformity with the foregoing international legal obligations any future detention of or criminal proceedings against any other German national in its territory, whether by a constituent, legislative, executive, judicial or other power, whether that power holds a superior or subordinate position in the organization of the United States, and whether that power's functions are of an international or interna1 character..."[69]

It is a fact that the Federal Government of the United States has no power to *issue relevant orders as opposed to requests*, to the Commonwealth of Virginia and State of Arizona insofar as the Constitution of the United States does not allow such interference with respect the internal criminal justice systems of the two federating states.[70] In *Breard vs. Greene*, the US Supreme Court held: "Last night the Secretary of State sent a letter to the Governor of Virginia requesting that he stay Breard's execution. If the Governor wishes to wait for the decision of the ICJ, that is his prerogative. But nothing in our existing case law allows us to make that choice for him."[71]

The Federal Government observed with respect to the *Breard* case, that it had indeed issued a "request" to the Governor of Virginia and that it had filed a brief in the US Supreme Court.[72] In effect, then, it was being argued that these states had autonomy to such a standard that it precluded the President of the United States from ordering the Governors of the two states to stay the carrying out of the death penalty. The International Court issued temporary interim measures of relief to both Paraguay and Germany but the offenders in both cases were in fact executed. In the *La Grand* (*Interim Protection*) case, the Court observed:

"Whereas the international responsibility of a State is engaged by the action of the competent organs and authorities acting in that State, whatever they may be; whereas the United States should take all measures at its disposal to ensure that Walter LaGrand is not executed pending the final decision in these proceedings; whereas, according to the information available to the Court, implementation of the measures indicated in the present Order falls within the jurisdiction of the Governor of Arizona; whereas the Government of the United States is consequently under the obligation to transmit the present Order to the said Governor; whereas the Governor of Arizona is under the obligation to act in conformity with the international undertakings of the United States..."[73]

---

68 See *Paraguay vs. USA, ICJ Reports 1998,* 248; and *Germany vs. USA, ICJ Reports 1999,* 11; and ibid, *2001*, 466.

69 *ICJ Reports 1999*, 11.

70 This, of course, does not exclude other mechanisms as for example filing petitions in the US Supreme Court: see next in text.

71 523 US 371-378, *per* Justice Souter.

72 See Agent of the United States of America to the Court's Registrar of the International Court, 15 April 1998: Correspondence of the Case. *Cf.*, The Agent of Paraguay to the Registrar of the International Court, 28 April 1998.

73 *ICJ Reports 1999*, 16.

In the main case, the International Court held:
"The review of the above steps taken by the authorities of the United States with regard to the Order of the International Court of Justice of 3 March 1999 indicates that the various competent United States authorities failed to take all the steps they could have taken to give effect to the Court's Order. *The Order did not require the United States to exercise powers it did not have*: but it did impose the obligation to "take all measures at its disposal to ensure that Walter LaGrand is not executed pending the final decision in these proceedings [...].". The Court finds that the United States did not discharge this obligation."[74]
These observations show that while the autonomy of a unit will limit the nature, scope and effect of central or federal interference, two facts are inescapable. For one thing, any act of the unit which constitutes a breach of international law will engage the international responsibility of the State and not the autonomous unit; and for another, the sovereignty of the territorial State over the unit remains fully assured. There is no question that the United States does exercise internal sovereignty over all its fifty states, and hence the former is internationally responsible for the breaches of its autonomous units.
In more general terms, it follows that while it is true that the unit has autonomy over its territory, the territorial State cannot be seen as not exercising sovereignty over the unit. Thus, the point is that the existence of autonomy does not imply a lack of sovereignty of the territorial State over the unit. This is because the existence of autonomy is in fact a manifestation of sovereignty, and not a diminution thereof.
Another way of expressing this is by stressing that it is the link of sovereignty which dictates the strength of the power which the State exercises over the autonomous unit. Equally, if sovereignty is manifested by transferring a degree of power, it is equally manifested by asserting the right to take some of the power back. This is the argument certain States provide to justify the transfer of some aspects of sovereignty to the European Union. They argue that they have willingly granted the EU certain powers of supremacy but that in principle they can revert to the *status quo ante* whenever they wish to take up that opportunity.[75]
While this is not the place of course to dwell on the argumentation maintained by the United Kingdom with respect to the EU, this nevertheless throws an interesting question into high relief. It is true, of course, that the unit does not have sovereignty and that sovereignty may be vested in the mother State, but it is also true that both domestic and international law may impose restrictions on the removal or suppression of that autonomy. In other words, once a unit is given autonomy it could be argued that it cannot be suppressed, and if that is correct then that territorial state lacks supreme absolute power. It may be useful to recall the fact that it was President Milosevic's revocation of Kosovo's autonomy in 1989 which led in due course to the civil wars in Yugoslavia; and it was this revocation which gave an enormous fillip to the Kosovar independence movement. This movement succeeded in two stages, the first of which began in March 1999 when the United States and the United Kingdom

---

74 *Ibid.*, 2001, 488 and 508. Emphasis added.
75 See generally Colin Turpin, "*British Government and the Constitution*" (Third edition), Butterworths, London 1995, 310; and see Hoffmann J. in *Stoke on Trent City Council vs. B and Q PLC* [1991] Ch 48, 56.

executed air strikes from March and ended in May 1999 when the Yugoslav army was forced to withdraw from Kosovo; and then in February 2008 when the Kosovar Assembly declared its independence from Serbia.[76]

The Anglo-American onslaught was not of course a reaction to the suppression of Kosovar autonomy. It was justified by reference to the so-called right of humanitarian intervention, a matter which need not be addressed here. The question at this point is whether the suppression of autonomy vests the unit with a right to secede. It could be argued that any suppression, as opposed to incidental violations, of autonomy constitutes a breach of the fundamental legal basis on which the relations between the unit and the host or mother State are organised, leaving the unit free to consider itself not bound by the link of autonomy thereafter.

Two more incidents are worthy of similar consideration, one of them being the conduct of the Ethiopian Government with respect to Eritrea. According to General Assembly Resolution 390A (V) of 1950,[77] Eritrea was to be an autonomous federated unit with legislative, executive and judicial powers within the Ethiopian State structure. It felt a great sense of injustice when the Ethiopian Government began in November 1952 to dismantle this autonomous structure and set about systematically to turning federation into union and blatantly to interfere with the autonomous government in Eritrea.[78] This fanned Eritrea's desire for independence and led to a bloody and protracted war which finally culminated in 1991 following military success and internal turmoil in Ethiopia.[79]

The other example of suppression comes from the experience of the autonomous southern region of Sudan.[80] The civil war between Government forces and the Anya-Nya rebels began in 1955 and ended with the Addis Abba Peace Pact of 1972, bringing a limited measure of autonomy to Sudan's three southern provinces. However, in 1983, autocratic rulers in Khartoum imposed Sharia law in a predominantly Christian and animist south and dismissed its government. This led to an even greater round of bloodletting and gave birth to the Sudan Liberation Army. A series of agreements followed but it is the Comprehensive Peace Treaty of 2005[81] which governs the situation today. A key concession made by Khartoum is the right secured in Article 1, paragraph 3 of the Machakos Protocol of July 2002 whereby South Sudan has been accorded the right of self determination through a referendum to determine its future status. The referendum is to be held in 2011 and until then the "people of South Sudan have the right to control and govern affairs in their region and

---

76 Generally, see Hans-Joachim Heintze, *op. cit.* note 50, 29.

77 See Eritrea: Report of the United Nations Commission on Eritrea; Report of the Interim Committee of the General Assembly on the Report of the United Nations Commission on Eritrea, 2 December 1950. The resolution effectively laid out an outline of the fundamental principles of the projected constitution of Ethiopia.

78 See Ieuan LL. Griffiths, "*An Atlas of African Affairs*, (Methuen, London, 1984), 88-92; and Kaiyan H. Kaikobad, *op. cit.* note 16, 172-73.

79 See Kaiyan H. Kaikobad, *op. cit.* note 16, 173.

80 See Thomas Benedikter, *op. cit.* note 37, 259-70.; Kjell-Åke Nordquist, *op. cit.* note 41, 69-73; and 76; UN Press Release S/C 8306, 8 February 2005; and see "Sudan", in Joanne Maher (ed.), *op. cit.* note 28, vol. ii, 4242.

81 This agreement is in fact a compilation of agreements concluded over a number of years, including the Machakos Protocol of 2002.

participate equitably in the National Government", *vide* Article 1, paragraph 2. In short, the period 2005-2011 is thus an interim phase in which a high degree of autonomy is affirmed for the North and South.

The correct answer, thus, to whether suppression gives an automatic right to secede is clearly a nuanced one. The right to break away from the territorial State may be vested in that unit if the autonomous status has been negotiated with the host or territorial State; or where there has been some international institutional involvement in the creation of that autonomy, including the carrying out of plebiscites. A breach of the agreed conditions may be relied upon to argue that the basic fundamental basis of agreement has also ended leaving the unit free to reject the territorial State as its sovereign overlord. This is the position Eritrea can claim as its legal justification for breaking away from the Ethiopian State. Similarly, but by way of a hypothetical example, it could also be argued that if China were to revoke the autonomous status of Hong Kong before the lapse of the obligatory fifty years, it could reasonably vest the latter with the right to consider opting for the path of total independence.

Where, however, autonomy is a concession or gift, as it were, of the territorial State, then the revocation of autonomy does not necessarily vest the unit with the right to agitate for total independence. Thus autonomy which is created by way of domestic arrangements, especially where there are no domestic or international agreements, plebiscites or referenda to honour, may be revoked, provided always that the power to revoke such autonomy is vested in the executive by reference to domestic constitutional law.[82] Thus, as Heintze observed, although Chechnya provided a legal right to autonomy by Article 85 of the 1977 Soviet Constitution, "this system was nullified by the absolutist government of the Communist Party and its democratic centralism".[83] Subject to the following, any other interpretation would not be consistent with the notion of the absolute sovereignty of the territorial State.

Notwithstanding the above, and this is central to this analysis, it must be stressed that the right to secede is in fact a right of self determination, and to that extent it can also strongly be contended that that right cannot be denied by technicalities of this sort. If this argument were taken to its logical conclusion, it will clearly be applicable to any territorial situation, that is, whether or not the unit is affected by a breach of conditions; and even if there is no autonomous unit, but simply a constituent part of the State.

Thus, taking the hypothetical (as yet) case of Scotland, if this realm of the United Kingdom were to decide to break away therefrom, it would not be required as a matter of international law to claim and sustain the argument that London had varied or truncated certain powers accorded to the Scottish Administration or Parliament by way of the terms of the Scotland Act of 1998.[84] Indeed, on this view of the matter, while the actual exercise of the right of self determination may well be conditional, as

---

82 *Cf.* Hannikainen who writes, "It would be preferable if the State were not entitled to abolish the autonomy unilaterally." See "Self-Determination and Autonomy in International Law", in Markku Suksi, *op. cit.* note 41, 79 and 91.

83 See *supra* note 50, 15.

84 1998 Chapter 46.

for example the high potential for catastrophic regional instability[85] and/or the breach of fundamental *jus cogens* norms, as for example the perpetuation of apartheid,[86] there is no conditionality based exclusively on a breach of conditions on the basis of which autonomy may only be granted.

In other words, while a breach of such conditions may act as a major *de facto* condition justifying secession, this is not a vital legal condition precedent at all. All that Scotland would have to show is that its inhabitants were genuinely desirous of setting up an independent sovereign State and that there were no implications and ramifications of catastrophic regional instability or the violation essential peremptory principles of international law. Further examination of these issues would constitute venturing further afield and accordingly, it will suffice to note that in the final analysis, while a host of polemical issues arise when the question of the sovereignty of the territorial State is examined in the context of autonomy, the right of self determination is not dependent upon proof of suppression of autonomy.

E. The Reversion of Sovereignty and Title by Autonomous Units

An issue which must follow the one raised directly above is whether an autonomous unit automatically succeeds to title once the sovereign has relinquished such title without identifying the State or States to which such title was being transferred. In the vast, overwhelming majority of cases, the sovereign either cedes or transfers title or sovereignty to another State or a State being created at the time of transfer of power. This is how territorial adjustments were made in Europe, Near East and the Far East after the First and Second World Wars. Such transfers also take place during peacetime, and of course the decolonisation process which began to gather momentum during the nineteen-sixties does duty as an example. It is also the case that the realties of war and the geopolitics of the victors may at times simply be concerned with the divestiture of the vanquished State's colonial possessions leaving for later the question of attribution and allocation of title to those possessions.

An intriguing question no doubt, an autonomous unit within the empire ought to be able at least to argue that where no title-holder is identified to whom the transfer is made, then that autonomous unit automatically re-acquires title by way of the doctrine of reversion. This was one of the perceived strengths of Yemen in *Eritrea vs. Yemen* where it argued that the renunciation by Ottoman Turkey of title to certain territories and islands by way of Article 16 of the 1923 Treaty of Lausanne and the fact that "the future of those territories and islands" was to be "settled or to be settled by the parties concerned" meant that the Yemen, the autonomous unit of the Ottoman Empire, could put forward itself as having re-acquired sovereignty.[87] The Tribunal however was not impressed by this argument for a variety of reasons, one of them being that the doctrine of reversion was part of international law; that no reversion could occur back

85 Reference here is being made to situations not unlike the Kurdish desire for a united sovereign homeland. Although laudable and legitimate, the realisation of this claim would mean the territorial disruption of at least five States, with Turkey losing about one third of it s territory.

86 This has reference to the racial minority administration of the Rhodesian and South African Governments before the realisation of black majority rule.

87 Generally see 114 *ILR* 1, 38-45.

to Yemen because there were interruptions in the chain of title;[88] that Yemen was a mountain entity with little sway over the coast; and that the "concept of territorial sovereignty was entirely strange to an entity such as medieval Yemen."[89]

These findings are flawed in at least three ways. First, in principle there is nothing to preclude an entity from re-acquiring sovereignty over a parcel which was at any rate under its control albeit as an autonomous entity, a suzerain, if not sovereignty. The whole point in autonomy as was seen above is to have various shades of power and self government, and it would be bizarre if the sovereign entity departed without identifying the successor that the autonomous entity were unable to fill the gap as it were. International law abhors a vacuum of sovereignty and if there were no reversions as the Tribunal has contended it would constitute inviting friction among States.

Secondly, to deny reversion in principle as a doctrine of international law is to partially negate the essence of self determination. If it did indeed was a non-existent notion in international law, there would be no plausible explanation or justification in terms of law as to the reversion of Ifni to Morocco and Walvis Bay to Namibia, both former enclaves administered by Spain and South Africa.[90]

Thirdly, it is difficult to believe that Yemen's contentions regarding the exercise of sovereignty on the coasts and the hinterland were rejected because it was quite simply a medieval entity and a stranger effectively to the notion of sovereignty. It is hard to believe this because this observation was made in 1998, in the dying years of the twentieth century. At any rate, findings such as these have been overtaken by the International Court of Justice. In the *Pedra Branca/Pulau Batu Puteh* (*Malaysia vs. Singapore*) case,[91] the Court had no difficulty in accepting that the Sultan of Jahore exercised sovereign authority over the Orang Laut, a seafaring community of Malays in the Straits of Singapore and that he had ancient original title over various islands, including the disputed islets of Pedra Branca/Pulau Batu Puteh.[92]

F. Limited International Personality

In principle, autonomous entities do not *ipso facto* and in principle have international legal personality, and this is one of the defining points of distinction between a sovereign State and an autonomous entity: the fact being that a sovereign State has international personality *ipso facto* and *ab initio*. Of course, whether a sovereign State can actually enter into international relations is a question which requires scrutinising two important legal facts, namely (a) the nature, scope and effect of internal and international law; and (b) matters *ratione materiae* and *ratione personae* flowing from category (a).

---

88 *Ibid.*, 40.

89 *Ibid.*, 45.

90 Generally, see GA Resolutions 2354 (XXII) of 19 December 1967; 2428 (XXII) of 18 December 1968; 32/9 D of 4 November 1977; 38/36A of 1 December 1983; and Security Council Resolution 432 of 27 July 1978; the South Africa-Namibia Agreement of 28 February 1994: 33 (1994) *ILM* 1528; and Kaiyan H. Kaikobad, "Self Determination, Territorial Disputes and International Law: An Analysis of UN and State Practice" in 1 (1996) *Geopolitics and International Boundaries* 15, at 45-46.

91 Judgment of 23 May 2008.

92 *Ibid.*, paragraphs 74-75.

As far as internal and international law is concerned it is amply clear in the light of the observations made in Section III above, namely the creation of autonomous units, and the observations to be made presently under subsection 7 below, that insofar as a unit is founded by virtue of international action or guarantee or sponsorship or all three, international law may or may not endow the unit with the right, limited or otherwise, to enter into legal relations with States and international organisations. Similarly, internal law may, as it is usually the case, preclude autonomous units the right to exercise full international legal personality, with the result that some units will by domestic arrangements have limited rights to enter, say, into international legal relations with States and international organisations. Thus, Aaland Islands has a limited presence in the European Community and Union, a situation arising out of a domestic decision to submit part of its jurisdiction to the powers of European Community and Union organs,[93] and both the Faroe Islands and Greenland have powers with respect to negotiations and treaty-making.[94]

As far as *matters ratione* in category (b) is concerned, this is an elaboration of the rights and obligations flowing from international legal principles, and to that extent, the Permanent Court's observations in the *Interpretation of the Statue of the Memel Territory*, are apposite with respect to *ratione materiae*. It was noted that the Four Powers, namely Great Britain, France, Japan and Italy agreed that by virtue of Article 5 of the Statute, the conduct of foreign relations was not among the items of competence of the Memel authorities and that "foreign relations are, under Article 7, within the exclusive jurisdiction of the Lithuanian Republic". Thus, the Permanent Court of International Justice held in this advisory opinion that to extent that attempts made by Memel authorities to secure the admission into Germany of Memel agricultural produce by negotiations with the former State fell within the sphere of foreign relations, such actions exceeded the competence of the authorities and thereby violated the Statute.[95]

By contrast, there is greater latitude in this respect for Hong Kong. The latter has Economic and Trade Offices in New York, Washington and San Francisco. This is of course a reflection of the Joint Declaration of 1984. Under Article 3, paragraphs 9 and 10, Hong Kong has the right to maintain economic links with other States, and may "conclude relevant agreements with states, regions and relevant international organisations."[96]

As far as matters *ratione personae* are concerned, there are clearly three actors involved, namely the host or territorial State, the autonomous entity and the entity with which relations are sought to be established. While the law, domestic or international, may allow such units that right, albeit limited as far as international law is concerned, the entity, that is the State with which legal relations are sought, would have to make a legal and political decision to enter into such relations, thus complementing the international personality of the unit. For international

93 See Hannikainen, *op. cit.* note 82, 93-94.

94 See Athanasia Spiliopoulou Åkermark, "The Procedural Position of Autonomous Regions Before International Judicial and Quasi-Judicial Organs", in Markku Suksi, *op. cit.* note 41, 139-140.

95 See *supra* note 59, 328.

96 See *supra* note 36. See further Article XI, Elaboration by China, Annex I to Joint Declaration, ibid, 243.

organisations, the constituent treaty would be relevant; that is to say, the right to admit non-State actors to membership of that international organisation will depend, *inter alia*, upon whether the treaty allows such actors to be admitted. Under Article 11, paragraph 2 of the Constitution of the Universal Postal Union of 1964,[97] any "sovereign country" may apply for admission to membership of the Union, but paragraph 3 allows a country which is not a member of the United Nations to be admitted to membership if at least two-thirds of member countries approve of such admission to membership. As Bowett noted in his classic study of international institutional law:

"Membership is not necessarily confined to States and even in those organisations where it is so confined a very variable concept of statehood is applied in practice: it would seem that a less rigorous interpretation of the term "State" is used when admission to certain specialised agencies is accorded than when admission to the United Nations is sought."[98]

Similarly, some autonomous units will have sufficient international personality to gain admission to membership of certain international organisations, but that would also depend on whether or not a non-State public, as opposed to private, entity may be allowed such membership. It is a fact that certain autonomous units may have limited international personality in that respect. For example, while Hong Kong, Macau, American Samoa, Greenland and Gibraltar have exercised a degree of international personality by being admitted to membership of the Universal Postal Union, none of the autonomous territories of the Russian Federation have similar membership status. Greenland actively participates in the negotiation of treaties which have the potential to affect its affairs. However, this is a concession based in international law. Aruba, an island in the Caribbean, has full autonomy from the Dutch Government[99] and participates as a member in a number of international organisations including the IMF, WMO, ILO and UPU, and is an associate member of UNESCO. However, none of the above has diplomatic representation abroad, save Hong Kong.

G. International and National Law

An autonomous territorial unit will be governed primarily by national legal systems, including constitutional laws, the laws of the territorial unit, but it is also the case that, as noted above, by relevant international law, especially where the United Nations has played a role in creating it.[100] Indeed, there may well be an element of either source of law. Here the Aaland Island issue is a good example.[101] The League of Nations decided in 1921 that the Islands would remain part of Finland insofar as international

97 611 *UNTS* 7; *UKTS* 71 (1966) Cmnd. 3142.

98 See Derek Willam Bowett, "*The Law of International Institutions*", (Stevens & Sons, London 1982), 385.

99 See Barry Turner (ed.), *op. cit.* note 21, 1144.

100 Generally see Markku Suksi, "On the Entrenchment of Autonomy", in Markku Suksi, *op. cit.* note 41, 151.

101 For a brief general background, see P. M. Brown, "The Aaland Islands Question", 15 (1921) *AJIL* 268.

law did not at that time accept the notion of self determination.[102] However, the Council decided that Aaland's existing autonomy would be strengthened within the Finnish State structure. Accordingly, the latter Government entered into an agreement with Sweden in 1921 with respect to various areas of mutual concern, including Swedish language provisions in schools and supervisory functions of the League.[103] The League approved this compact in 1921 and these instruments were incorporated into the Autonomy Act of 1922.

Similarly, while South Tyrol was granted special autonomous status on the basis of Italian constitutional law,[104] the fundamental instrument behind the autonomy is the Paris Agreement of 1946 between Italian and Austrian Governments.[105] By contrast, the other fifteen Regions of Italy with various autonomous powers and legislative and executive powers were created by ordinary statute.[106] Eritrea was not governed by international law but General Assembly Resolution 390A was an international instrument which could not be ignored, not least because constitutional provisions relevant to Eritrea were included therein. Similarly, China cannot ignore the two international agreements providing Macau and Hong Kong with their respective powers of autonomy; indeed the Parties are bound by the terms of the treaties of 1987 and 1984. Nor can the Finnish Government ignore the fact that one of the sources of the autonomy exercised by the Aaland Islands is based in the 1921 League of Nations decision to align the Islands with Finland but not without autonomy for the Islanders.

IV. RIGHTS AND OBLIGATIONS OF THE TERRITORIAL STATE AND THE AUTONOMOUS UNIT

In the light of the above observations, it is possible to itemise the salient rights and obligations of both the central authorities within the State, that is, the State which bears the burden of autonomy, and the autonomous unit. Importantly, for current purposes, these are rights and obligations in terms of international law.

A. The Duty to Respect the Autonomy of the Territorial Unit

The central authorities are under a duty in international law to respect the autonomy of the unit. This includes all aspects of autonomy, that is, the duty to respect and honour the various powers allocated to the unit and the duty not to abolish or suppress the autonomy altogether. This proposition of law was discussed in subsection 4 of Section IV above. It suffices to note the following.

---

102 By doing so, it precluded union of Aaland with Sweden with whom the Islanders had a natural linguistic connexion. Generally, see James Crawford, *op. cit.* note 3, 22, note 87; 44-45; and 85-89; Jan H. W. Verzijl, "*International Law in Historical Perspective*", Vol. i, Martinus Nijhoff, Leyden 1968, 328-32; Joshua Castellino, *op. cit.* note 58, 19-20; Hannikainen, *op. cit.* note 82, 80 and 95; Thomas Benedikter, *op. cit.* note 37, 137-47; Kjell-Åke Nordquist, op. cit. note 41, 77; and Markku Suksi, *op. cit.* note 100, 166-67.

103 See Markku Suksi, *op. cit.* note 100, 157.

104 See Thomas Benedikter, *op. cit.* note 37, 88.

105 *Ibid.*, 91-92; also see Margaret Carlyle, "The Territorial Provisions of the Peace Treaty with Italy", in Arnold Toynbee and Veronica Toynbee (eds.), *op. cit.* note 11, 453 and 458-63; Hannikainen, *op. cit.* note 82, 87, and note 20; and Hans-Joachim Heintze, *op. cit.* note 50, 20.

106 See Hannikainen, *op. cit.* note 82, 87.

First, the duty to respect the autonomy of the unit is in some circumstances the duty to respect commitments made in the form of treaties or other binding instruments or engagements, national, international or quasi-international. Accordingly, where the latter is the legal basis of the autonomy, then the rule of *pacta sunt servanda* applies as declared in Article 26 of the Vienna Convention on the Law of Treaties; [107] or analogous variations thereof. Secondly, denial of such powers or suppression of such status may have a number of different legal results, depending of course on the legal bases of the autonomy.

Thus where the autonomy is based, created, guaranteed or sponsored by national or international agreements, institutions and instruments, then any substantial violation of the autonomy may lead at worse to a *de facto* nullification of the legal bases of autonomy, the result of which could arguably constitute freeing the unit from its obligations of autonomy leading to independence. At best, it would constitute suspending the autonomy regime or part thereof to the benefit of the autonomous unit. Here the analogy is derived from Section III of the Vienna Convention on the Law of Treaties. Article 60 stipulates that where one of the Parties effects a material breach of the treaty, the other Party is entitled to invoke the breach as a ground for termination of the treaty or suspending its operation in whole or in part. Eritrea and Sudan are perhaps the best examples of this proposition of the law.

B. The Duty not Take Forcible Action against Autonomous Units

This duty, which flows from the above, has reference to forcible action, in particular armed force, depriving peoples of the right of self determination and in particular autonomy exercised *de jure*. This view is predicated on the fact that an autonomous status freely agreed with full consent of the territorial unit can, in all the right and appropriate circumstances, be regarded as having exercised the right of self determination. The UN General Assembly Resolution of 1970, usually referred to as the Declaration on Friendly Relations and Co-operation among States,[108] contains detailed provisions on the scope, nature and effects of the principle of equal rights and self determination of peoples, one of which stipulates as follows:

The establishment of a sovereign and independent State, the free association or integration with an independent State or the emergence into any other political status freely determined by a people constitutes modes of implementing the right of self determination by that people.[109]

It is amply clear that the words and phrases used are wide and general enough to include the creation or emergence of an autonomous unit within the State as an act of self determination. The next paragraph[110] of this principle provides that every State "has the duty to refrain from any forcible action which deprives peoples referred to above" in the elaboration of the right of self determination. The key sense here is that any *forcible action* against the realisation by a people of its right of self determination, whether or not it is the status of autonomy or otherwise, is forbidden. While it would

107 *UKTS* No. 58 (1980), Cmnd. 7964.

108 Resolution 2625 (XXV) of 24 October 1970.

109 The 4th paragraph of the principle. Importantly, this status is not to be confused with territory of a non self governing territory of a colony: see the 6th paragraph.

110 The 5h paragraph of the principle.

appear that the use of armed force is in fact forbidden, the truth is that on many occasions, governments of States do not need to use forcible action. It is the case that a simple legislative act may be enough to deny a unit of its autonomous status. The latter may of course re-act by taking up arms against the central authorities, as for example the way Eritrea and Kosovo reacted to their respective denial of autonomy, and as a further response, the central powers may have to resort to the use of armed force. However, this scenario may not necessarily develop; or it may be short-lived or fizzle out. Nor is it the case that the use of armed force by the centre in these circumstances always and necessarily constitutes forcible action; it could also be seen as more akin to maintaining law and order than the forcible repression of autonomy.

While it may be appropriate to restrict the interpretation and application of this right to forcible action, it may not necessarily be the most useful because it would tend to apply the law to only one kind of action depriving the unit of its right of self determination, that is, forcible action. It is submitted that the rule should be applied to any kind of action which tends to deprive the right of self determination, including autonomy. There are three reasons.

First, there is little or no sense in being side-tracked, as it were, in blind alleys debating semantics and whether or not the impugned acts constitute forcible action. Secondly, the essence of the whole notion of self determination of peoples is to furnish them opportunities freely to determine their political, economic and social future and development, and accordingly any kind of interpretation of the provision which frustrates this legal ideal, as it were, is to defeat the very object and purpose of the right. Thirdly, the term "forcible" has to be read and treated in the context in which it appears in that paragraph. The point that the drafters were obviously trying to emphasise was that forcible action on both sides was unacceptable; that if the peoples were denied, for current purposes, their autonomy then that was not a licence to seek support which contravened in effect Article 2, paragraph 4 of the UN Charter. In other words, support must be (i) consistent with all acts which do not constitute an unlawful use of armed force and (ii) consistent with acts which seek or are based on pacific means of settlement of the problems arising from denial, including creating awareness, dissemination of information and organising political supporting events. In short, the term forcible action ought to be interpreted in such a way that this qualification is marginalised.

C. *The Duty to Respect the Sovereignty of the State*

This is a corollary duty on the autonomous unit. Where the territorial or host State is obliged to respect the autonomy of the unit, it follows plainly that the autonomous unit must respect the sovereignty, and in particular the territorial integrity, of that State. A breach of this duty could be regarded as a breach of one of the essential conditions of its autonomous status. The tragedy of East Pakistan is a case in point. In December 1970, free and fair elections were held in Pakistan. The major political party of Pakistan's eastern wing, an autonomous federated province of Pakistan, began clamouring for far-reaching extensive autonomy, and indeed for autonomy which would have negated the notion of a federation and the sovereignty of a united Pakistan. This resulted in a prolonged deadlock with political parties in West

Pakistan, and by early 1971, East Pakistan was in open revolt. The Pakistan army was obliged to put an end to this state of affairs and in March 1971 it decided to act.[111] Islamabad took the position that the use of armed force was necessary to preserve the unity of the State.

Similarly, the secessionist movements in the various republics of Yugoslavia in the early 1990s were the direct cause of the Yugoslav army coming into action in Slovenia and Croatia. The same is true for the Ethiopian armed campaigns to keep Eritrea from breaking away from the State which finally ended in 1991 with the latter securing independence from Ethiopia; and while Nigeria's use of armed force to resist Biafra's unilateral action for independence between 1967 and 1970,[112] was similar to the above, the territorial State in this case could not be defeated. It is interesting to note that it was the announcement regarding the re-organisation of the federal republic which triggered the Biafra conflict in 1967.[113] Whereas Nigeria was then grouped in four regions, it was when the Government decided to create twelve states out of those regions with devolved powers that the war to save the unity of Nigeria began.

It is this aspect of the matter which causes the acutest of problems for autonomy. For even if it is agreed that the autonomous unit must respect the sovereignty of the State there may be difficulty in deciding what constitutes the appropriate remedy where the unit does not wish to respect the territorial sovereignty of the host State. If it automatically vests the territorial State with the right to use armed force to resist all independence movements, then it negates the right of self determination; and if the autonomous unit has the right to seek full independence, then it negates the right to respect the sovereignty of the State in question. It is this conundrum which views the right of self determination as being incompatible with the right of territorial integrity.[114]

For purposes of reconciliation of these two competing principles, it would be tempting to create a hierarchy and to elevate one principle over the other. However hierarchies of this kind are essentially subjective in character. Nor is it easy to justify placing a principle at a higher or lower level. It is believed that a better way of reconciling these two principles without being too artificial or convoluted is to identify the notion of forcible action as a key guiding criterion. In broad general terms, then, the State must respect, as a matter and obligation of law, the autonomy of its unit/units; and the latter must respect, again as a matter and obligation of law, the sovereignty of the State to which it belongs. Accordingly, any respect for the unit's autonomy will be lost or

---

111 For a standard account of the conflict, see Richard B. Lillich and Frank C. Newman, "*International Human Rights: Problems of Law and Policy*", (Little, Brown and Co., Boston and Toronto 1979), Chapter VIII. It is standard in the sense that it fails to record the "orgy of killing, terror and destruction" which the armed militia of East Pakistan, the *Mukhti Bahini*, began to carry out soon after the election results in December 1970. Indeed to those who were observing events as they unfolded on a day-by-day basis, including the author of this piece, the Pakistan army was re-acting as opposed to acting, to this unchecked killing of Punjabis who bore the main brunt of the action by the armed brigands. This is of course no defence in law but it puts the issue in correct perspective. Most accounts of the crisis are defective because they are built on earlier defective accounts. For a detailed study, see Joshua Castellino, *op. cit.* note 58, Chapter 5.

112 See Heather A. Wilson, "*International Law and the Use of Force by National Liberation Movements*", (Clarendon Press, Oxford 1988), 85-87.

113 *Ibid.*, 85; and see Ieuan LL. Griffiths, *op. cit.* note 20, 78-79.

114 See Heather A. Wilson, *op. cit.* note 112, 87-88.

forfeited if the unit decides to and does employ armed force to assert its independence from the unity of the State as a remedy against an actual or perceived challenge to the autonomy of the unit.

The same rule applies *mutatis mutandis* when viewed from the other side. Thus, any respect, as a matter and obligation of law, for the State's territorial sovereignty and integrity is lost or forfeited where the State decides to and does employ armed force to assert its authority on the unit as a remedy against an actual or perceived challenge to the territorial sovereignty of the State. It follows that where no forcible action is used by either side, the unit will have the right to pursue independence if its autonomy is denied in a non forcible way, and the State will have the duty to let the unit seek independence provided it does so by way of non forcible, peaceful and constitutional means. At the same time, until that objective is achieved the State will have the right to demand that its sovereignty, especially internal sovereignty be respected as a matter and obligation of law. The chief merit of this approach is the fact that both principles can work side by side without causing grief and hatred for the other Party.

Again, a word of caution is necessary here. The propositions set out above are valid in only broad general ways because it is possible to think of territorial regimes and situations which do not fully satisfy the paradigm developed above. For it is the case that certain situations are so replete with complications of all kinds, both political and legal, that to apply the rules set out above would lead to unsatisfactory or unrealistic results. Autonomous units, for example, which are characterised by gross and systematic abuses of human rights and by policies of apartheid would find themselves in perpetual states of hopelessness and defeat if in fact they were to fail to use force to change such policies. It would follow that the use of armed force would be justified and moreover it seems that it would be legal as well, for it is the case that Article 7 of the Definition of Aggression provides as follows:

Nothing in this Declaration, and in particular Article 3, could in any way prejudice the right of self determination, freedom and independence, as derived from the Charter of peoples forcibly deprived of that right and referred to in the Declaration on Principles of International Law concerning Friendly Relations and Co-operation among States in accordance with the Charter of the United Nations, particularly peoples under colonial and racist regimes or other forms of racial alien domination; nor the right of these peoples to struggle to that end and to seek and receive support, in accordance with the principles of the Charter and in conformity with the above-mentioned Declaration.[115]

D. Duty Not to Abuse Autonomy

Closely related to the above is the duty not to abuse the autonomy granted to the unit. Thus the unit's laws and enforcement autonomous agencies ought not to be used in such a way as to further nefarious activities of the unit. It was widely believed that both Kosovo and the Chechnyans were heavily involved in arms smuggling and illicit drug trafficking. This trade was deemed necessary for purposes of fighting their wars against the lawful authorities, that is, to finance their breakaway movements. There

115 General Assembly Resolution 3312 (XXIX), 14 December 1974.

are of course confirmed reports on the Kosovo Liberation Army attacking police officers.[116]

E. The Duty to Ascertain the Wishes of the Population:

Plebiscite, Elections and Consultation

This is an important development in the law of self determination. The position taken here is that international law requires some sort of objectively verifiable ascertainment of the wishes of the population, be it an autonomous unit, an ethnic entity or even an existing State,[117] provided of course that there is some concern among peoples such as the above with respect to issues of self determination. Another way of saying this is that if there is some evidence that the population or peoples are seeking to exercise their right of self determination, then an opportunity of ascertaining their wishes ought to be provided.

This process of ascertainment can be a varied affair. The plebiscite is usually the first technique which comes to mind but that is neither the only one nor necessarily the best way to ascertain the wishes of the population. A simple general election in which the issue of self determination of a province is a key central issue of one or more political parties is also a technique of ascertainment of wishes. In September and December 1962 elections were held for the North Borneo Legislative Council, and the results showed that the population of North Borneo wished to merge with Malaya. In 1963, the UN Mission to Malaya endorsed the conduct of the elections as free and fair and consequently in 1963 the region was merged with Malaysia.[118] Similarly, the elections for delegates to the proposed Constituent Assembly of Namibia organised and supervised by the UN Transition Assistance Group (UNTAG) in Namibia in 1989 turned out in favour of SWAPO and confirmed the freedom struggle as a legitimate *vox populi*. Within ten days, the South African army had withdrawn from Namibia.

In other jurisdictions a *mushwara* or informal consultation process, not unlike the process carried out in West Irian in 1969,[119] will be given due weight in all the appropriate circumstances; as was the simple United Nations fact-finding mission which went to Bahrain in 1970 to ascertain the wishes of the people with respect to whether they wished to remain independent of, or integrate with, Iran, the State which

---

116 See Satish Nambiar, "India: An Uneasy Precedent", in Albrecht Schnabel and Ramesh Thakur (eds.), *op. cit.* note 7, 260 and 263.

117 See Thomas M. Franck, "The Emerging Right to Democratic Governance", 86 (1992) *AJIL* 46, 52 *et seq.*; and James Crawford, " Democracy and International Law", 64 (1993) *BYIL* 113, 123-24.

118 Generally, see Report of the UN Secretary General, 14 September 1963, as cited in 1963 *UN Yearbook* 41-43; Kaiyan H. Kaikobad, *op. cit.* note 90, 28; UK Mission to North Borneo, Cmnd. 1974, 1 August 1962. Similarly, when Party Quebecois fought and lost the general election of 2000 in Canada, it was also a vote against the separation of Quebec from the Canadian Federation as an independent State: generally, see Andre Bernard, "The Bloc Quebecois", in John H. Pammett and Christopher Dornan (ed.), *The Canadian General Election of 2000*, (Dundurn Press, Toronto 2001), 139 *et seq*.

119 Generally, see S. K. N. Blay, "Self-determination *Versus* Territorial Integrity in Decolonisation, 18 (1986) *New York Journal of International Law and Politics* 441, 450-55; UN GA Resolution 2504 of 19 November 1969; and Kaiyan H. Kaikobad, *op. cit.* note 90, 32.

had long-standing claims over Bahrain.[120] The UN Secretary General's personal special representative who carried out the survey reported that the overwhelming majority of Bahrainis favoured independence.[121]
There is ample practice to indicate that the ascertainment of wishes today is a requirement in terms of international law, as opposed merely to being a matter of practicality or pragmatism. It is well known that plebiscites were employed to determine territorial allocation at the end of the Great War of 1914-1918, although the conduct of such plebiscites was not based on *opinio juris*.[122] It is in the period following the end of the 1939-1945 War and the beginning of the end of colonialism in which plebiscites began to be seen as more than just a practical solution, and perhaps as a requirement of law. It appears that UN General Assembly practice is consistent with the requirement of holding plebiscites in matters of self determination. In Article 2 of the resolution entitled Right of Peoples and Nations to Self Determination of 1952, the General Assembly stipulated that Member States shall facilitate the exercise of this right by "the peoples of such Territories [namely non-self governing and Trust territories] according to the principles and spirit of the Charter of the United Nations in regard to each territory and to the freely expressed wishes of the peoples concerned, the wishes of the people being ascertained through plebiscites or other recognised democratic means, preferably under the auspices of the United Nations".[123]
In the Resolution 1541 (XV) dealing with the principles which should guide members in determining the existence of the obligation to transmit information to the General Assembly under Article 73(e) of the Charter, the former declared: "Free association should be the result of a free and voluntary choice by the peoples of the territory concerned expressed through informed and democratic processes."[124] The same is provided for the integration of non-self governing territories and there is reference in Principle XI (b) that such ascertainment should be based on universal adult suffrage. Similarly, the Friendly Relations Declaration stipulates that all peoples have the right freely to determine without external interference, their political status.[125] Indeed, the United Nations has organised or endorsed or approved plebiscites in Togoland in 1956 which then joined Ghana;[126] in Northern Cameroons in 1961[127] which then

120 Generally, see Husain M. Al-Bahrana, "The Fact-Finding Mission of the United Nations Secretary General and the Settlement of the Bahrain-Iran Dispute, 22 (1973) *ICLQ* 541; and Kaiyan H. Kaikobad, *op. cit.* note 90, 22.
121 See 1970 *UN Yearbook* 285, 286.
122 Modern plebiscites were used as early as the nineteenth century; and nine were provided for in the Versailles Treaty of 1919: See Norman Hill, "*Claims to Territory in International Law and Relations*", (Oxford University Press, Greenwood Press Reprint, Westport, Connecticut, 1945/1976), 187. He is critical of the process from the political point of view.
123 Resolution 637 A (VII), 16 December 1952. Note that the chapeau of the resolution refers to these propositions as recommendations.
124 See Principle VII, Annex to the Principles, Resolution 1541 (XV), 15 December 1960.
125 See the first paragraph under this principle.
126 See Resolutions 1044 and 1045 (XV) of 13 December 1956.
127 See GA Resolution 1608 (XV) of 21 April 1961. Generally, see Kaiyan H. Kaikobad, *op. cit.* note 90, 28-29.

joined Nigeria; in Western Samoa in 1961;[128] in Djibouti in 1977;[129] and in East Timor/Timor Leste in 1999,[130] all of them subsequently becoming independent.

Finally *Opinion No. 4*[131] delivered by the Arbitration Commission of the International Conference on Yugoslavia (also known as the Badinter Arbitration Commission) on 11 January 1991 is relevant for it stressed the importance of ascertaining the wishes of all the people of Bosnia, that is the Serbs as well as the Bosnians. The Commission noted that the Bosnian Serbs had voted in a plebiscite but that was outside the institutional framework of the Socialist Republic of Bosnia-Herzegovina.[132] No plebiscite was in evidence; there was merely an amendment of the Constitution of 1990 which stated that the SRBH comprised of Muslims, Serbs and Croats among others living on its territory; but that the Commission was "of the opinion that the will of the peoples of Bosnia-Herzegovina to constitute the SRBH as a sovereign and independent State cannot be held to have been fully established".[133] Subsequently, a referendum was held in February 1992 which by a majority vote decided in favour of the creation of an independent State.[134]

F. The Right to Seek Assistance Consistent with the Principles of the UN Charter

Where there is forcible action constituting a denial of the right of self determination or autonomy in particular, autonomous units enjoy the right to seek assistance from other States provided it is consistent with the principles and purposes of the Charter. This position is based in the sixth paragraph of the Friendly Relations Declaration. Accordingly, this rules out intervention by the use of armed men and smuggling of weapons for use by men across boundary lines and which grave and serious acts of violence which could be seen as being assimilated to invasion, attack and bombardment. Furthermore, Article 3(g) of the Declaration on Aggression stipulates that acts of this kind would constitute aggression. Finally, the last paragraph of the Friendly Relations Declaration stipulates that nothing in the resolution shall be construed as authorising or encouraging any action which would dismember or impair the territorial integrity of or political unity of sovereign and independent States.[135] It follows that an aggrieved autonomous entity will be limited to ensuring that its movement of autonomy does not impair the territorial integrity of the mother or host State.

---

128 See GA Resolution 1626 (XVI) of 18 October 1961.

129 See GA Resolution 32/1 of 20 September 1977 which admits Djibouti to membership of the United Nations; also see 1977 *UN Yearbook* 870.

130 See Security Council Resolution 1272 of 25 October 1999. The referendum was also approved by the Indonesian People's Consultative Assembly (the legislature): "Timor-Leste" in Maher (ed.), *Europa World Yearbook 2009* (note 28), 4448.

131 92 *ILR* 173.

132 *Ibid.*, 177.

133 *Ibid.*, 178.

134 Note separate to the *Opinion*, 178.

135 See S. K. N. Blay (note 119), 448-49.

G. The Right to Autonomy as an Expression of Indigenous Peoples Rights (Where Applicable)

This has reference to the fact that indigenous persons have a right of both self determination and autonomy. The 2007 United Nations General Assembly Declaration on the Rights of Indigenous Peoples provides in Article 3 that indigenous peoples have the right of self determination. [136] It provides, "By virtue of that right they freely determine their political status and freely pursue their economic, social and cultural development." Furthermore, Article 4 states as follows:

Indigenous peoples, in exercising their right to self-determination, have the right to autonomy or self-government in matters relating to their internal and local affairs, as well as ways and means for financing their autonomous functions.

It follows that to the extent that the resolution is indicative of the direction in which customary international is developing, this is a right as opposed to a privilege.

V. AUTONOMY AND THE KASHMIR DISPUTE: CONCLUDING REMARKS

In the light of the above observations, it is possible to apply the law relative to autonomy in the matter of the Kashmir dispute in the following way.

Kashmir, as a distinct entity with a majority Muslim population, has, in principle the right of self determination; and this would mean the right freely to determine without external influence or control, its future, permanent political status, and one aspect of this would be either meaningful autonomy from the Indian federal government or complete sovereign independence if it so chooses. India is obliged to conduct a plebiscite or a referendum allowing the Kashmir people to decide whether they wish to (i) become independent; (ii) autonomous; (iii) keep the *status quo*; (iv) or devise any other kind of territorial settlement, including a condominium or merger with Pakistan. Pakistan has of course granted Kashmir full autonomy as a step in the settlement of the dispute/conflict. India's obligations stem from the customary international law relative to self determination; and not the right of minorities. The Government of India have a duty to carry out the wishes of the population and respect and maintain the autonomy of Kashmir, if that is what is decided.

The administration and population of Kashmir are obliged not to conduct themselves in any way which would constitute abusing the autonomy of Kashmir. If Kashmiris decide to opt for autonomy as opposed to sovereign independence, then the administration in Srinagar, and the population at large is obliged not to embark on a struggle for sovereign independence. The Government of India are obliged not take forcible action depriving the population of the autonomy it will/may have opted for. Where the Indian Government decides to take forcible action against the autonomous unit, then Kashmir would have the right to seek assistance consistent with the principles and purposes of the UN. However, it is not the case that the Kashmiri nation has to demonstrate the violation or breach of the conditions of autonomy; ultimately, the right of sovereign independence vests in Kashmir without qualifications other than (i) the creation of regional instability; and (ii) the violation of fundamental *jus cogens* rules. The existence of a sovereign independent Kashmir will

---

136 General Assembly Resolution 61/295 of 2 October 2007.

not create regional instability. On the contrary, when Kashmir finally emerges as an independent State, regional stability will greatly be enhanced insofar as vexed problem between two nuclear States will finally be put to rest. Nor is there any question of a violation of any peremptory rule of international law in the matter of either an autonomous or sovereign independent State.

Finally, it must always be borne in mind that although a distinct territorial unit, Kashmir is not a homogenous entity; there are at least five sizeable ethnic groups, including the Kashmiri-speaking Kashmiris, the Punjabi-speaking Kashmiris; Sikhs, Ladakh/Chinese and Pukhtuns; the notion of self may not easily be ascertained.

CHAPTER 8

Set-Up and Challenges of National Human Rights Commissions in India and Nepal*

Emma Lantschner**

I. INTRODUCTION

National Human Rights Institutions (NHRI) are a quite recent phenomenon in the range of bodies dealing with the promotion and protection of human rights. Most of them are fewer than twenty years old.[1] In 2010, 65 NHRI all over the world were found to be in line with the Paris Principles on the status and functioning of NHRI as defined in October 1991.[2] According to these principles, such institutions need to be independent (in terms of legal basis, budget, and regarding their members), members need to be an expression of the diversity and plurality in a country, and the mandate of the institution should be as broad as possible.[3] NHRI can be organized as a collegial organ in the form of a commission or as an individual organ in the form of an ombudsperson. Both types can either have a general mandate or be assigned a special purpose.[4] Examples for the latter are the national commissions for women or language issues or ombudspersons dealing only with persons belonging to national minorities.

In South Asia, only the National Human Rights Commissions (NHRCs) of India and Nepal as well as Afghanistan's Independent Human Rights Commission have the status of being in compliance with the Paris Principles (A status). However, as will be seen below, this status is currently being questioned by the Sub-Committee on

---

* This article is a revised and updated version of "National Human Rights Commissions in India and Nepal: State of Affairs and Challenges Ahead", published in 8 *European Yearbook of Minority Issues* (2010), 523-539.

** Emma Lantschner is assistant professor at the Centre for Southeast European Studies at the University of Graz. In 2009, she undertook a study visit to Nepal and India to do research on the National Human Rights Commissions of these two countries in the framework of the Eurasia-Net project, lead by the European Academy Bolzano/Bozen (EURAC). This article is partly based on interviews carried out during this study visit.

1 UN Office of the High Commissioner for Human Rights, "Survey on National Human Rights Institutions: Report on the findings and recommendations of a questionnaire addressed to NHRIs worldwide", July 2009, 4.

2 The Paris Principles were defined at the first International Workshop on National Institutions for the Promotion and Protection of Human Rights in Paris 7-9 October 1991, adopted by Human Rights Commission Resolution 1992/54, 1992 and General Assembly Resolution 48/134, 1993.

3 See Paris Principles, A(2), B(1-2).

4 For more nuanced distinctions of the types of NHRI see, e.g., Valentin Aichele, *Nationale Menschenrechtsinstitutionen in Europa* (Deutsches Institut für Menschenrechte, Berlin, 2004), 12-13; International Council on Human Rights Policy, *Performance & Legitimacy: National human rights institutions* (International Council on Human Rights Policy, Versoix, 2nd ed. 2004), 3-4; Linda C. Reif, "Building Democratic Institutions: The Role of National Human Rights Institutions in Good Governance and Human Rights Protection", 13 *Harvard Human Rights Journal* (2000), 1-69, at 5-13.

Accreditation (SCA) of the International Coordination Committee of NHRI (ICC). Sri Lanka and the Maldives have observer (B) status, which means that their institutions are either not fully in line with the Paris Principles or insufficient information has been provided to make a determination. Other South Asian states either have no such commission or they have no registered status at the International Coordinating Committee of NHRIs.

The present article assesses the functioning of the NHRCs of India and Nepal, starting with an overview of the technical aspects related to their legal bases, composition, and mandate (II) and then presents a more substantive analysis of the major challenges encountered by these two bodies in their day-to-day work (III).

II. Formal Preconditions

A. Legal Bases

According to the Paris Principles, NHRI should be based on a law or even on the constitution of a country. The obvious purpose of this provision is to de-link the existence, mandate, and composition of the institution as much as possible from the arbitrary decisions of changing governments.

The NHRC in India is based on the Protection of Human Rights Act of 1993. The NHRC was immediately established and is thus one of the most longstanding institutions. However, from the beginning, the first NHRC detected a discrepancy between the aims and objectives of the Act and the means foreseen by the Act to reach these goals. Although a high-level Advisory Committee made suggestions as to the amendment of the Act already in 1999 and the Commission's proposals based on this work were submitted to the government in 2000, it was only in 2006 that the law was finally amended.[5] Quite a number of proposed changes have not found their way into the new law.[6] How they still hamper the functioning of the Commission will be analyzed in part III of this article.

Nepal's Commission has its original foundation in the 1997 National Human Rights Commission Act. However, due to the political instability in the country, the Commission was set up only in 2000.[7] After the turbulences connected to the killing of the king in 2001, the new king's dismissal of the government in 2005 to command the war against Maoists, and the democracy movement in 2006 which finally ended with the abolishment of the monarchy in 2007,[8] the Interim Constitution of the same year made the NHRC a constitutional body, partly amending also the law of 1997.[9] In

5 Protection of Human Rights (Amendment) Act, 2006, No. 43 of 2006. Virendra Dayal, "Evolution of the National Human Rights Commission, 1993-2002: A Decennial Review", 1 *Journal of the NHRC* (2002), 40-71, at 42.

6 See Human Rights Documentation Centre, "Wasted Opportunity to Reform India's NHRC", *Human Rights Features* (2007).

7 See Bipin Akhikari, *Building Capacity of National Human Rights Institutions: The Case of Nepal* (Right to Education Foundation, Kathmandu, 2004), 22.

8 For an account of Napali recent history, see Manjushree Thapa, *Forget Kathmandu: An Elegy for Democracy* (Penguin, New Delhi, 2007).

9 See Part 15 of the Interim Constitution of Nepal (Arts. 131-133) is specifically dealing with the National Human Rights Commission of Nepal.

late 2009, the Commission's compliance with the Paris Principles was under review by the responsible Sub-Committee on Accreditation of the ICC.[10] The Sub-Committee was not in the position to come to a conclusion as the work on a review of the NHRC legislation was still pending at the Nepalese Parliament. The NHRC of Nepal, therefore, had to undergo another review in early 2010 during which it should have been established whether the status of being compliant with the Paris Principles can be maintained or whether the Commission will be downgraded.[11] During its March 2010 session, the SCA recommended the ICC to give the Nepalese Commission "B" status accreditation, if in the course of one year it is not in a position to provide evidence that it is still in conformity with the Paris Principles. During this period the NHRC retains it's "A" status. This decision reflects concerns of the SCA over the non-implementation of previous recommendations as well as over certain provisions of the still not adopted draft law. One of the criticized key issues concerned the definition of "human rights" as it would make reference only to domestic law and not all human rights instruments.[12] Other concerns will be discussed in the following sections.

B. Composition

The Paris Principles require that the composition of NHRI and the appointment of its members "shall be established in accordance with a procedure which affords all necessary guarantees to ensure the *pluralist representation* of the social forces (of civilian society) involved in the protection and promotion of human rights".[13] These social forces include NGOs, trade unions, social and professional organizations, different philosophical and religious thoughts, academic experts, and members of parliament. Also, the General Observations of the ICC Sub-Committee on Accreditation emphasize in this context the importance "to maintain consistent relationships with civil society".[14] In terms of selection and appointment of the members of the Commissions, the SCA attaches great importance, amongst other things, to a transparent process and broad consultation throughout the process.[15]
The UN Survey on NHRI[16] noted that only half of the Commissions under consideration indicated that their founding law included a provision on pluralism. The laws establishing the NHRCs of India and Nepal are a case in point. Neither of the legal bases emphasized the importance of diversity in the Commission. In the case of

---

10 Documents of these bodies as well as a list of accredited NHRI and their status of accreditation can be retrieved at <http://www.nhri.net/>.
11 See International Coordinating Committee of National Institutions for the Promotion and Protection of Human Rights, Report and Recommendations of the Session of the Sub-Committee on Accreditation, Geneva, 16-18 November 2009, para. 4(4).
12 See International Coordinating Committee of National Institutions for the Promotion and Protection of Human Rights, "Report and Recommendations of the Session of the Sub-Committee on Accreditation (SCA)", Geneva, 29 March – 1 April 2010, 13.
13 See Paris Principles, B(1), emphasis added.
14 See ICC Sub-Committee on Accreditation, General Observations, adopted by the International Coordination Committee of National Human Rights Institutions for the Promotion and Protection of Human Rights (ICC) by email after the SCA meeting of March 2009, Geneva, June 2009, para. 2(1).
15 *Ibid.*, para. 2(2).
16 See UN Office of the High Commissioner for Human Rights, *op.cit.* note 1, 50.

Nepal, this has changed with the Interim Constitution which now foresees that "the representation from all fields including women" needs to be maintained in the appointment process.[17] The draft NHRC law has been criticized by the SCA for not providing for a procedure that ensures pluralistic representation among the Commissioners.[18] The Indian and Nepalese Commissions attach great importance to the prestige of the members of the Commissions. The Indian Act, for instance, foresees that the chairperson of the NHRC is a former Chief Justice of the Supreme Court,[19] the highest position in the judiciary of a country. Also according to the Nepalese Act of 1997, the chairperson of the Commission had to be a former judge of the Supreme Court, albeit not necessarily a Chief Justice.[20] Here again the Interim Constitution brought a change in that it foresaw that "a person who hold[s] a high reputation and has rendered outstanding contribution being actively involved in the field of protection and promotion of human rights and social work" can be appointed to chair the NHRC.[21] These characteristics are also preconditions for being appointed to the position of one of the four ordinary members in the Nepalese NHRC. In this point, the Indian NHRC differs slightly because two out of the remaining four members have to be a former judge of the Supreme Court and a former chief justice of a high court. The other two members are appointed from among persons who have knowledge or practical experience with human rights issues.

The focus on judges can be seen from two perspectives: on the one hand, a judge—and in particular a former Chief Justice of the Supreme Court—knows the law, is used to procedures and knows how to move in a legal environment. A person of this rank might also have the necessary leverage to push for systemic changes. On the other hand, as has been criticized by human rights activists, the judges often lack a strong background in human rights and do not really know the situation on the ground. The overrepresentation of judges—as well as retired high ranking government servants, whose independence might be questioned—has been seen critically by human rights organizations. For instance, the appointment of a former Director of the Central Bureau of Investigation and lifelong employee of the India Police Service has been heavily criticized in a recent report because, according to some, his bias is unavoidable.[22] Since the establishment of the Indian NHRC there has been no trade unionist, no NGO representative, no academic or member of parliament represented. Also, the current composition does not reflect diversity in other respects because it is composed of only male, upper-caste Hindu commissioners.[23]

---

17 Interim Constitution of Nepal, 2007, Art. 131(2). The meaningful participation of women to ensure plurality is also emphasized by the General Observations of the ICC Sub-Committee on Accreditation, *op.cit.* note 14, para. 2(1).

18 See ICC, *op.cit.* note 12, 14.

19 See The Protection of Human Rights Act, Art. 3(2)(a).

20 See National Human Rights Commission Act, Art. 3(1)(a).

21 Interim Constitution of Nepal, Art. 131(1)(a).

22 See Emerlynne Gil and Pia Alexandra Muzaffar Dawson (eds.), *2009 ANNI Report on the Performance and Establishment of National Human Rights Institutions in Asia* (The Asian NGOs Network on National Human Rights Institutions [ANNI], Bangkok, 2009), 49-50, available at: <http://www.pwtn.org/2009_ANNI_Report.pdf>.

23 Interview with the director of the Asian Centre for Human Rights, Suhas Chakma, in New Delhi on 23 April 2009. View shared also by Gil and Muzaffar Dawson, *op.cit.* note 22, 49-51 and 53.

A difference between the composition of the Indian and Nepalese Commissions, which could also enhance the plurality of the former, lies in the fact that it has ex-officio members: the chairs of the National Commissions for Minorities, for Scheduled Casts, for Scheduled Tribes, and for Women.[24] What could be seen as a useful way of creating synergies between the national commissions has not proven to be successful in practice. In fact, despite previous invitations, for the last couple of years the chairpersons of the mentioned human rights institutions have not been invited to a joint meeting by the NHRC, which puts in doubt the commitment of the NHRC of India to put in practice the principle of cooperation as foreseen by the Paris Principles.[25]

The members of the NHRC of Nepal are appointed by the prime minister, on the recommendation of the Constitutional Council, consisting of the Chief Justice, the speaker of the parliament, and three cabinet ministers. As all of them are appointed by the prime minister or belong to the governing party, there is an imminent danger of the political interests influencing the Commission's composition.[26] As has further been noted by human rights organizations and the Sub-Committee on Accreditation of the ICC (the latter concerning the draft NHRC law), there is no broad consultation process during the appointment process to the current Commission and it could not be considered as transparent.[27] A parliamentary and public hearing apparently took place[28] but was not to the satisfaction of the civil society sector. Even more doubtful was obviously the appointment of the members to the previous commission. After the royal coup in 2005, the king appointed new commissioners without parliamentary oversight at all. These commissioners were, however, in office only for about one year because in 2006 they were forced to resign by the newly restored parliament.[29]

In India, the NHRC is appointed by the President after obtaining a recommendation by a Committee composed of governing and opposition politicians.[30] Although this composition balances better between the political forces in the country it still neglects the involvement of other actors. It has been criticized that the appointment process is a political bargaining instead of an open consultation process with civil society and other relevant players.[31]

In light of the aforementioned, it might be legitimate to put in doubt the conformity of the NHRCs of India and Nepal to the Paris Principles related to independent

---

24 According to the Protection of Human Rights Act, Art. 3(3), these members participate in all functions of the Commission except for the investigations into complaints of human rights violations.

25 See Gil and Muzaffar Dawson, *op.cit.* note 22, 57-58.

26 For criticism raised in that sense, see Bidhya Chapagain, "NGO Parallel Report on the Compliance with the Paris Principles of the National Commission of Human Rights of Nepal", September 2008, 4; ICC, *op.cit.* note 12, 13.

27 See Chapagain, *op.cit.* note 26, 5; ICC, *op.cit.* note 12, 14.

28 Interview with Commissioner K. B. Rokaya in Kathmandu on 15 April 2009.

29 Information from the website of the NHRC of Nepal at <http://www.nhrcnepal.org/>.

30 These are the prime minister, speaker of the House of the People, the minister of home affairs, the leader of the opposition in the House of the People, the leader of the opposition in the Council of States and the deputy chairman of the Council of States. See Protection of Human Rights Act, Art. 4(1).

31 Interview with Colin Gonsalves, Executive Director of Human Rights Law Network, New Delhi, on 21 April 2009.

Commissioners,[32] reflecting the plurality of a country and appointed through a transparent and inclusive process.

C. Funding

One way to ensure the independence and autonomy of a body is by providing it with the necessary financial means. The Paris Principles foresee in this context that NHRCs should get adequate funding with the purpose of enabling it to have a staff and premises, to be independent from the government and to not "be subject to financial control which might affect its independence."[33] The Interim Constitution of Nepal is silent on this point,[34] and the issue appears to be controversial during the drafting process of the new act regulating the NHRC. In late 2009, members of the NHRC and of civil society alike criticized the fact that the government intended not only to delete the adjectives "independent and autonomous" as a description of the Commission from the draft bill, but also that it was reluctant to equip it with the necessary financial autonomy so that it could, for instance, recruit its own staff.[35] If this is not the case, the NHRC "cannot function independently as expected by the civil society and on a par with the international standards."[36] This state of affairs has also been criticized by the SCA in its report of March 2010. It found that there was a lack of guarantees of the NHRC's independence and autonomy, that "draft Bill does not provide for sufficient operational independence" and that there was "no provision to ensure that the NHRC is provided with adequate funding to fulfill its mandate."[37] According to the same report of the SCA, the "NHRC is greatly under-staffed" as "less than 50 percent of envisaged staff positions are filled, and nearly 90 percent of these are temporary contracted staff."[38] This causes a permanent staffing crisis to the detriment of the functioning of the NHRC.

The financial autonomy of the Indian NHRC is spelled out in Article 32 of the underlying Act. However, Article 11 foresees that the Central Government shall "make available" to the Commission the staff required "for the efficient performance of the functions of the Commission." This makes the Commission dependent on the government, as it is the latter to chose how many staff and whom to make available to the Commission. This results in a situation in which many officers working at the

---

32 In general, it has been found that the independence of NHRIs in Asia is at a decline, due to highly politicized selection processes and the silencing of human rights defenders in this context. Statement of the Asian Network on National Human Rights Institutions (ANNI), 14th Annual Meeting of the Asia Pacific Forum of National Human Rights Institutions, 5 August 2009, Amman, Jordan.

33 See Paris Principles, B(2).

34 See Chapagain, *op.cit.* note 26, 3.

35 See "Nepal: Draft bill raises Commission's concern", *Ekantipur News*, 12 October 2009; Ananta Raj Luitel, "Is draft bill trying to weaken NHRC?", *The Himalayan Times Online,* 21 October 2009.

36 NHRC Chair Kedar Nath Upadjyaya, quoted in the article "Toothless draft raises NHRC hackles", *The Kathmandu Post*, 11 October 2009.

37 See ICC, *op.cit.* note 12, 13-14.

38 *Ibid.*, 14. According to the information provided by Commissioner Rokaya, the state had increased the budget of the NHRC in 2009 for 85 percent (which allowed for an increase of staff from 165 to 310) and it was never necessary to ask for funding from external donors. Other sources say that the NHRC could not function if it was not supported, also financially, by a capacity building project of the UNDP.

commission come there "with a certain mind-set", which is characterized by "deep resistance to change, bureaucratic procedures of work and very heavy accumulated backlog of bad practices."[39] Their knowledge about and commitment to human rights is limited and they are not trained once they join the commission.[40] It is also highly questionable whether this is in line with the General Observations of the ICC Sub-Committee on Accreditation. The Sub-Committee notes that for the sake of guaranteeing the independence of the commission it should be good practice that the number of seconded staff does not exceed 25 percent and in any case is never more than 50 percent of the workforce at the commission.[41] How easy it is to weaken a commission if it completely depends on the secondments by the government is shown by the Commission for Scheduled Tribes, in which 40 percent of the required staff is missing. In addition, although the number of senior staff was increasing over the last year, the lower-level posts remained vacant or were even abolished, which considerably reduces the functionality of the Commission.[42]

D. Mandate

National Human Rights Commissions have to be independent to be able to carry out their mandate in a way most conducive for the promotion and protection of human rights. The Paris Principles foresee that the mandate should be as broad as possible. As has already been mentioned, the SCA criticized the draft NHRC law of Nepal as the definition of "human rights", making reference only to domestic law and not to all human rights instruments, limits the mandate of the Commission.[43] In operative terms, the mandates of both Commissions are quite broad. They include the task to inquire, *suo motu* or on a petition by the victim or another person on his or her behalf, into a complaint of violation of human rights. In addition, they have the task to give advice to the governments by reviewing legislation concerning the protection of human rights as well as studying international treaties and giving recommendations to the government for their effective implementation. Finally, they undertake research and spread human rights literacy among the population. Both commissions have the task to cooperate with civil society.[44]

If the draft NHRC law is adopted by the Nepalese parliament in its current form there is no requirement for the government "to seek the Commission's opinion on the formulation of, or amendments to, legislation regarding human rights an on matters relating to Nepal becoming a partner to international or regional human rights treaties."[45] Similar as under the current legislation, the draft law is ambiguous concerning the NHRC's jurisdiction over acts related to the Nepalese Army. In this

---

39 See B. P. Joshi, "National Human Rights Commission – Need for Review", Common Wealth Human Rights Initiative (unpublished), 2, at <http://www.humanrightsinitiative.org/>.

40 *Ibid.*

41 See ICC Sub-Committee on Accreditation, *op.cit.* note 14, para. 2(4).

42 Interview with a senior official of the National Commission for Schedules Tribes, on 30 April 2009. Similar problems persist in other NHRI all over the world, as identified in the UN OHCHR's Survey on National Human Rights Institutions, *op.cit.* note 1, 52.

43 See ICC, *op.cit.* note 12, 13.

44 For details, see The Protection of Human Rights Act, Art. 12; Interim Constitution of Nepal, Art. 132.

45 See ICC, *op.cit.* note 12, 14.

context the SCA stressed that it is important "that the NHRC is fully able to look into all alleged human rights violations, regardless of which State officials are responsible, including all army officers and personnel."[46]

The next chapter examines the question of what challenges currently appear for the NHRCs in fulfilling their mandate.

III. Challenges for the NHRCs of India and Nepal

Considering the overwhelming diversity, economic disparities and internal conflicts existing in India and Nepal, it is not hard to imagine that both National Human Rights Commissions are faced with tremendous challenges. India's population of 1,16 billion is more than twice that of the European Union. More than 100 languages are spoken compared with about 92 in Nepal. Both countries are mainly Hindu (about 80 percent in both) but are also home of members of several other religious denominations. Although both countries are officially secular, religion—as well as the caste system—still plays an important role. How the NHRCs of India and Nepal have managed to deal with these challenges while putting into practice their mandate will be explored in this chapter.

A. Investigating into Individual Complaints

The National Human Rights Commissions are not there to substitute the court systems in both countries. Rather, they should constitute an additional, more easily accessible and faster possibility for victims of human rights violations to get redress. The judicial system in India and Nepal has been able to address important cases of human rights violations.[47] Nevertheless, in both countries there is a pervasive regime of impunity. For instance, serious human rights violations by security forces, such as torture or extrajudicial killings are rarely prosecuted, which gives the perpetrators the feeling of being above the law and results in yet other violations of human rights.[48] Thus, NHRCs are sometimes addressed by persons who hope that the Commissions are more forceful in fighting human rights violations. However, local human rights organizations are not satisfied with the record of the NHRCs in this context.

Regarding the Indian Commission, they criticize the way in which investigations into complaints are carried out and the lack of transparency. On receiving a complaint, the NHRC requests a report from the alleged perpetrators. In many cases, it is the same person who is accused of the violation of human rights who conducts the investigations and writes the report for the Commission. Often, the Commission closes the case after receiving such a report without giving the victim the possibility to react to it and without inquiring into the correctness of the facts stated in the report.[49] Only in 6 percent of the cases has the Indian Commission carried out its own

46 *Ibid.*

47 Positive in this context the assessment of the Asian Centre for Human Rights, *India Human Rights Report 2008* (Asian Centre for Human Rights, New Delhi, 2008), viii.

48 For India see, *ibid.*, vii and 68-69; *id.*, *India Human Rights Report 2009* (Asian Centre for Human Rights, New Delhi, 2009), iv-v and 83-84. For Nepal see, Chapagain, *op.cit.* note 26, 3.

49 See the Asian NGO Network on National Institutions (ANNI), *2008 Report on the Performance and Establishment of National Human Rights Institutions in Asia* (Asian Forum for Human Rights and

investigations, a situation which is also connected to the fact that it has quite limited investigation capacities. In some cases, the reports recognized that torture had taken place and the Commission nevertheless dismissed the case.[50] Furthermore, often individuals or organizations who have lodged the complaint on their behalf are not informed about the closure of the case, or that the cases have not even been registered without providing reasons for this action to the complainants.[51]

Another criticism of human rights organizations concerns the reluctance of the Indian NHRC to recommend compensation for the victims of human rights violations. From the more than 637,000 cases filed with the Commission until 2006[52], the victims had been paid compensation only in 716 cases. In addition, the amounts recommended are very low and can hardly be considered a deterrent for perpetrators of human rights.[53] The record concerning recommendations for prosecution is even worse. Again, until 2006, "the NHRC had recommended disciplinary action in 223 cases and prosecution in 74 cases against state actors". It is also remarkable that in the two and a half years preceding this date, only two disciplinary actions or prosecutions were recommended.[54]

Although certainly not serving as an excuse for the deficiency in the complaint-handling procedure, the amount of complaints the NHRC of India has to deal with every year needs to be taken into consideration. The workload increased from 496 complaints in the first year of its existence to 82,233 cases in the period of April 2006 to March 2007.[55] About 32,000 cases were still pending so that the Commission had to deal with more than 114,000 cases in the period under consideration by the last Annual Report. The number of complaints rose further to 94,559 in 2008.[56] The Secretary General of the Indian NHRC acknowledged that the slow pace in which individual complaints are dealt with is one of the weaknesses of the Commission.[57]

The huge backlog of cases might be easier to handle if there existed some sort of decentralization. The Protection of Human Rights Act 1993 provides in Article 21 that the state governments may constitute State Human Rights Commission (SHRC). Up until now, 18 such Commissions have been established.[58] The mandate of the SHRC

Development, Bangkok, 2008), 61-62. This experience has also been reported in an interview by the director of the Asian Centre for Human Rights Suhas Chakma.

50 Interview with Suhas Chakma.

51 The Asian NGO Network on National Institutions (ANNI), *op.cit.* note 49, 63. For recommendations against all these practices see, Recommendations following the National Consultation on Strengthening National Human Rights Commission, organized by Public Advocacy Initiatives for Rights and Values in India (Pairvi), Asian Centre for Human Rights (ACHR) and People's Watch Tamil Nadu (PWTN), New Delhi, 29-31 January 2007.

52 Lacking more updated figures, the ones of 2006 have been used.

53 See Human Rights Documentation Centre, "India's NHRC Fails to Use its Meagre Powers", *Human Rights Features* (2007).

54 *Ibid.*

55 See National Human Rights Commission, Annual Report 2006-2007, 1, at <http://nhrc.nic.in/>. This report is the last Annual Report publicly available.

56 See "India: NHRC receives 94,000 complaints in 2008", *Hindustan Times*, 15 March 2009.

57 Interview with Akhil Kumar Jain, Secretary General of the NHRC of India, in New Delhi on 29 April 2009.

58 These are in the states of Andhra Pradesh, Assam, Bihar, Chhattisgarh, Gujarat, Himachal Pradesh, Jammu & Kashmir, Karnataka, Kerala, Mahrashtra, Mahya Pradesh, Manipur, Orissa, Punjab, Rajasthan, Tamil Nadu, Uttar Pradesh and West Bengal.

is, with one exception,[59] exactly the same as the one of the NHRC, whereas the sphere of competence is limited to matters in which states have exclusive or concurrent legislative competence.[60] This means, at least in theory, that each type of Commission has a field of competence and that the National Human Rights Commission has not been conceived as a last instance commission. However, many people prefer to address the NHRC instead of the SHRC[61] due to, at least in some cases, a lack of trust in the effectiveness of the Commissions at the state level. Appointments to the SHRC are reported to be "extremely political" and staff members are not sufficiently trained to properly fulfill their task.[62] The theoretically separate spheres of competence do not prevent that both Commissions are sometimes requested to decide on cases which require the use of similar concepts or approaches. However, the Act does not give the NHRC any supervisory power over the SHRC. This leads to a situation in which important guidelines or instructions issued by the NHRC are ignored by SHRC so that decisions are reached that do not reflect the approaches taken by the NHRC. The proposals of the NHRC for the amendment of the Protection of Human Rights Act in 2000 recommended a hierarchical relationship between National and State HRC to remedy this situation, but it was not adopted into the amended Act. There seems to be some tacit convention of respect of the chairs of the SHRC (former Chief Justices of High Courts) *vis-à-vis* the chair of the NHRC (former Chief Justice of the Supreme Court) which allows the latter to invite the former to reconsider decisions in case they are not in line with the views of the NHRC.[63] This can, however, be hardly satisfactory in lack of an institutionalized mechanism of coordination. The last published Annual Report of the NHRC, covering 2006-2007, gives an account of the initiative of the NHRC to organize annual meetings with all SHRC to foster "mutual discussions [...] keeping in view the social, cultural and linguistic diversity" that the Indian society comprises.[64] Although this is a positive first step, the collaboration between National and State HRC needs to be further strengthened with the aim of increasing the quality of work of SHRC, ensuring the consistency of the jurisprudence of the Commissions and raising the awareness of people for human rights and the mechanisms available for their protection. The annual meetings of the NHRC with all SHRC could well serve as a platform to find the appropriate ways and means for this purpose.

By doing so, the outreach of the NHRC could also be improved. The statistics of 2008 show that 58.39 percent of the cases filed with the Indian NHRC have come from Uttar Pradesh, the state adjacent to New Delhi where the Commission is seated.[65] Since 2007, the Indian NHRC has been trying to raise awareness about its existence

---

59 The exception consists of Art. 12(f): to study treaties and other international instruments on human rights and make recommendations for their effective implementation.

60 See The Protection of Human Rights Act, Art. 21(5).

61 This is possible as Art. 32 of the Indian Constitution can be applied *mutatis mutandis* also to the NHRC.

62 See the Asian NGO Network on National Institutions (ANNI), *op.cit.* note 49, 67.

63 Interview with Virendra Dayal, former member of India's NHRC, in New Delhi on 28 April 2009.

64 See NHRC, Annual Report 2006-2007, 179.

65 *Op.cit.* note 48. The ratio of Uttar Pradeh is, however, decreasing: in 2006-2007, 63 percent of all registered cases came from that state. See NHRC of India, Annual Report 2006-2007, 294.

by organizing sittings in state capitals.[66] For that purpose, and to better spread human rights literacy across the country, it would also be recommended to establish regional offices of the NHRC across the country.[67]

This has been done by the NHRC of Nepal in an attempt to improve the outreach of the NHRC of Nepal also to the remote and hardly accessible parts of the country. Five regional and three subregional offices were created.[68] In the period from July 2007 to June 2008 a total of 16 regional-level and 74 local-level training events or meetings were organized to promote the idea of human rights.[69]

The success of NHRCs depends also on the willingness of the state authorities to follow suit to the recommendations of the Commissions. In the case of Nepal, the record is not all too positive.[70] Out of the 149 recommendations made by the Commission to the government in the period between 2000 and June 2008, the government has fully acted only on 16 cases and partially on another 35 cases. The lowest performance by the government is shown on recommendations related to violations committed by the police (28 out of 29 remained unimplemented), killings by Maoists (11 out of 13 unimplemented) as well as disappearances and torture by security forces (9 out of 11 unimplemented). The government does not even respond to communications from the Commission requesting to follow-up on the recommendations.[71] According to Article 132(2)(h) of the Interim Constitution, the NHRC has the possibility "to publicize the names of the official, person or bodies not following or implementing the recommendations and directions" adopted by the NHRC "and to record them as human rights violators." So far, the NHRC has never made use of this possibility to blacklist human rights perpetrators.[72] The currently debated new law on the NHRC would foresee an obligation of the government to implement NHRC recommendations within a three months period or, in case of failure, report back to the Commission giving reasons for the non-implementation.[73]

B. *Monitoring of Legislation and Cooperation with Civil Society*

Apart from investigating into individual complaints, the NHRCs have the mandate to advise the states concerned regarding the effective implementation of legislation concerning human rights and recommend necessary reforms or amendments thereto.[74] Although these provisions, in particular the Indian one, could be restrictively interpreted in the sense that the NHRCs have a say only on the implementation or

---

66 See the Asian NGO Network on National Institutions (ANNI), *op.cit.* note 49, 57-58.

67 In this sense see also Recommendations following the National Consultation on Strengthening National Human Rights Commission, *op.cit.* note 51.

68 Eastern Regional Office, Biratnagar; Central Regional Office, Janakpurdham; Western Regional Office, Pokhara; Mid-Western Regional Office, Nepalgunj; Far-Western Regional Office, Dhangadi. Subregional Offices were created in Khotang, Jumla and Rupendehi. In the interview with Commissioner Rokaya, he announced a sixth subregional office.

69 See NHRC of Nepal, Annual Progress Report: July 2007–June 2008, 2, available at: <http://www.nhrcnepal.org/>.

70 See Kamal Raj Sigdel, "Govt apathy riles NHRC", *The Kathmandu Post*, 15 April 2009, 1.

71 See Chapagain, *op.cit.* note 26, 10-11.

72 See Raj Luitel, *op.cit.* note 35.

73 See "Nepal: Draft bill raises Commission's concerns", *Ekantipur News*, 12 October 2009.

74 The Protection of Human Rights Act, Art. 12(d); Interim Constitution of Nepal, Art. 132(2)(f).

amendment of laws that are already in force, it seems to be clear that their review of any legislation dealing with human rights is required already at the drafting stage.

As the legal system in Nepal is undergoing considerable reform after the end of the Maoist insurgency and the people's movement, the NHRC of Nepal is currently focusing on the monitoring of new legislation. It has for instance given recommendations to the government during the drafting of the bill on the Truth and Reconciliation Commission and on the Disappearances bill. These recommendations have, at least partly, been considered by the government.[75] As has already been mentioned, the Commission was also involved in consultations concerning the new bill on the NHRC; however, the government has made changes to the agreed draft afterwards, which again raised the concern of the NHRC[76] and of the SCA. In the context of law-making the SCA criticized in particular that the current draft law does not require the government to ask for the Commission's opinion when drafting or amending legislation related to human rights or Nepal's ratification of human rights treaties.[77] The NHRC of Nepal is involved in the making of the new constitution of Nepal, with the aim to ensure that it becomes a human rights friendly document. The NHRC has further been mandated to monitor the human rights related implementation of the Comprehensive Peace Agreement concluded between the Maoists and the government to end the war.[78] In this context, the parties pledge "to accept the reports submitted by the above-mentioned bodies [among them also the NHRC], to provide the information requested by them, and to implement the suggestions and recommendations given by them on the basis of consensus and dialogue."[79] With this provision, the Commission would have quite a strong leverage. It seems, however, that it has not had much effect.

In general, the NHRC seems to be satisfied with the government when it comes to its involvement in the reviewing and commenting on existing and draft legislation. According to the information provided by the Commission, it also seeks to involve the civil society sector when making recommendations to the government.[80] Prominent human rights organizations in Nepal are, however, not satisfied with the level of involvement afforded to them by the NHRC.[81] The relationship between the NHRC and human rights organizations was severely damaged by the instalment of a procoup Commission by the king in 2005. Organizations and activists were skeptical about its

---

75 Interview with Commissioner K. B. Rokaya.

76 See "Nepal: Draft bill raises Commission's concern", *Ekantipur News*, 12 October 2009. According to information provided in ICC, *op.cit.* note 12, 13, the "NHRC organized a meeting with parliamentarians in February 2010 to lobby for a revised bill, and have participated in other events organized by civil society organizations advocating for appropriate legislation for the NHRC."

77 See ICC, *op.cit.* note 12, 14.

78 Comprehensive Peace Agreement (CPA) 2006, signed by Prime Minister Girija Prasad Koirala and Maoist chairman Prachanda, 21 November 2006, Art. 9(4).

79 *Ibid.*, Art. 9(5). In this context, the NHRC published in 2007 the "Summary of the Report on the Status of Human Rights under the Comprehensive Peace Agreement" and in 2009 the report "Three-Year of Comprehensive Peace Accord: Summary Report of 2006-2009", both at <http://www.nhrcnepal.org///publication/doc/reports/3-year_CPA.pdf>.

80 Interview with Commissioner K. B. Rokaya.

81 See Chapagain, *op.cit.* note 26, 6; as well as interview with Bidhya Chapagain, Chief of Human Rights, Monitoring and Advocacy Department of INSEC (Informal Sector Service Centre) in Kathmandu on 17 April 2009.

independence and autonomy. Nevertheless, they were convinced of the use of such a commission. When the Commission seats remained vacant for more than a year after the commissioners appointed by the king stepped down, they organized, together with NHRC personnel, a campaign entitled "Save the National Human Rights Commission". However, still today, NGOs and human rights organizations feel that there are too few instances of coordinated activities initiated by the Commission and no mechanisms facilitating regular interaction.[82] One of the aims of a UNDP led project dedicated to the capacity development of the NHRC[83] is to link the Commission with the civil society sector and to create a framework for good working relations between the NHRC and other human rights stakeholders in the country. Efforts, in this sense, are reflected in the strategy of the NHRC for the period 2008-2010, in which it envisages a "[f]unctional and goal-oriented collaboration with NGOs, civil society and human rights defenders for the promotion and protection of human rights of people and for the effective implementation of state commitment on it in action."[84] In the context of cooperation with international human rights organizations the SCA commented critically, that the draft bill would foresee that "foreign institutions" who plan to implement human rights programmes in Nepal have to "seek consent of the Commission". In the view of SCA this is "inappropriate" as "such a provision should stress cooperation and engagement with all human rights partners, and it would be preferable for the provision requiring such institutions to work in cooperation with the NHRC, and vice-versa."[85]

According to the Annual Report 2006-2007 of the Indian NHRC, "[t]he promotion and protection of human rights cannot gather momentum without the fullest co-operation between the Commission and the NGOs"[86] For that purpose, the NHRC established a Core-Group of NGOs already in 2001, which functioned until 2004 and was finally re-established in 2006. Since then, it has met five times although the NGOs consider that at least two meetings per year should be held. From the NGOs perspective, there is a feeling that the NHRC is unwilling to convene the Core Group of NGOs or to invite it to regional meetings of NHRI.[87]

C. *International and Regional Cooperation of NHRCs and the Role of SAARC*

When it comes to the monitoring of the states' performance regarding the implementation of international treaties, the situation in India and Nepal is comparable. In India, the NHRC neither provided input nor participated in deliberations during the process of preparing the country's periodic reports to various UN treaty bodies. Although the recent reports of India to the UN Committee on the International Convention on the Elimination of All Forms of Racial Discrimination (CERD) deny the existence of racial discrimination in India, the NHRC has remained

82 *Ibid.*, as well as interview with Bidhya Chapagain.
83 Information about the project is available on the website of UNDP, available at <http://www.undp.org.np/governance/projects/cdnhrc/index.php?ProgramID=22>.
84 See NHRC of Nepal, Strategic Plan–2008-2010, 9.
85 See ICC, *op.cit.* note 12, 14.
86 See NHRC of India, Annual Report–2006-2007, 177.
87 See Gil and Muzaffar Dawson, *op.cit.* note 22, 53-55.

silent on the domestic implementation of CERD.[88] It seems, however, that the NHRC was involved in the review of India under the Universal Periodic Review, presenting its own country paper.[89] In Nepal, the Commission regrets in its 2004 Annual Report that several reports to UN treaty monitoring bodies had been sent by the government without inviting the council of the NHRC.[90] The following report remains silent on the issue. Conversely, it needs to be acknowledged that in 2007, the Commission published a study of the domestication status of the International Covenant on Civil and Political Rights in Nepal and in 2009 a report on the status of child rights in Nepal.[91] In July 2010, the NHRC of Nepal submitted together with the National Women Commission and the National Dalit Commission a joint report in the framework of the Universal Periodic Review. The review with regard to Nepal is supposed to take place during the January/February 2011 session.[92]
Both NHRCs are members in the Asia-Pacific Forum (APF), a regional organization composed of national human rights institutions from across the Asia Pacific.[93] In the occasion of the APF meeting in 2008, the chair of the NHRC of India announced that his NHRC proposes to organize a conference on capacity building of NHRI for the countries belonging to the South Asian Association of Regional Cooperation (SAARC) in an attempt to share experiences and broaden understanding of human rights issues in the SAARC region.[94] The meeting, which was the first of this kind, finally took place on 16-18 April 2009 in Delhi.[95] The participating NHRI agreed to:

- work toward national capacity building through sharing of experience, information and best practices on human rights;
- take steps to promote human rights awareness, and toward this end, hold conferences at least once in two years, apart from exchanges of visits, training programs and bilateral or regional cooperation between the NHRIs;
- work together to identify and cooperate on capacity building for dealing with human rights issues like human rights awareness, human trafficking and migrant labour;

---

88 *Ibid.*, 60.
89 Conference Paper of the Conference of NHRIs of South Asian Countries on "Human Rights Awareness and National Capacity Building", organized by the NHRC India in New Delhi on 16-18 April 2009, 20 and 40.
90 See NHRC of Nepal, Annual Report 2004, 77.
91 Both documents are available on the website of the NHRC of Nepal at <http://www.nhrcnepal.org>.
92 A coalition of 238 Nepalese NGO also submitted a report in July 2010 entitled "Nepal NGO Coalition Submission to the United Nations Universal Periodic Review. Tenth session of the UPR Working Group of the Human Rights Council", available at:
http://www.inseconline.org/pics/1278390005.pdf.
93 See http://www.asiapacificforum.net
94 Opening Remarks of Mr. Justice S. Rajendra Babu, Chairperson, National Human Rights Commission, India, chairing the session on "Regional Co-operation between National Human Rights Institutions", 13th Asia Pacific Forum Meeting, Kuala Lumpur (Malaysia), 28-31 July 2008.
95 Although an invitation to participate at least in the inauguration of this conference was extended to Indian NGOs, this invitation was not repeated after the conference had to be postponed. Gil and Muzaffar Dawson, *op.cit.* note 22, 54.

- work collectively at UN fora, including the Human Rights Council, for an independent status for NHRIs, distinct from NGOs;
- appeal to the respective governments to support and provide necessary wherewithal to NHRIs to ensure that they become fully compliant with Paris Principles, which includes administrative and financial autonomy.[96]

It is important for NHRCs to function with fearlessness and independence also in the international cooperation. They must encourage states not to hide from international monitoring bodies but to cooperate with them unreservedly. Their highest priority must be to uphold universal standards.[97] This is particularly important considering that for the time being there is no regional mechanism for the protection of human rights. The question arises, whether the time is ripe for such a mechanism in South Asia.

Some think that it is not realistic to believe that states could agree on such a mechanism in the near future. It is felt that the direction is rather the opposite: laws are being tightened, police are given increased rights to infringe on civil rights under the guise of fighting terrorism, impunity is not countered by courts with sufficient determination and the mistrust among states of the region is still widespread. Others consider that there still persist too many ways of thinking. Whereas in Europe, after the Second World War there was a strong political desire for an overarching understanding of human rights, in South Asia the situation is different. It is felt that the making of formal institutions has to be preceded by a greater accommodation on the political side and by more coherent ideas about the kind of standards that need to be protected.[98]

Few are optimistic about the establishment of a South Asian human rights mechanism, albeit only in the middle term. The South Asian Centre for Human Rights has given some thought to the idea of a regional human rights document. It noted that the serious human rights problems encountered in South Asia show a high level of common patterns. Apart from an imperatively needed reform of the security forces, the judiciary must act against the compounding problem of impunity for human rights violations much more strongly. According to that study, the added value of a regional mechanism is in its "capacity to contextualize international standards and to enhance their cross-cultural appeal and applicability." Such a mechanism could "address human rights issues of particular shared concern in the SAARC region." The study, therefore, recommends the SAARC countries to "establish a Working Group of Eminent Persons of South Asia to explore the possibility of drafting a South Asia Human Rights Convention with full and active participation of civil society groups

---

96 See Resolution of the Conference of NHRIs of South Asian Countries on "Human Rights Awareness and National Capacity Building" at New Delhi on 16-18 April 2009, at: <http://www.nhri.net/latest_news/nhrc.htm>, as well as in Gil and Muzaffar Dawson, *op.cit.* note 22, 54-55.

97 Intervention of Virendra Dayal at the Conference of NHRIs of South Asian Countries on "Human Rights Awareness and National Capacity Building" at New Delhi on 16-18 April 2009, on file with the author.

98 Interview with Virendra Dayal and Colin Gonsalves.

and other stakeholders". The study further recommends NHRIs in South Asia to establish a South Asian subregional mechanism.[99]
During the SAARC Summit in Colombo, Sri Lanka, from 27 July to 3 August 2008, nothing like that was established or even discussed. SAARC has so far been reluctant in labelling the issues it is dealing with as human rights. There is no doubt about the fact that the SAARC Convention on Combating the Crime of Trafficking in Women and Children for Prostitution, its Convention on Regional Arrangements on the Promotion of Child Welfare in South Asia as well as the Social Charter are human rights related.[100] What is more, the president of the Maldives asserted during the 13th SAARC summit in 2005 that "it is time that an autonomous SAARC Centre for Human Rights, based on civil society, is established. Such a Commission could promote international standards, facilitate co-operation among lawyers and jurist, and share expertise and resources in the advocacy of human rights and democracy in the region".[101] Not dealing with sensitive issues among the member states, which apparently allows for more friendly cooperation seems, however, to be an approach which still persists in the organization. Consequently, SAARC has played no role so far in forging regional guidelines or a regional platform for the work of the NHRIs in South Asia.
The second recommendation of the Asian Centre for Human Rights addressed to the NHRCs requested them to establish a South Asian subregional mechanism. Also this can be implemented only with the participation of the states. However, even if the cooperation of NHRCs, as started with the first meeting in 2009, should not receive an institutional roof any time soon, it is already a first step toward approaching the many viewpoints on human rights issues persisting in the various countries.

IV. Concluding Remarks

As the presentation of the functional preconditions and day-to-day challenges of the NHRCs of India and Nepal have shown, one can conclude that the problems both commissions are dealing with are, to a large extent, similar. In both countries, widespread impunity for human rights violations persists. Regarding Nepal, one is tempted to look for explanations by pointing to the fact that it is a young democratic state which has only recently ended a war and is still struggling to set up functioning structures and institutions. Indeed, it has been said that the problem in Nepal is not so much that the state violates human rights but the absence of the state.[102] The point of departure of India is different: it has been an established democracy for more than 60 years. Nevertheless, the state has not managed to operationalize the principles as laid down in the constitution and break impunity. Of course, the NHRCs of India and Nepal cannot be the left alone with the burden of fighting this state of affairs. However, some structural changes might help to deal with the Sysiphusian struggle.

---

99 See Asian Centre for Human Rights, *South Asia Human Rights Index 2008*, 2008, 183-185, at <http://www.achrweb.org/reports/SAARC-2008.pdf>.
100 For more on these Conventions and the organization in general, see the article of Ugo Caruso in this volume.
101 Quoted in Asian Centre for Human Rights, *op.cit.* note 99, 184.
102 *Ibid.*, 15.

First, the financial independence and autonomy of both institutions must be ensured. It would be a missed opportunity for Nepal, if the upcoming law regulating the NHRC would be reluctant to speak out clearly in that sense. Regarding the Indian Commission, the fact that its entire staff is seconded by the government needs serious reconsideration. Second, both Commissions need to take the principles of plurality and transparency more seriously and, among other considerations, give room for the appointment of representatives of NGOs, human rights organization and other sectors of civil society to the commission.

In the case of India, a better coordination between the NHRC and the State HRC would further be recommendable. First of all, State Human Rights Commissions should be set up in all states. They should further be strengthened in terms of qualified staff and independent Commissioners and be conceived at sort of "first instance" commissions with the aim to lower the number of complaints filed with the National Human Rights Commission. The NHRC could serve as a kind of appeal Commission but would have more time to dedicate to conceptual work and proposals for systemic change. Alternatively, it could be envisaged to establish regional offices of the NHRC whose staff could carry out investigations on behalf of the NHRC, could be present during the interrogations of suspects to make sure that no inhuman or degrading treatments take place, and could more regularly visit prisons or clinics in which people are detained for the purpose of treatment to see how detainees are kept. They could furthermore engage in awareness raising activities covering a wider geographical scope than what is possible from the centre in Delhi.

A closer cooperation with other human rights institutions would also be beneficial for the sake of not only reducing the workload of the NHRC but also for ensuring a coherent jurisprudence throughout the human rights institutions of the country.

A better and coordinated outreach of human rights institutions—an issue equally important for Nepal—would also contribute to an increasing awareness by people of the role and function of each commission. In this way, it could be avoided that the Commission is getting a high number of complaints for which it is not responsible.

In terms of regional cooperation, it is encouraging to see the interest of the NHRIs of South Asia to work together in improving their work and promoting the awareness of human rights. Although it seems unrealistic to expect that a regional human rights mechanism will be established any time soon, all efforts in that sense are to be strongly supported. The NHRCs of South Asia, in cooperation with the civil society sector, could play an important role, first, by engaging in serious discussions including experts and human rights activists on possible differences and obstacles hindering a common approach in human rights issues so far, and second, by pushing their respective governments as well as SAARC toward putting human rights issues high on the agenda of all states involved and starting a debate on such an instrument at the governmental level. An improved functioning of National Human Rights Institutions in South Asia could thus, if not create heaven on earth, be a major blessing in helping to keep away the furies of hell.[103]

---

103 See Dayal, *op.cit.* note 97, inspired by Dag Hammarskjold who said: "The UN was not created to take earth to heaven, but to save it from going to hell!"

CHAPTER 9

Comprehensive Security in South Asia: SAARC and the Applicability of OSCE Standards*

Ugo Caruso**

I. INTRODUCTION

Today, the presence of specific regional mechanisms is relevant to the management of human and minority rights issues. This is of particular importance for South Asia, a region where, despite the existing regional institutional framework provided by the South Asian Association for Regional Cooperation (SAARC), a mechanism dedicated to the protection of human and minority rights is still missing. This research aims to contribute to the academic discussion on the applicability of European experiences and the implementation of higher standards of protection within the South Asian context by investigating whether the experience of the Organization for Security and Cooperation in Europe (OSCE) is relevant to future possible SAARC developments. To that end, a detailed study of SAARC structure and legal instruments will emphasize the difficulties encountered by the association in its implementation process. The results of such a study should contribute to an assessment of whether a comprehensive OSCE-style security-oriented approach would be suited to a SAARC regional instrument for human and minority rights protection.

II. AN OVERVIEW OF SAARC

A. *SAARC Structure and Decision-Making Bodies*

The South Asian Association for Regional Cooperation was established in December 1985, with the formal adoption of its charter by its seven founding members—namely Bangladesh, Bhutan, India, Maldives, Nepal, Pakistan, and Sri Lanka. The association is committed, *inter alia*, to promoting the welfare of the people of South Asia and to improving their quality of life; to accelerating economic growth, social progress and cultural development in the region; and to providing all individuals with the opportunity to live in dignity and to realize their full potential.[1] In 2005, official

---

* This article has first been published in 8 *"European Yearbook of Minority Issues"*, (Martinus Nijhoff Publishers, Leiden 2010).

** The author is a Researcher and PhD candidate at the University of Frankfurt am Main, Faculty of Law, Wilhelm Merton Centre for European Integration and International Economic Order. The present article is the result of a study visit conducted by the author in July-August 2009 to the SAARC secretariat in Kathmandu in the context of the EU-funded Eurasia-Net project.

1 As from the Art. 1 of the SAARC Charter, the remaining objective of the association shall be: "to promote and strengthen collective self-reliance among the countries of South Asia; to contribute to mutual trust, understanding and appreciation of one another's problems; to promote active collaboration and mutual assistance in the economic, social, cultural, technical and scientific fields; to

membership was extended to Afghanistan, which become the eighth official SAARC member state.

Cooperation within the framework of the association is governed by respect for the principles of sovereign equality, territorial integrity, political independence, non-interference in the internal affairs of other states and mutual benefit.[2] However, it is foreseen that SAARC regional cooperation should complement rather than substitute bilateral and multilateral cooperation, and should not be inconsistent with bilateral and multilateral obligations.[3] According to Article 10 of the SAARC Charter, decisions are taken on the basis of unanimity and no bilateral and contentious issues can be included in the deliberations.[4] Informal political consultations can also be undertaken with the aim of enhancing political cooperation.[5]

As to its internal structure, SAARC operates through meetings of heads of state or government, held on an annual basis or more frequently if deemed necessary by the member states.[6] The association also has a Council of Ministers, generally convened twice a year, and mandated to formulate policies and review the progress of cooperation.[7] A Standing Committee of Foreign Secretaries is responsible for overall monitoring and coordination, and for projects and financing approval. Technical committees are responsible for the implementation, coordination and monitoring of the programme in their respective areas of cooperation,[8] and action committees can also be created to oversee implementation of projects involving more than two, but not all, member states.[9]

Coordination and implementation of SAARC activities and decisions fall under the responsibility of a poorly staffed SAARC secretariat, established in 1987 in Kathmandu, Nepal, which functions as an interlocutor between the association and other international organizations.[10] The SAARC secretary general has repeatedly

---

strengthen cooperation with other developing countries; to strengthen cooperation among themselves in international forums on matters of common interests; and to cooperate with international and regional organizations with similar aims and purposes."

2 See Art. 1(b) of the SAARC Charter, Dhaka, Bangladesh, 8 December 1985.

3 *Ibid.*, Art. 2.

4 See Muhammad Jamshed Iqbal, "SAARC: Origin, Growth, Potential and Achievements", 27(2) *Pakistan Journal of History and Culture* (2007), 127-140, at 133-134.

5 See the 9th SAARC Summit Declaration, Male, Maldives 12-14 May 1997, Art. 8. See also Mohammad Mohsin, "The Twelfth SAARC Summit: Quest for Durable South Asian Cooperation", 12(1) *South Asian Survey* (2005), 35-46, at 38-39.

6 To date, 15 summits have been convened: Dhaka (1985), Bangalore (1986), Kathmandu (1987), Islamabad (1988), Male (1990), Colombo (1991), Dhaka (1993), New Delhi (1995), Male (1997), Colombo (1998), Kathmandu (2002), Islamabad (2004), Dhaka (2005), and New Delhi (2007), Colombo (2008).

7 The Council of Ministers can establish additional mechanisms within the SAARC structure. See Art. 4 of the SAARC Charter, *op. cit.* note 2.

8 For instance, the Committee on Economic Cooperation, composed of secretaries of commerce, supervises economic regional cooperation.

9 See Art. 7 of the SAARC Charter, *op. cit.* note 2. For instance, the South Asian Growth Quadrangle (SAGQ) comprising Bhutan, Nepal, the North-Eastern part of India and Bangladesh, was endorsed by the 9th SAARC Summit of May 1997 as a subregional initiative under SAARC.

10 The secretariat comprises the secretary general, several directors, and the general services staff. The secretary general is appointed by the Council of Ministers on the principle of rotation, for a non-renewable tenure of three years.

requested that SAARC member states strengthen the secretariat and furnish it with sufficient resources to cope with a significantly expanded agenda.[11] In addition, SAARC regional centres have been set up on the basis of key priority areas for the region, such as agriculture, tuberculosis, documentation, meteorological research, and human resources development.[12]

Although SAARC's early years were devoted to its institutional establishment and development, on the occasion of the 3rd SAARC summit in Kathmandu in November 1987 its members promptly agreed to move away from a focus on internal structures and to expand the association's activities into concrete areas of cooperation.[13] The focus was then on ensuring "more tangible benefits from SAARC to the people of the region";[14] SAARC leaders believed that the association's long-term perspective should be to focus on the formulation and implementation of more concrete and action-oriented programmes to expand and strengthen areas of regional cooperation and to better coordinate national policies and approaches to common regional problems.[15]

Although well established on paper, SAARC has faced numerous obstacles in moving from declaration to implementation, and numerous shortcomings in the SAARC institutional infrastructure have emerged. For instance, though the SAARC Charter, in Article 3, clearly declared that "the Heads of State and Government shall meet once a year or more often as and when considered necessary by the member states", in SAARC's 25-year lifespan only 15 summits have been held.[16] Curiously, in spite of ex-Article 10 of the SAARC Charter, which explicitly stated that "bilateral and contentious issues shall be excluded from the deliberations", bilateral and political issues were most the common reason for postponing SAARC summits.[17] Previously, India-related issues were the main reason for postponement; the postponement of the 11th SAARC summit, for instance, demonstrates the dominant position of India–Pakistan bilateral issues *vis-à-vis* other SAARC member states.[18] It is also worth

---

11 See Report by the Secretary General to the 9th SAARC Summit, Male, 12-14 May 1997, in SAARC Documents, "Milestones in the Evolution of Regional Cooperation in South Asia", Vol. VI (August 1995-July 1998)", prepared by the SAARC secretariat, Kathmandu, Nepal, January 2004, 28-29, 315.

12 The regional centres are: the SAARC Agricultural Information Centre (SAIC) in Dhaka, the SAARC Meteorological Research Centre (SMRC) in Dhaka, the SAARC Tuberculosis Centre (STC) in Kathmandu, the SAARC Documentation Centre in New Delhi, the SAARC Human Resources Development Centre (SHRDC) in Islamabad, the SAARC Information Centre in Nepal, the SAARC Costal Zone Management Centre (SCZMC) in Male, the SAARC Forestry Centre in Thimphu, the SAARC Disaster Management Centre in New Delhi, the SAARC Energy Centre in Islamabad, and the SAARC Cultural Centre in Colombo.

13 See Mohan P. Lohani, "Two Decades of SAARC: An Overview", in Gopal Pokharel, Anjan Shakya and Ballav Dhala (eds.), *Expansion of SAARC, Challenges and Opportunities* (Institute of Foreign Affairs, Kathmandu, Nepal, 2008), 164.

14 See the 3rd SAARC Summit Declaration, Kathmandu, Nepal 12-14 November 1987, 19.

15 See Lohani, *op. cit.* note 13, 165.

16 See Art. 3 of the SAARC Charter, *op. cit.* note 2. The annual SAARC summits should in any case be considered an excellent confidence-building opportunity towards achieving a better understanding of the respective member states' position in the region.

17 See Art. 10 of the SAARC Charter, *op. cit.* note 2.

18 It is worth recalling that the 5th summit was postponed because of the reluctance of Sri Lanka to host the event in spite of the continued presence of the Indian Peacekeeping Force (IPKF) in its

noting that the recurrent policy of bilateralism pursed by larger member states, especially India, in its relationships with neighbouring countries, has adversely influenced the regional approach embodied by SAARC.[19] Due to its gag on bilateral and contentious issues, the association has been heavily constrained in its ability to contribute in a valuable way to a discussion of sensitive regional issues, such as terrorism.[20] This policy of non-interference, and the continuous delaying of SAARC summits, has raised questions about the credibility of the SAARC process, and about the advisability of decision-making by unanimity.

A more substantial evaluation of the work of SAARC suggests that coordination, monitoring and implementation occur outside the framework of a responsible dedicated entity within the SAARC structure. The effective dispensation of time and resources is a recurrent problem in the implementation of SAARC activities, as are persistent duplication of efforts and the lack of a culture of accountability.[21] 23 years after its inception, on the occasion of its 15th summit, South Asian leaders were still emphasizing the need to consolidate and ensure effective implementation of all SAARC programmes and mechanisms.[22] In this context, it should be recalled that although the declaration of the 1st SAARC summit formally recognized that the existence of a peaceful and secure region was a prerequisite for achieving all subsequent SAARC objectives, the association has never embarked on security-related activities.[23] On human rights issues, for instance, there has been no concerted efforts to tackle this matter effectively, apart from a collective resolve expressed at the 1997 Male summit "to take all necessary steps to achieve the objective of promoting and protecting human rights".[24] Besides, though specific studies have been conducted on determinate issues, for instance the SAARC Regional Multimodal Transport Study (SRMTS), no studies have been conducted on the state of human and minority rights in South Asia.[25]

By contrast, developments have occurred at the international level. The association has granted observer status to several countries, including China, Japan, South Korea, Iran, Mauritius, USA, Australia and Myanmar.[26] The same status was also granted to several United Nations (UN) entities, as well as to international financial bodies and

---

territory. The 6th summit was postponed because of the Bhutanese political problems coming from the expulsion of Lhotsampas from Southern Bhutan. The 7th summit was postponed because of security concerns expressed by the Indian government after the demolition of the Babri Mosque in the state of Uttar Pradesh in December 1992.

19 See Mohsin, *op. cit.* note 5.

20 See South Asia Centre for Policy Studies (SACEPS), "SACEPS Focus on South Asia", *SACEPS Newsletter*, Vol. 1, No. 1, January 2009, 10.

21 See Institute of Policy Studies (IPS), Sri Lanka, *Assessing and Reformulating SAARC Road Map*, SACEPS Paper No. 18 (South Asia Centre for Policy Studies (SACEPS), Kathmandu, Nepal, December 2008), 49.

22 See the 15th SAARC Summit Declaration, Colombo, Sri Lanka, 2-3 August 2008, Art. 4. See also Anjan Shakya, "The Challenges and Opportunities of SAARC", in Pokharel *et al.*, *op. cit.* note 13, 206.

23 See the 1st SAARC Summit Declaration, Dhaka, Bangladesh, 8 December 1985, Art. 4.

24 See the 9th SAARC Summit Declaration, Male, Maldives, 12-14 May 1997, Art. 63.

25 For further information about the SRMTS, see Mahendra Lama, "Monitoring of SAARC Policies and Programmes", SACEPS Policy Paper No. 18 (SACEPS, Kathmandu, 2008), Art. 53.

26 See Shakya, *op. cit.* note 22, 209.

organizations.[27] In addition, regular dialogue with other regional organizations such as the Association of South-East Asian Nations (ASEAN), the Economic Cooperation Organization (ECO) and the Pacific Islands Forum Secretariat (PIFS) have been held with the aim of promoting cooperation among subregional organizations.[28] Finally, SAARC was granted observer status with regard to the UN at the 59th General Assembly session.[29] Although these developments have expanded the scope of SAARC's framework for international and regional collaboration, formal comprehensive guidelines for constructive and mutually beneficial cooperation with the observers are still missing.[30] The absence of defined parameters for cooperation has proved detrimental in moving beyond the simple exchange and capacity-building programmes agreed with some of the observers to date.[31] The same concerns have already been expressed by the secretary general of SAARC who stated , in 2004, that collaboration with states outside the region could not be entertained in the absence of modalities or institutional mechanisms for defining such relations.[32]

B. An Attempt to Revitalize the SAARC Process: The SAARC Group of Eminent Persons

In 1997, in a significant development during the 9th SAARC summit, its leaders commissioned a 12-member Group of Eminent Persons (GEP), consisting of independent and experienced personalities from the member states, to undertake a comprehensive appraisal of SAARC and identify measures to enhance the effectiveness of the association in achieving its objectives. Tasked with evaluating SAARC's performance from its inception, the GEP submitted a report to the 10th summit in Colombo, in which it examined various options for revitalizing the SAARC process and tried to develop a long-term vision for the association for the year 2000

---

27 Memoranda of understanding have been signed to promote collaboration with the: United Nations Conference on Trade and Development (UNCTAD), United Nations Children's Fund (UNICEF), United Nations Development Programme (UNDP), United Nations Economic and Social Commission for Asia and Pacific (UNESCAP), United Nations Drug Control Programme (UNDCP), International Telecommunications Union (ITU), World Health Organization (WHO), United Nations Fund for Women (UNIFEM), Canadian International Development Agency (CIDA), European Union (EU), World Bank, Asian Development Bank (ADB), Joint United Nations Programme on HIV/AIDS (UNAIDS) and South Asia Cooperative Environment Programme (SACEP). Guidelines and procedures for establishing fruitful cooperation with UN and its agencies a well as ASEAN, the EC and the ADB were agreed in 1992 against the background of the 6th SAARC summit. See Report by the Secretary General to the 17th Session of the Standing Committee, Dhaka, Colombo, 7-9 December 1992, in SAARC Documents, "Milestones in the Evolution of Regional Cooperation in South Asia", Vol. IV (November 1991-April 1993)", prepared by the SAARC secretariat, Kathmandu, Nepal, September 1993, Art. 8, 182.

28 See Iqbal, *op.cit* note 4, 137.

29 See the 13th SAARC Summit Declaration, Dhaka, Bangladesh, 12-13 November 2005, Art. 49.

30 See Deepak Dhital, "The Importance of Project-Based Cooperation in SAARC", in Pokharel *et al.*, *op. cit.* note 13, 68.

31 *Ibid.*, 69.

32 See Analytical Report by the SAARC Secretary General at the 30th Session of the Standing Committee, Islamabad 18-19 July 2004, in SAARC Documents, "Milestones in the Evolution of Regional Cooperation in South Asia", Vol. VII (March 1999-January 2004), prepared by the SAARC secretariat, Kathmandu, Nepal, January 2004, Art. 64, 377.

and beyond.[33] The report also included a comprehensive package to manage SAARC's transition from a free trade area to a customs union by 2010, and to an economic union by 2020.[34] Although it noted positive achievements—for instance, the successful establishment of schemes for promoting greater personal contact, and the development of systems for exchanging information and sharing experiences under the so-called "Integrated Programme of Action (IPA)"—the GEP also highlighted the main evolutionary difficulties faced by the association.[35] In particular, the GEP noted that the gradual development of a comprehensive agenda for the association led to growing concerns about the social aspect of SAARC evolution and recommended the development of a social charter.

Broadly speaking, the GEP was of the opinion that SAARC's achievements over the years, while significant, have fallen short of its founding objectives. Too often, cooperation has been hindered by a lack of political will and hampered by periodic political bilateral confrontations.[36] Furthermore, the GEP agreed that, despite the positive developments noted, SAARC was still very far from maturing as a regional economic grouping. It felt that progress made through negotiations under the SAARC Preferential Trading Agreement (SAPTA) had been very limited, and SAARC countries had consequently failed to develop collective leverage in global economic negotiations or to constitute an effective voice in global economic fora. Overall, the GEP was of the opinion that the association had made little headway in realizing its primary objectives, namely to promote the welfare of the peoples of South Asia and to improve their quality of life. Even on the IPA, the GEP was unanimous in its opinion that the impact of activities carried out under its auspices had been compromised by an *ad hoc* selection process, the short-term nature of those activities, and their inability to generate and implement regional programmes for harnessing South Asian countries.[37] The GEP concluded its report by stressing the need to reinforce member state commitment to moving "beyond formalistic proclamations" and attaining effective formal implementation of the fundamental goals and objectives set out in the SAARC Charter.[38]

Though a committed approach was strongly recommended by the GEP, the report was never given appropriate consideration; it was never even fully discussed at the inter-

---

33 In order to facilitate the work of the group, the secretariat of SAARC prepared and presented a comprehensive set of background papers: among the others a paper on "SAARC—An Overview of Achievements and Challenge Ahead", a paper on "Poverty Eradication—the SAARC Dimension", and two other papers on "Social Agenda of SAARC" and "SAARC—The Main Institutional Issues" were delivered. For further information, see SAARC Documents, "Milestones in the Evolution of Regional Cooperation in South Asia", Vol. VI (August 1995-July 1999), prepared by the SAARC secretariat, Kathmandu, Nepal, October 1998, 344-345.

34 See SAARC Group of Eminent Persons (GEP), "SAARC Vision Beyond the Year 2000: Report of the SAARC Group of Eminent Persons established by the 9th SAARC summit", 6(1) *South Asian Survey* (1999), 119.

35 The GEP went further in identifying the elements of a possible plan of action for the SAARC agenda, along with a set of recommendations for consideration. For further information, see Mohsin, *op.cit.* note 5, 38-39.

36 See SAARC Group of Eminent Persons (EGP), SAARC Vision beyond the year 2000 *op.cit* note 34, 15.

37 *Ibid.,* 16.

38 *Ibid.,* 18.

governmental level, let alone endorsed in its entirety.[39] Efforts to implement the recommendations set out in the report were undertaken only on an *ad hoc* basis.[40] Furthermore, contrary to the suggestions formulated in the GEP report, SAARC member states made no pledge at the summit level to provide adequate human resources to the secretariat or existing national focal points (Naps).[41]

C. *SAPTA, SAFTA and the Future South Asian Economic Union*

The SAARC Preferential Trading Agreement (SAPTA) was signed in 1993 and entered into force on 7 December 1995. Overall reciprocity and mutual advantage were the basic principles for pursuing equitable benefit for all SAARC member states, and negotiation of a tariff regime was to be achieved through a step-by-step process and periodic reviews. However, SAPTA was confined solely to the issue of tariff cuts. Significant trade imbalances were recurrent between member countries and intra-SAARC trade was usually of a bilateral nature.[42]

In 2002, the association considered the possibility of developing a free trade regime in South Asia. Then, at the 12th SAARC summit in 2006, South Asian leaders took the pragmatic initiative to adopt a framework arrangement on a South Asian Free Trade Agreement (SAFTA), together with other major decisions such as an additional protocol to the SAARC Convention on Suppression of Terrorism and a SAARC Social Charter.[43] SAFTA agreed to eliminate barriers to trade, facilitate the cross-border movement of goods, promote conditions of fair competition and ensure equitable benefits for all contracting states. Furthermore, since the ultimate goal of SAARC was the creation of the South Asian Economic Union, preferably by 2020, SAFTA was actually concluded and signed very quickly, although it was acknowledged that the kind of treaty required to cover "substantially all the trade" under Article XXIV of the General Agreement on Tariffs and Trade (GATT) 1994 was still a way off.[44] At the 15th SAARC summit in 2008, leaders pledged to improve and implement SAFTA by taking concrete measures to improve trade, including mutual recognition of standards, the adoption of common tariff nomenclatures and the harmonization of customs procedures.[45]

Despite significant efforts, SAFTA has yet to become fully operational. Although the region is experiencing high economic growth, intraregional trade rate is less than 5 percent of the total regional trade.[46] Moreover, representation of the private sector

---

39 By that time, the Council of Ministers requested the SAARC Secretary General to glean the report and extract measures that could be implemented at the high level. The report prepared by the SG and endorsed by the Standing Committee of the Foreign Secretaries were considered "inappropriate" by the Council of Foreign Ministers and sent back to be presented again in 1998. For further information, see Sridhar K. Khatri, "Vision and Strategy for a Third Decade of SAARC", in Pokharel *et al.*, *op.cit.* note 13, 185.

40 See South Asia Centre for Policy Studies (SACEPS), *SACEPS Focus on South Asia Vol. 1 No. 1* (SACEPS Newsletter, Kathmandu, Nepal, January 2009), 1.

41 See Institute of Policy Studies (IPS), *op.cit.* note 21, 50.

42 See Lama, *op.cit* note 25, 22.

43 See Mohsin, *op.cit.* note 5, 37-38.

44 *Ibid.*, 38-39.

45 See the 15th SAARC Summit Declaration, Colombo, Sri Lanka, 2-3 August 2008, Art. 27.

46 See Gyan C. Acharya, "SAARC: A Nepalese Perspective", in Pokharel *et al.*, *op.cit.* note 13, 102.

within the SAPTA–SAFTA negotiations and implementation process has been minimal.[47]

D. IPOs, Poverty Eradication Activities and the Decade of Implementation

The respective foreign ministers, at their first meeting in New Delhi in August 1983, formally launched the first SAARC Integrated Programme of Action in particular areas of cooperation such as agriculture and rural development health and population activities; women, youth and children; environment and forestry; science and technology and meteorology; human resources development; and transport. High-level working groups were also established to strengthen cooperation in information and communication technology, biotechnology, intellectual property rights, tourism, and energy. Each IPA is implemented through a technical committee, established to help member states build up or reinforce their national capabilities in identified IPA areas; committees can also undertake coordinated programmes and activities at the national and regional levels.[48]

However, practice has indicated that technical committees have been unable to coordinate and harmonize their work, leading to duplication and compartmentalization of activities.[49] In 1992, the Standing Committee of Foreign Secretaries further observed that "[m]any of these [IPOs] fell short of achieving their intended purpose due to various reasons, including inadequate preparation, inappropriate representation and lack of adequate follow-up on the part of Member States".[50] The same standing committee also labelled SAARC mechanisms for effective coordination, particularly between sectors at the national level or between the technical committees at the regional level, as inadequate.[51]

In 1998, an Independent Expert Group on IPA was constituted to review the functioning of the IPOs. In its report, the group observed that much of the energy and resources dedicated to implementation had been directed towards short-term activities, with limited impact, and that inadequate attention had been paid to ensuring relevance and sustainability. Moreover, the group identified severe resource shortages, a lack of internal coordination and non-implementation of decisions as some of the key impediments adversely affecting the performance of the IPOs.[52] The process for monitoring and evaluating IPOs was also criticized for not having been conducted on a continuous basis.[53]

---

47 See Lama, *op.cit.* note 25, 24.

48 The Technical Committees were reduced from eleven to seven under the reconstituted SAARC Integrated Programme of Action (IPA) of 2000.

49 See Lama, *op.cit.* note 25, 4.

50 See Report of the 1st Special Session of the Standing Committee of Foreign Affairs Colombo 27-29 April 1992, in SAARC Documents, "Milestones in the Evolution of Regional Cooperation in South Asia, Vol. IV (November 1991-April 1993)", prepared by the SAARC secretariat, Kathmandu, Nepal, September 1993, Arts. 44, 53.

51 *Ibid.*, (h), 56.

52 See Report of the Secretary General to the 25th Session of the Standing Committee Colombo 25-26 July 1998, in SAARC Documents, "Milestones in the Evolution of Regional Cooperation in South Asia", Vol. VI (August 1995-July 1998), prepared by the SAARC secretariat, Kathmandu, Nepal, October 1998, 5, 345.

53 See SACEPS, Recommendation to the 15th SAARC Summit (SACEPS, Colombo, 2008), 16.

On poverty-related issues, at the 6th Summit in Colombo SAARC leaders created the Independent South Asian Commission on Poverty Alleviation (ISACPA), mandated to conduct an in-depth study of the diverse experiences of poverty alleviation among the seven countries. At the 7th summit in Dhaka, ISACPA presented a report entitled "Meeting the Challenge", which aimed to tackle the scourge of poverty in South Asia. Among other issues, the report acknowledged that in many cases conflict and militancy were at least partially the result of the inability of regional economies to grow rapidly enough to satisfy the newly-awakened aspirations of the people.[54] The same report also noted the *ad hoc* nature of consultations held with the poorest groups in each country and the absence of comprehensive social mobilization programmes to enable South Asian populations to contribute to regional growth and human development. By adopting the ISACPA report, SAARC leaders pledged to halve poverty by 2002 through the adoption of an Agenda of Action which would, *inter alia*, embrace the implementation of proper development strategies at the macro and micro levels.[55]

In 1995, the 8th SAARC summit approved the establishment of a 'three-tiered mechanism' for dealing with poverty issues. That mechanism was composed of a first tier, comprising the secretaries of the governments concerned with poverty eradication and social development in SAARC countries; a second tier involving finance/planning secretaries; and a third tier consisting of finance/planning ministers. However, at the 11th SAARC summit in 2002, the first and unrealistic deadline for poverty reduction was adjusted, and it was actually agreed that the Independent South Asian Commission on Poverty Alleviation (ISACPA) would be reconvened to review progress made in cooperation on poverty alleviation and to suggest further appropriate and effective measures. The reconstituted ISACPA finalized its report, entitled "Our Future Our Responsibility. Road Map towards a Poverty Free South Asia", in December 2002.

On minority issues, the 2002 report properly underlined the minimal effective representation of minorities in local government bodies and their lack of access to a number of basic social services, and noted minimal participation in economic and political activities by disadvantaged groups such as schedule castes, ethnic, racial and linguistic minorities, indigenous people and refugees.[56] In January 2004, the 12th SAARC summit commended the work of the commission, and decided that ISACPA should continue its advocacy role and set out a series of 'SAARC Development Goals (SDGs)' in the areas of poverty alleviation, education, health and environment, with a blueprint for their implementation over the next five years.[57] In 2004, the commission submitted its report, "An Engagement with Hope", in which it identified 22 such

54 See Independent South Asian Commission on Poverty Alleviation (ISACPA), Meeting the Challenges (SAARC 1992), 10. See also Mohan Lohani, "Comprehensive Security in South Asia", in Dev Raj Dahal and Nishchal Nath Pandey (eds.), *Comprehensive Security in South Asia* (Manohar Publisher, New Delhi, 2006), 203-214.

55 See Lohani, *op.cit.* note 13, 166. For further information about the Agenda of Action see the 7th SAARC Summit Declaration, Dhaka, Bangladesh, 10-11 April 1993, Art. 10.

56 See Independent South Asian Commission on Poverty Alleviation (ISACPA), *Our Future Our Responsibility. Road Map towards a Poverty-Free South Asia* (SAARC, 2003), 27 and 68.

57 See the 12th SAARC Summit Declaration, Islamabad, Pakistan, 4-6 January 2004, Art. 13. The summit went further to declare poverty alleviation as "the overarching goal of all SAARC activities".

SDGs.[58] SDG 6 on "Reducing social and institutional vulnerabilities of the poor, women and children" dealt with "disadvantages suffered by marginalized and socially excluded people".[59]

In January 2007, the ISACPA then finalized the SDG indicators in its report, "Taking SDGs Forward".[60] The report, endorsed by the 14th SAARC summit, actually included representation of excluded group (dalits/tribals/indigenous people) within local governance structures among the indicators of Goal 6. Furthermore, access to free legal aid for marginalized groups was among the indicators of Goal 7, to "Ensure access to affordable justice".[61] As suggested by the ISACPA report, SDGs will only serve their purpose if governments pay due attention to the observed gaps and to the changes needed to safeguard the rights of everyone, especially the poorest and most vulnerable groups.[62] Although the formulation of SDGs did indeed represent a valuable effort to localize the UN Millennium Development Goals (MDGs), the implementation of their indicators and monitoring mechanisms has yet to be properly established in practice.[63] In this context, an officially agreed timeframe for the implementation of each target/sub-targets at the country level would certainly help to internalize the SDGs within respective national planning processes.[64]

In 2005, during the 13th summit in Dhaka, SAARC leaders declared 2005-2015 to be the "SAARC Decade of Poverty Alleviation"; in this context, a two-tiered mechanism consisting of ministries and secretaries replaced the former and ineffective three-tier mechanism, and was mandated to serve "as an exclusive forum for focused and comprehensive examination of poverty-related issues".[65] The summit went further, calling for the association to "focus on formulation and implementation of concrete regional programmes and projects".[66] Simultaneously, the so-called 'SAARC Development Fund (SDF)' was established as an umbrella financial institution for all SAARC projects and programmes, and to attempt to overcome the shortcomings of the previous South Asian Development Fund (SADF).[67] Finally established in August 2008 at the 15th summit meeting, the SDF operates through three distinct 'windows': the Social Window, focused on poverty alleviation and social development; the Infrastructure Window, covering projects in areas such as energy, power, transportation, telecommunications, environment and tourism; and the Economic Window devoted primarily to non-infrastructural funding.[68] Furthermore, SDF could mobilize and generate funds from both internal and external sources. SAARC leaders

---

58 See Independent South Asian Commission on Poverty Alleviation (ISACPA), "An Engagement with Hope", SAARC Development Goals (SDGs), 2005-2010 (SAARC 2004).
59 *Ibid.*, 13.
60 See Independent South Asian Commission on Poverty Alleviation (ISACPA), "Taking SDGs Forward", SAARC Development Goals (SDGs) (2007-2012), (SAARC, 2007), 27 and 68.
61 *Ibid.*, 14
62 *Ibid.*, 54, 22.
63 See Gyan C. Acharya, "SAARC: A Nepalese Perspective", in Pokharel *et al.*, *op.cit.* note 13, 104.
64 SACEPS, "SACEPS Focus on South Asia", *SACEPS Newsletter, Vol. 1 No. 1*, January 2009, 9.
65 See the 13th SAARC Summit Declaration, Dhaka, Bangladesh, 12-13 November 2005, Art. 10.
66 *Ibid.*, Art. 9.
67 SADF was established in 1996 with the merger of two earlier funds: the SAARC Fund for Regional Project (SFRP) and the SAARC Regional Fund (SRF).
68 See Dhital, *op.cit.* note 30, 67.

recommended that the Social Window of development be put into practice at the earliest possible occasion.[69]

As noted above, in April 2007 SAARC heads of state and government emphasized that, in the third decade of its existence, SAARC should move urgently from a declaratory to an implementation phase;[70] this official sentiment heralded the arrival of the popularly labelled "SAARC Decade of Implementation".[71] In this normative context of refocusing the association on results-based work, there were also calls for a review of existing SAARC mechanisms, its secretariat and its regional centres.[72] It was also foreseen that the 'Third Decade' would contribute to a dynamic following up of the relationship between SAARC and the national authorities responsible for the implementation of SAARC conclusions.[73]

III. SAARC Legal Instruments of Protection

A. The SAARC Regional Convention on Suppression of Terrorism

Signed at the 3rd SAARC summit in Kathmandu in November 1987, the SAARC Regional Convention on Suppression of Terrorism (SRCST) came into force on 22 August 1988 upon ratification by all member states.[74] A SAARC Terrorist Offences Monitoring Desk (STOMD) was established in Colombo in 1995, and mandated to collate, analyse and disseminate information about terrorist incidences, tactics, strategies and methods.[75] It was also to update the convention to meet the obligations incumbent upon member states as a result of UN Security Council Resolution 1371 (2001) and the International Convention for Suppression of Financing Terrorism. Additionally, at the 12th summit in Islamabad in January 2004, SAARC member states supplemented the SRCST with an Additional Protocol, which sought to strengthen the convention by criminalizing the provision, collection or acquisition of

---

69 See *ibid.*, 132. However, thanks to the Indian voluntary contribution of USD 100 million, pilot projects have been launched in three basic agree areas: empowerment of women, improving healthcare for women and children and enhancing capacity in school education.

70 See 14th SAARC Summit Declaration, New Delhi, India, 3-4 April 2007, Art. 10.

71 See Dhital, *op.cit.* note 30. Moreover, attention devoted to reconsidering the SAARC agenda came from the "Vision document for SAARC's Third Decade". Formulated to enable SAARC to adapt to the rapidly evolving global scenario, the idea behind such a document was to provide SAARC and its member states with the possibility of expanding and deepening cooperation in different sectors within the context of a broader framework.

72 See Shafi Sami, "SAARC Future Directions", in Pokharel *et al.*, *op.cit.* note 13, 131.

73 *Ibid.*, 131

74 For instance the convention provides for a list of terrorist offences (ex-Arts. 1, 2); provisions for extradition (Art. 3) and mutual assistance (Art. 8). Furthermore, as a result of the convention each of the SAARC countries had to enact domestic enabling legislation to facilitate the implementation of its critical provisions, including extradition for those involved in terrorist activities.

75 Following the SAARC Legal Experts Meeting in 1999, three key elements were identified for successful implementation of the convention: 1) creation of offences listed in Art. 1 of the convention as extraditable offences under SAARC members' domestic law; b) treatment of such offences as "non-political offences" for the purposes of extradition; c) ensure of extraterritorial (criminal) jurisdiction in the event of extradition not being granted (Arts. 4-6).

funds for the purpose of committing terrorist acts.[76] The Additional Protocol came into force on 1 January 2006 following ratification by all SAARC member states. However, implementation of the convention and its additional protocol yielded poor results, and raised the issue of the effectiveness of the two legal instruments. Bilateral difficulties in interstate relations were seen to result from a lack of sincerity and commitment to the regional goal of suppression of terrorism.[77] Furthermore, as already highlighted in the GEP report, some of the countries were very late to enact the enabling national legislation giving effect to the convention.[78] In fact, these unexpected delays were identified as the major obstacle to implementation of the convention as a whole. In 2001, the then secretary general released an analytical report to the 27th session of the Standing Committee opining that "the implementation of the SAARC Convention on the Suppression of Terrorism and the related Convention on Narcotic Drugs and Psychotropic Substances has not been effective".[79] A year later, SAARC leaders reiterated the need to "accelerate the enactment of enabling legislation within a definitive time-frame for the full implementation of the Convention".[80] In 2005, the 13th SAARC summit declaration spelt out member state agreement on the early and effective implementation of the additional protocol to the convention.[81] Yet in 2008, variations in the definition of terrorism and the absence of bilateral agreements on extradition were common elements of country-level implementation evaluations.[82] This was exacerbated by the seemingly contradictory relationship between the prohibition of including bilateral and contentious issues within SAARC deliberations, and the strong cross-border and bilateral character of the terrorist acts in South Asia. For instance, India and Pakistan did not show much interest in implementing the convention because of their seemingly contrasting views on cross-border terrorism.[83] Ambiguities in the implementation process were also encountered with regard to the 2004 additional protocol to the convention. The implementation of Article 17, for instance, was widely debated; as terrorists acts were usually grounded in ethnic and religious elements, the inclusion of the latter made the workability of the additional protocol even more difficult.[84]

---

76 See Art. 1 of the Additional Protocol to the SAARC Convention on Suppression of Terrorism, Islamabad 2004.

77 See Sugeeswara Senadhira, "China and South Asia: Possible Cooperation between SCO and SAARC", in Pokharel *et al.*, *op.cit.* note 13, 31.

78 See GEP, *op.cit.* note 34, 16.

79 See Analytical Report by the SAARC Secretary General at the 27th Session of the Standing Committee, Kathmandu, 30 December 2001-1 January 2002, in SAARC Documents, "Milestones in the Evolution of Regional Cooperation in South Asia", Vol. VII (March 1999-January 2004), prepared by the SAARC secretariat, Kathmandu, Nepal, January 2004, 15, 336.

80 Please refer to the 11th SAARC Summit Declaration, Kathmandu, Nepal, 2002, Art. 44. The same concern was expressed at almost all of the 15 SAARC summits to date.

81 See 13th SAARC Summit Declaration, Dhaka, Bangladesh, 12-13 November 2005, Art. 38.

82 See Lama, *op.cit.* note 25, 11.

83 See Sugeeswara Senadhira, "China and South Asia: Possible Cooperation between SCO and SAARC", in Pokharel *et al.*, *op.cit.* note 13, 30.

84 Art. 17 of the Additional Protocol to the Convention on the Suppression of Terrorism states that "the member countries are not under obligation to extradite or provide legal assistance if the requested state party has substantial ground to believe that extradition has been requested for the purpose to punish a person for his race, religion, nationality, ethnic group or political opinion and the request would cause prejudice to that person's position for any of these reasons." On this point, see Smruti S.

B. *The SAARC Convention on Preventing and Combating Trafficking in Women and Children for Prostitution, and on Regional Arrangements for the Promotion of Child Welfare*

The Convention on Preventing and Combating Trafficking in Women and Children for Prostitution was signed in 2002 to promote cooperation in the various aspects of prevention, interdiction and suppression of trafficking in women and children. The treaty also deals with the repatriation and rehabilitation of victims of trafficking, and prohibits the use of women and children in international prostitution networks.[85] A specific Regional Task Force was established in 2006 to oversee implementation of the treaty; however, the convention is also experiencing operational difficulties at the country level.[86] Furthermore, the convention was triggered by the general demand of NGOs and civil society organizations, but no effective roles were assigned to these organizations.[87] To date, no serious regional follow-up initiatives have been taken.[88] The Convention on Regional Arrangements for the Promotion of Child Welfare was signed in 2002, with the aim of forming appropriate regional arrangements to assist SAARC member states in facilitating, fulfilling and protecting the rights of South Asian children.[89] As with the other conventions, its implementation has proved challenging, and to date no regional initiatives have been undertaken to that end.[90] In July 2004, the SAARC secretary general was still asking remaining SAARC member states to expedite the ratification process.[91] One year later, however, SAARC heads of state and government expressed satisfaction that both conventions had been ratified by all member states.[92]

C. *The SAARC Social Charter*

The first mention of a SAARC social charter initiative was at the 10th summit, held in Colombo, Sri Lanka, in 1998. Six years later, the SAARC Social Charter was finally signed at the 12th Summit in Islamabad in 2004.[93] The charter has a broad range of

---

Pattanaik, "Strategies for developing Comprehensive Security in South Asia", in Pokharel *et al.*, *op.cit.* note 13, 148.

85 See Art. 2 of the SAARC Convention on Preventing and Combating Trafficking in Women and Children for Prostitution, Kathmandu, Nepal, January 2002.

86 See Lama, *op.cit* note 25, Art. 22, 14.

87 See South Asia Centre for Policy Studies (SACEPS), *SACEPS Focus on South Asia Vol. 1 No. 1* (SACEPS Newsletter, Kathmandu, Nepal, January 2009), 10.

88 See Sridhar K. Khatri, "Vision and Strategy for a Third Decade of SAARC", in Pokharel *et al.*, *op.cit.* note 13, 186.

89 See Art. 2 of the Convention on Regional Arrangement for the Promotion of Child Welfare, Kathmandu, Nepal, 2002.

90 See Lama, *op.cit.* note 25,14.

91 See Analytical Report by the SAARC Secretary General at the 30th Session of the Standing Committee, Islamabad 18-19 July 2004, in SAARC Documents "Milestones in the Evolution of Regional Cooperation in South Asia", Vol. VII (March 1999-January 2004), prepared by the SAARC Secretariat, Kathmandu, Nepal, January 2004, 46, 374.

92 See the 13th SAARC Summit, Dhaka, Bangladesh, 12-13 November 2005, 26. The two conventions entered into force on November 2005 after the last ratification by Nepal.

93 The 12th SAARC Summit Declaration mentioned that: "[W]e hail the signing of the SAARC Social Charter as a historic development, which would have a far-reaching impact on the lives of

objectives, including for instance poverty eradication, population stabilization, empowerment of women, youth mobilization, human resource development, and promotion of the rights and wellbeing of children.[94] Furthermore, the social agenda of SAARC is focused on addressing issues of population planning and disadvantaged groups.[95]

Implementation of the charter is facilitated by national coordination committees (NCCs) or "appropriate national mechanism as may be decided in each country."[96] Furthermore, information on such mechanisms are exchanged between states parties through the SAARC secretariat, and at the regional level "appropriate SAARC bodies" are tasked with reviewing implementation of the charter. To ensure full workability of the provisions and a transparent broad-based participatory process, the charter also requires the formulation of national plans of action, or modification of any already in existence, by SAARC member states.[97] South Asian leaders rightly concluded at the 13th SAARC summit that realizing the objectives of the charter would be crucial to enabling SAARC to meet the hopes and aspirations of the South Asian people and to visibly improve their quality of life. In this context, it was foreseen that national implementation efforts would be complemented by regional programmes and projects in areas requiring a collective regional response, while member states should expeditiously complete preparation of their respective national strategies and plans of action.[98] On this point, in 2002 the SAARC secretary general stressed that the Social Charter was not intended to be merely declaratory but to serve as a means of promoting effective action.[99] By 2007, however, implementation of the charter had to a large extent been left to civil society organizations. While directing NCCs to formulate concrete programmes and projects to complement national implementation efforts, the 14th SAARC summit declaration underscored the vital role to be played by civil society organizations in driving forward implementation of the Social Charter.[100] Further exposing its fragile internal structure, SAARC was not able to address the absence of effective results in its implementation process, preferring to rely instead on support from external civil society organizations.

It should also be underlined that no monitoring instruments outside the official SAARC framework were in place at the time of writing. Additionally, many of the themes and targets of the Social Charter are common to those of the SAARC Development Goals (SDGs), indicating an apparent duplication of efforts and a

---

millions of South Asians. Issues covered under the Charter, such as poverty alleviation, population stabilization, empowerment of women, youth mobilization, human resource development, promotion of health and nutrition and protection of children are key to the welfare and well being of all South Asians."

94 See the 12th SAARC Summit Declaration, Islamabad, Pakistan, 4-6 January 2004, Art. 18.

95 See Mohsin, *op.cit.* note 5.

96 See Art. 10 of the SAARC Social Charter, Islamabad, Pakistan, 4 January 2004. The first meeting of the heads of NCCs was held in Islamabad, Pakistan, in 2006, to review the country-wise status on the preparation of the national plans of action to implement the charter.

97 *Ibid.*

98 See the 13th SAARC Summit, Dhaka, Bangladesh, 12-13 November 2005, 23.

99 See Analytical Report by the SAARC Secretary General at the 27th Session of the Standing Committee, *op.cit.* note 80, 6, 335.

100 See the 14th SAARC Summit Declaration, New Delhi, India, 3-4 April 2007, Art. 7. For further information see Lama, *op.cit.* note 25, 201.

consequent misuse of SAARC resources. No clear institutional or operational mechanisms have been set up by SAARC to synergize the two sets of activities.[101] Ultimately, although the Social Charter was conceived as an inclusive participatory process, most member states failed to involve policy makers and civil society in its implementation.[102]

IV. Comprehensive Security in South Asia

A. SAARC and the Rise of a New Regionalism

With the decline of the traditional security paradigm, which prioritized interstate military threats, the post-Cold War era has witnessed the increased ability of non-state actors to intervene in the global security architecture.[103] The resultant shift in international approaches towards security has also impacted on regional systems of cooperation. The desire to reduce political and military conflicts through heightened economic interdependence, cooperation and integration, and the development of a notion of comprehensive security, has led to consideration of both traditional and non-traditional threats. Thus, the political, economic and socio-cultural dimensions of security have come to be included within a new approach to security characterized by comprehensiveness.[104] In this context, these substantial new security concerns have not only influenced the institutional development of international and regional organizations, but have contributed to the modelling of their tools and competences.
Nowadays, systems of regional military cooperation—previously focused on external enemies or efforts to contain the risks of confrontation through regional arms control agreements and military confidence- and security-building measures—are increasingly characterized by regional institutions with a strong economic character;[105] in other words, regional economic cooperation or integration is increasingly regarded as having important security dimensions or implications. As illustrated by the European experience, economic cooperation may be initiated by a

101 In August 2002, the proposal to form a committee on social cooperation to take stock of cooperation in the social sector was advanced by the SAARC secretary general. See Analytical Report by the SAARC Secretary General at the 28th Session of the Standing Committee, Kathmandu 19-20 August 2002, in SAARC Documents "Milestones in the Evolution of Regional Cooperation in South Asia", Vol. VII (March 1999-January 2004), prepared by the SAARC secretariat, Kathmandu, Nepal, January 2004, 1, 348.
102 See Sridhar K. Khatri, *Labour Migration, Employment and Poverty Alleviation in South Asia*, SACEPS Paper No. 15 (SACEPS, Kathmandu, 2009), 33-35. On this point it is worth recalling that the document entitled "SAARC Vision 2015: An Agenda of Implementation for the Third Decade", presented before the 5th Special Session of the Standing Committee invites "all stakeholders, including the private sector, Media and civil society organizations, including the NGOs, to contribute to the achievement of the objectives of the SAARC Social Charter".
103 See Mahendra Lama, "SAARC Dynamics of Emerging New Regionalism", in Pokharel *et al.*, *op.cit.* note 13, 110.
104 See Nazir Hussain, "Re-Thinking the South Asian Security Traditional and Non-Traditional Paradigm Debate", 8(1) *Pakistan Vision* (2007), 157-171, at 159-160.
105 See Alyson J.K. Bailes and Andrew Cottey, Regional Security Cooperation in the Early 21st Century, in *SIPRI Yearbook 2006 Armaments, Disarmament and International Security* (Stockholm International Peace and Research Institute), 204.

desire to reduce the probability of political or military confrontation between the states involved, but lead to a win–win situation in which common interests are realized under the auspices of a new framework of regional economic integration.[106] Beyond the purely economic dimension, the regionalism of today has thus succeeded in broadening its security agenda to include both traditional and non-traditional security threats, thus creating a new comprehensive paradigm for security. This latter development, initiated in Europe through the comprehensive security framework developed by the OSCE in the 1990s, has incorporated economic and environmental issues alongside traditional political military security concerns and democracy and human rights.[107]

Although primarily a European development, the Asian continent has also witnessed the evolution of similar, but distinct, trends. For instance, the experience of the Association of Southeast Asian Nations (ASEAN) clearly demonstrates how an Asian regional organization, originally created with an economic development agenda, was able to incorporate security-related functions; the recognized interconnectedness of economic development with peace and security issues can thus not be regarded as an exclusively European affair.[108]

Since SAARC's very inception, the close correlation between economic development and peace and security has been well understood; however, no initiatives have been undertaken to provide the association with early warning systems or crisis management tools.[109] Though conscious of the importance of fostering mutual understanding and meaningful cooperation among member states for achieving its core objectives—peace, freedom, social justice and economic prosperity—the association has been unable to agree on a common framework for regional security.[110]SAARC activities in this context continue to be characterized by the ongoing paradox, in which the primary position of the human security segment is recognized within the association's charter, its objectives and its conventions, but here is a persistent absence of meaningful correspondence between the normative

---

106 *Ibid.*, 211.

107 *Ibid.*, 212.

108 In 2004, ASEAN adopted a plan of action to establish an ASEAN security community with an early warning system and preventive diplomacy functions. These developments reflected a broadening and deepening concept of security, which now is widely viewed as including 'human security' and the interrelatedness between security, development and human rights. For further information see Craig Collins, Erik Friberg and John Packer, *Overview of Conflict Prevention Capacities in Regional, Sub-regional and Other Inter-governmental Organisations* (European Centre for Conflict Prevention, International Secretariat of the Global Partnership for the Prevention of Armed Conflicts, The Hague, 2006), 11.

109 It is worth recalling that at the 1st SAARC Summit Declaration: "The Heads of State or Governments reaffirmed that their fundamental goal was to accelerate the process of economic and social development in their respective countries through the optimum utilization of their human and material resources, so as to promote the welfare and prosperity of their peoples and to improve their quality of life. They were conscious that peace and security was an essential prerequisite for the realization of this objective." See the 1st SAARC Summit Declaration, Dhaka, Bangladesh, 7-8 December 1985, Art. 4.

110 See Art. 2 of the SAARC Charter, *op.cit.* note 2. See also, Madhukar SJB Rana, "Comprehensive Security for South Asia: Conceptualisation towards a Regional Strategy", in Pokharel *et al., op.cit.* note 13, 46.

standards developed and their effective implementation at the country level.[111] The real challenge for SAARC today is thus to develop a security policy that is capable of effectively balancing politico–military, economic, and human security issues.

B. Comprehensive Security in South Asia

In the South Asian context, the partition and creation of nation-states had a long-lasting impact on the definition of state (in)security. The formation of states against a background of bloody partitions actually resulted in state security being prioritized high above human security. From the post-1947 period, for instance, states perceived their existence as a way of advancing their own politico–strategic objectives, and expanded the role of military security strategy within their external relations.[112] Consequently, interstate relations became increasingly oriented towards military security, creating a situation in which South Asian countries were forced to respond to post-Cold War realities by holding on to Cold War conceptions of security.[113]

However, with the decline of military confrontation in the region and the emergence of socioeconomic and political problems, states were slowly forced to develop a more comprehensive approach towards security.[114] On the importance of SAARC considering social dimension issues, the secretary general stated in his 2002 report to the 27th session of the standing committee that: "Economic growth figures do not guarantee overall national or regional development unless accompanied by social equity and effective measures of poverty alleviation. The promotion of economic growth, whether nationally or collectively, is, therefore, not an end in itself. It is intrinsically related to the region's development agenda including its vital social and human dimensions."[115]

According to this scenario, the primary interest of South Asian in military security has hampered the development of SAARC, which since its inception has been characterized by the absence of a common security threat perception. The association's prohibition on addressing bilateral and contentious issues also proved detrimental to SAARC's regional institutional development: its security spectrum was trapped at both the intra- and interstate levels within the fragile confines of Indo–Pakistani rivalry.[116] The situation is exacerbated by the growing importance of the religion–politics nexus in South Asia. Aside from their predominant role in the core conceptions of nation-states, religious values have frequently been invoked as justification for political action, triggering religious conflicts with demonstrated

---

111 Please refer to the analysis of the SAARC conventions, *infra*. In addition, see Art. 1 of the SAARC Charter, *op.cit.* note 2.

112 See Pattanaik, *op.cit.* note 84, 143. For instance, interstate wars between India and Pakistan in 1949, 1965, 1971 and the Sino–Indian war of 1962 made the states, and especially India and Pakistan, increasingly oriented towards military security.

113 See Khalida Ghaus, "The Changing Security Spectrum of South Asia: Consequences for SAARC", in Pokharel *et al.*, *op.cit.* note 13, 159.

114 For instance, the open nuclearization of the India–Pakistan relationship caused both sides to argue for stability in their respective relations.

115 See Analytical Report by the SAARC Secretary General at the 27th Session of the Standing Committee, *op.cit.* note 80, 5, 335.

116 See Hussain, *op.cit.* note 105, 162.

influence at the intra- as well as interstate level.[117] Furthermore, on the issue of terrorism for instance, the coherent and effective implementation of standards previously agreed within the framework of SAARC proved extremely problematic, and the region was consequently exposed to international intervention, with no sizeable role for SAARC. On all these issues, little space was devoted to consideration of human security elements and, regrettably, SAARC member states continue to ignore the importance of the human security dimension, which paradoxically could play a pivotal role in channelling efforts to forge a comprehensive security paradigm for South Asia.[118]

In resolving this current state of affairs it could prove significant to work, with essential support from India, on the implementation of a new SAARC security regionalism, complete with effective crisis management tools and capable of generating a favourable win–win situation for all member states.[119]

C. Comparison With and Lessons From the OSCE Experience[120]

1. OSCE and SAARC Approaches towards Security

The OSCE was the first organization to conceive and adopt a comprehensive approach towards security, recognizing it a multifaceted phenomenon, indivisible and beneficial to all participating states, and demanding a multidimensional approach.[121] The comprehensiveness of the OSCE security vision is evident in its inclusion of both military and non-military security aspects, paralleled by an emphasis on democratic institutions, respect for the rule of law, fundamental freedoms and human rights, including minority rights, and economic wellbeing and stability.[122] This thematic inclusiveness was officially recognized in the 1975 Helsinki Final Act, which made explicit the complementarity of political and military security goals within the framework of broad organizational aims.[123] In 1990, the Charter of Paris for a New

117 *Ibid.*, 159.

118 See Khalida Ghaus, "The Changing Security Spectrum of South Asia: Consequences for SAARC", in Pokharel *et al.*, *op.cit.* note 13, 158.

119 See Lama, *op.cit.* note 104, 112-113.

120 Established as a multilateral forum to promote dialogue between east and west, the organization was first established as the Conference on Security and Cooperation in Europe (CSCE). Until 1990, the CSCE functioned as a series of meetings and conferences, at which norms and obligations were elaborated and information on their implementation was reported periodically. Determined to give more political impetus to the CSCE, it was agreed at the 1994 Budapest Summit that the CSCE would be renamed the Organization for Security and Cooperation in Europe (OSCE). The CSCE was built on political commitments without a founding legally-binding treaty; the change in name was an important political step but was not intended to revise its legal status. To date, the legal personality of the OSCE in public international law is very much debated. For further information, please see Sonya Brander, "Making a Credible Case for a Legal Personality for OSCE", *OSCE Magazine*, March-April 2009.

121 For further information see OSCE Secretariat Conflict Prevention Centre, "The OSCE Concept of Comprehensive and Cooperative Security: An Overview of Major Milestones", Vienna, 17 June 2009.

122 See Thomas M. Buchsbaum, "East Asian Security: Can the OSCE's Experience Be Helpful?" in Institute for Peace Research and Security Policy at the University of Hamburg (ed.), *OSCE Yearbook 2003* (Nomos Publishers, Baden Baden, 2003), 351-353.

123 See Final Act of the Conference on Security and Cooperation in Europe, Helsinki, 1 August 1975, Art. 3, 13.

Europe reaffirmed that "security is indivisible and the security of every participating state is inseparably linked to that of all the others".[124] New impetus was given to traditional military threats through continued negotiation on confidence- and security-building measures (CSBMs) and the Treaty on Conventional Armed Forces in Europe (CFE).[125] CSCE peacekeeping activities were also foreseen "in cases of conflict within or among participating states to help maintain peace and security in support of an ongoing effort at a political solution".[126] The growing importance of environmental and economic security issues was reflected in the established in 1992 of the Economic Forum, renamed the Economic and Environmental Forum (EEF) in 2006.[127] On this latter point it is worth noting that the forum has been very active in advocating for the economic and social integration of persons belonging to national minorities; the third preparatory seminar to the 13th OSCE Economic Forum was entitled "Integrating Persons belonging to National Minorities: Economic and Other Perspectives".[128] The increased activity of the EEF prompted participating states to establish the Office of the Coordinator of OSCE Economic and Environmental Activities (OCEEA) in November 1997, with the overarching objective of strengthening security and stability in the OSCE region by promoting international cooperation on economic and environmental issues. Combating corruption, the financing of terrorism, trafficking in human beings and other forms of transnational organized crime were also among the activities foreseen for the OCEEA.

As to SAARC, although the association has since its very inception formally recognized that a peaceful and secure region is a prerequisite for the achievement of its core objectives, no security-related activities or studies have as yet been undertaken .[129] Efforts towards the establishment of a South Asian Economic Union have revealed that economic development is severely hindered by political constraints, thereby widening the gap between more influential countries such as India and Pakistan and the rest of SAARC member states. The 'isolated' approach currently evident in the implementation of the political and economic dimensions of SAARC strategy should now be replaced by a more holistic methodology that enables coherent progress on the association's politico–military and economic–environmental pillars. However, before this process can begin, member states must state their clear commitment to the advancement of SAARC, and take action to combat the bilateral tensions and lack of timely implementation of programmatic and legal instruments that have been identified by critics as central blocking points to regional development.

---

124 See CSCE Charter of Paris for a New Europe, Paris, 19-21 November 1990, Art. 5.
125 *Ibid.*, 8.
126 See CSCE Helsinki Document 1992, "The Challenge of Change", Helsinki Summit Declaration, 9-10 July 1992, III, 17.
127 The CSCE foreign ministers decided at the Prague Council meeting on 30 January 1992 to establish an annual economic forum.
128 See OSCE Office of the Coordinator of OSCE Economic and Environmental Activities, Consolidated Summary 3rd Preparatory Seminar to the 13th OSCE Economic Forum, "Integrating Persons belonging to National Minorities: Economic and other Perspectives", Kyiv, Ukraine, 10-11 March 2005.
129 See the 1st SAARC Summit Declaration, Dhaka, Bangladesh, 8 December 1985, Art. 4.

2. *Institutional Development*

In order to properly address the expansion of its thematic areas of intervention, the OSCE has been involved in a continuous process of restoration of its institutional capabilities. In 1990, the Charter of Paris for a New Europe officially established a CSCE secretariat responsible for administering the organization.[130] The charter further strengthened the OSCE process by creating new institutions and structures, such as the Conflict Prevention Centre and the Office for Free Election in Warsaw (later to become the Office for Democratic Institutions and Human Rights).[131] In 1992, with the Helsinki Document, "The Challenges of Change", decisions were taken to develop new structures and instruments to strengthen early warning, conflict prevention and crisis management.[132] In this framework, it worth drawing attention to the creation of the OSCE High Commissioner on National Minorities, an "instrument of conflict prevention at the earliest possible stage"[133] and the establishment of the CSCE Forum for Security Cooperation.[134] In 1994, through adoption of the Code of Conduct on Politico–Military Aspects of Security, OSCE participating states committed themselves to maintaining only such military capacities as were commensurate with legitimate individual or collective security needs and, with respect to intrastate relations, to provide for democratic control of armed and security forces and their compliance with international humanitarian law. Through that code of conduct, participating states also agreed to prevent and combat terrorism.[135] The decision of the Forum for Security Cooperation formalized voluntary participation in activities related to the Code of Conduct by the OSCE Partners for Cooperation.[136] Through the Rapid Expert Assistance and Cooperation Teams (REACT),[137] the OSCE was able to quickly deploy skilled civilian and police expertise to field operations, while the Platform for Cooperative Security[138] aimed at strengthening cooperation between the

---

130 See CSCE Charter of Paris for a New Europe, Paris, 19-21 November 1990, E, 16.

131 *Ibid.*, 13.

132 See CSCE Helsinki Document, *op.cit.* note 127, I.

133 *Ibid.*, I(2). The High Commissioner provides "early warning" and, as appropriate, "early action" at the earliest possible stage in regard to tensions involving national minority issues.

134 See CSCE Helsinki Document 1992, *op. cit.* note. 127, V. Since its creation, the forum has agreed on a number of documents and decisions on arms control, disarmament and confidence-building measures, and in 2003 produced the OSCE Document on Stockpiles of Conventional Ammunition (SCA). Outlined in its tasks by the Programme of Immediate Action in the Annex to Chapter V of the Helsinki Summit, the forum immediately adopted the so-called "Stabilizing Measures for Localized Crisis Situations", the "Principles governing Conventional Arms Transfers", the "Global Exchange of Military Information (GEMI)" and the "Principles Governing Non-Proliferation".

135 See OSCE Code of Conduct on Politico–Military Aspects of Security, adopted at the 91st Plenary Meeting of the Special Committee of the CSCE Forum for Security Cooperation, Budapest, 3 December 1994.

136 See OSCE Ministerial Council Helsinki 2008, Report of the Chairmanship of the Asia Contact Group (Spain) to the Helsinki Ministerial Council on the 2008 Work with the Asian Partners for Cooperation, Helsinki, Finland, 2 December 2008, 4. See also OSCE Office of the Secretary General, Consolidated Summary of the 2008 OSCE–Afghanistan Conference on Strengthening Cooperation between the OSCE and its Asian Partners for Cooperation to Address Challenges to Security, Kabul, Afghanistan, 9-10 November 2008, 10.

137 See OSCE Charter for European Security, Istanbul, 19 November 1999, Art. 42.

138 See OSCE Charter for European Security, Istanbul, 19 November 1999, Operational Document—The Platform for Cooperative Security.

OSCE and other international and regional organizations; the Charter for European Security took important steps to advance the OSCE's structural capability.[139]

By contrast, the establishment of the SAARC secretariat was not incorporated within the SAARC charter; the Secretariat is in fact the result of a memorandum of understanding signed in November 1987 between SAARC founding members in accordance with Article 8 of the SAARC charter.[140] Repeated requests for structural improvements have not been properly addressed by SAARC member states; an under-resourced secretariat is thus faced with the growing demands of an expanding association. In addition, the principles of subsidiarity and proportionality currently in force in the European context have not received official recognition nor been correctly applied within the SAARC context. While strict adherence to the principle of unanimity in decision-making process has hindered the development of a coherent SAARC position on many issues, this problem was redressed in the OSCE by the introduction of the 'consensus-minus-one' procedure and the adoption of specific human dimension instruments, such as the Vienna and Moscow mechanisms.[141] In fact, the European experience has led to growing acceptance that strict adherence to unanimity will result, at least in certain cases, in deadlock.

Finally, analysis of the problems encountered in the implementation of SAARC decisions, programmes and legal instruments seems to indicate a general resistance to revitalizing the association through a structural amendment of its charter and rules of procedure. The strategy pursued by European regional organizations, that is, to embark on a constant process of institutional advancement through the development of consecutive and coexistent legal (e.g. EU treaties) and political instruments (e.g. OSCE charters) of a constitutional and non-constitutional nature, has to date not been considered by SAARC.

3. *Human and Minority Rights Concerns*

The OSCE, built solely on political commitments and without a founding legally binding treaty, was nevertheless the first organization to link peace and security to respect for human rights through its 1975 Helsinki Final Act. The latter also included the principle of equality before the law of all persons belonging to national minorities, to be respected by all states parties to the organization.[142] The 1990 Copenhagen Document on the Human Dimension of the then CSCE clearly stated that "protection and promotion of human rights and fundamental freedoms is one of the basic purposes

---

139 An Operation Centre was also established to plan and deploy OSCE field operations. See OSCE Charter for European Security, Istanbul, 19 November 1999, 43.

140 See Memorandum of Understanding on the Establishment of SAARC Secretariat, 17 November 1987 Bangalore, India.

141 The 'consensus-minus-one' procedure was introduced at the 2nd CSCE council in Prague on 30 and 31 January 1992 ("Prague Document on Further Development of CSCE Institutions and Structures") where it was decided that in cases of a state's "clear, gross and uncorrected violation" of CSCE commitments, decisions could be taken without the consent of the state concerned. This exception was invoked in July 1992 to suspend Yugoslavia from the CSCE.

142 Furthermore, the Final Act also states that states parties should afford people belonging to national minorities the full opportunity for actual enjoyment of their human rights and fundamental freedoms. See Final Act of Helsinki, Final Act of the Conference on Security and Cooperation in Europe, Helsinki, 1 August 1975, Art. VII, 6.

of government"; the document further defined respect for the rights of persons belonging to national minorities as an essential factor for peace, justice, stability and democracy in the participating states.[143] As noted above, two years later the OSCE created a specific institution on minority-related issues, the OSCE High Commissioner on National Minorities, mandated to function as an "instrument of conflict prevention at the earliest possible stage".[144] Furthermore, the 1992 Helsinki Document also remarked the close relation of human and minority rights with peace and security issues by clarifying that "gross violations of CSCE commitments in the field of human rights and fundamental freedoms, including those related to national minorities, pose a special threat to the peaceful development of society, in particular in new democracies".[145] In the 1994 Budapest Document, "Towards a Genuine Partnership in a New Era", participating states clearly defined the protection of human rights, including the rights of persons belonging to national minorities, as an essential foundation of democratic civil society.[146] Two years later in Lisbon, participating states reaffirmed their determination to fully respect and implement commitments relating to the rights of persons belonging to national minorities as an important contribution to security.[147]

An analysis of SAARC performances in human and minority rights reveals an association only weakly committed to this key issue, unable to translate relevant policy summit declarations into reality . For instance, at the 6th SAARC summit, heads of states and government observed that civil and political rights on the one hand, and economic and social rights on the other, were interdependent and of equal importance. They further underlined the need to view the efforts of states to guarantee human rights holistically, by pursuing development for all citizens in conditions of stability, which in turn would guarantee the enjoyment of human rights for all persons.[148] Later, in 1997, member states collectively resolved "to take all necessary steps to achieve the objective of promoting and protecting human rights"[149] and, on the 50th Anniversary of the Universal Declaration of Human Rights, reaffirmed their commitment to further advancing human rights and fundamental freedoms in the region by strengthening the relevant national institutions.[150] In addition, the association has been unable to properly implement the standards developed during its regional conventions.

Today, a specific mechanism for dealing with human and minority rights issues in South Asia is a priority. However, even if SAARC is considered the appropriate forum for the design and implementation of such a mechanism, great uncertainty would persist as to whether this should be developed within the framework of a top-

---

143 See Copenhagen Meeting on the Conference on the Human Dimension of the CSCE, Copenhagen, 29 June 1990, 1 and 30.

144 See CSCE Helsinki Document 1992, *op.cit.* note 127, Art. I(2).

145 *Ibid.*, Art. 12.

146 See CSCE Budapest Document 1994, "Towards a Genuine Partnership in a New Era", 5 December 1994, Art. VIII, 2.

147 See OSCE Lisbon Document 1996, Lisbon Declaration on a Common and Comprehensive Security Model for Europe for the Twenty-First Century, 3 December 1996, Arts. 10, 11.

148 See the 6th SAARC Summit Declaration, Colombo, Sri Lanka, 21 December 1991, Art. 7.

149 See the 9th SAARC Summit Declaration, Male, Maldives, 12-14 May 1997, Art. 63.

150 See the 10th SAARC Summit Declaration, Colombo, Sri Lanka, 29-31 July 1998, Art. 75.

down or a bottom-up approach; to date, neither of these two options has guaranteed positive outcomes. An analysis of the implementation record for SAARC conventions suggests uneven results: although in some cases the development of legal instruments has been primary triggered by NGOs or civil society organizations, the latter have been marginalized during the implementation phase. By contrast, in a top-down process, where particular conventions have been designed to address common member state concerns, their entry into force and subsequent implementation have been regrettably delayed and ineffective. Furthermore, the current reluctance on the part of member state to deal with human and minority rights issues through SAARC structures should raise new questions about the advisability of pursuing a soft-law approach in developing a mechanism dedicated to the protection of those rights rather than a hard-law implementation process.

In any event, an absolute precondition for moving forwards on this issue is the full commitment of all member states to the empowerment of SAARC. The association should be considerably reinforced, both in its secretariat and accountable instruments, to guarantee satisfactory monitoring activities, and to permit follow-up and ultimately sanctionatory procedures. The eventual development of an instrument of regional human and minority rights protection would certainly advance a more people-centric approach of SAARC, and go a long way to redressing the state-centric focus of the association in evidence today.

4. CBM/CSBMs

OSCE Confidence-Building Measures (CBMs) and Confidence- and Security Building Measures were first identified as available organizational tools in the 1975 Helsinki Final Act.[151] Refined by the 1986 Stockholm and 1990 Vienna Document,[152] CBM/CSBMs were further developed in the 1990 Treaty on Conventional Armed Forces in Europe and the 1992 Treaty on Open Skies.[153] In 1996, a Framework for Arms Control was set up within the framework of the OSCE Lisbon Document.[154] Three years later, the Vienna Document on Negotiations of Confidence- and Security-Building Measures further complemented OSCE resources.[155]

---

151 See Hans-Georg Wieck, "European Experience of Conflict Resolution and Confidence Building and its Relevance for South Asia", in Rajendra K. Jain (ed.), *India, Europe and South Asia* (Radiant Publishers, New Delhi, 2006), 110.

152 The Stockholm Document provided, for the first time in the history of modern arms control, for compulsory inspections as a means of verification. The Vienna Document introduced new communication and consultation measures, qualified the 'third generation of CSBMs' such as the points of context for hazardous incidents of a military nature and a communication network for transmitting computerized information.

153 Even though these were not CSCE/OSCE documents in a formal sense, both treaties were nevertheless closely associated with the organization as they were negotiated in conjunction with talks among CSCE participating states on confidence-building measures.

154 See OSCE Lisbon Document 1996, Framework for Arms Control, 3 December 1996, III, 17. The framework was designed to create a web of interlocking and mutually reinforcing arms control obligations and commitments, and to channel arms control efforts into a comprehensive structure.

155 See OSCE Vienna Document 1999 of Negotiation on Confidence- and Security-Building Measures, 16 November 1999. A number of mechanisms of the Vienna Document 1990 are contained in the Vienna Document 1999: the mechanisms for consultation and cooperation as regards unusual

In the context of SAARC, particular CBMs were undertaken against the background of the association, but were never listed as being among its available tools[156], and peace agreements concluded in the region were bilateral in nature and often the result of third party intervention.[157] This inability of SAARC to formally internalize CBSMs among its available tools resulted, for instance, in an extensive number of bilateral CBMs being concluded between India and Pakistan, the implementation of which was not always straightforward.[158] As in the case of human and minority rights issues, enhancement of SAARC capabilities is primarily contingent on the sincerity of the political commitments of its member states. Studies conducted by the OSCE on the applicability of OSCE CSBMs in different regions indicated that negotiating partners should agree initially on a broader set of political commitments to guarantee the political framework in which implementation of the CSBMs could then occur.[159]

V. The Relevance of Afghanistan

The history of Afghan membership within SAARC clearly suggests the incredible results that can be achieved when India and Pakistan converge to pursue particular objectives.[160] Officially recognized as a SAARC member state in 2007, Afghanistan

---

military activities; the mechanism for cooperation as regards hazardous incidents of a military nature, and the voluntary hosting of visits to Dispel concern about military activities.

156 For instance, the Lahore Declaration of 1999 reaffirming India and Pakistan's commitment to find a peaceful resolution to the issues of Jammu and Kashmir has been designed and agreed in the frame SAARC.

157 For instance, the 1997 Chittagong Hill Tracts Peace Accord was signed between the government of Bangladesh and the Parbatya Chattagram Jana Sanghati Samity (PCJSS) was possible due to the positive role played by India. The 2002 Ceasefire Agreement between the government of Sri Lanka and the Liberation Tigers of Tamil Eelam (LTTE) was facilitated by the Norwegian government which also took part, together with Sweden, Finland, Denmark and Iceland, in monitoring the ceasefire agreement through the Sri Lanka Monitoring Mission. For further information see Satish Nambiar, "Military Confidence-Building Measures in the India-Pakistan Context", in Dev Raj Dahal and Nishchal Nath Pandey (eds.), *Comprehensive Security in South Asia* (Manohar Publisher, New Delhi, 2006), 203-214.

158 See Coalition for Action on South Asian Cooperation (CASAC), "South Asian Cooperation: From Commitment to Implementation", CASAC Discussion Paper I, New Delhi, November 1998), 1. For instance, the list of CBMs adopted by India and Pakistan includes the Liaquat-Nehru Pact (151), the Indus Water Treaty (1960), Tashkant Agreement (1966), Simla Agreement (1972), Salal Dam Agreement (1978), Establishment of the Indo–Pakistan Joint Commission (1982); Agreement Concerning Non-Attack on Nuclear Sites and Exchange of Information on Nuclear Installations (1988), Air Space Violations Agreement (1991), Agreement for Prior Notification of Military Exercises (1991), Joint Declaration on Prohibition of Production and Deployment of Chemical Weapons (1992), Establishment of a Hot-Line between Air Forces of India and Pakistan and Between Commanders on Both Sides of the Line of Control (1993), Naval Communication Agreement (1993), Lahore Memorandum of Understanding (1999), Agreement on the Pre-Notification of Flight Testing of Ballistic Missiles (2005), Agreement on the Establishment of a Hot-Line between the Maritime Security Agencies (2005), Kashmir Trade Accord (2006), Agreement on Reducing the Risk from Accidents Relating to Nuclear Weapons (2007), Indo–Pack Judicial Committee (2008), Joint Indo–Pakistani Anti-Terror Mechanisms (2009).

159 See the OSCE–IFANS/MOFAT Workshop on the Applicability of OSCE CSBMs in Northeast Asia Revisited", Seoul, Korea, 22-23 September 2003, 30.

160 See Syed A. Husain, "Afghanistan in SAARC: Challenge More Than Opportunity", in Pokharel *et al.*, *op.cit.* note 13, 6.

has key geopolitical importance in connecting SAARC to the Central Asian countries. For example, the 2002 Kabul Declaration on Good Neighbourly Relations, signed by Afghanistan and its six neighbours—China, Pakistan, Tajikistan, Turkmenistan, Uzbekistan, and Iran—was a significant step towards achieving a peaceful and stable region through constructive and supportive bilateral relationships based on the principles of territorial integrity, mutual respect, friendly relations, cooperation and non-interference in each other's internal affairs.[161] When the OSCE included Afghanistan among its Partners for Cooperation on 3 April 2003, SAARC was presented with an opportunity to move closer towards the cooperative security architecture of the OSCE.[162] With due consideration for the 1975 Helsinki Final Act, which notes the close link between peace and security in Europe and in the world as a whole, and the 1999 Charter for European Security, which states that "the OSCE is the inclusive and comprehensive organization for consultation, decision-making and co-operation in its region", Afghanistan will play a pivotal role in exposing SAARC to the comprehensive security approach employed by the OSCE. The association could surely gain from a comparative analysis of the 2002 Charter on Preventing and Combating Terrorism and the 2003 OSCE Strategy to Address Threats to Security and Stability in the Twenty-First Century: the latter aims, *inter alia*, to intensify OSCE cooperation with its Mediterranean and Asian Partners for Cooperation;[163] moreover, the formal recognition by the 2003 strategy of the cross-dimensional nature of modern threats to security and stability would provide SAARC with a good template for any of its future security-related activities.[164]

The same is true of the formal OSCE reference to the wide range of potential threats linked to systematic violations of human rights and fundamental freedoms, including the rights of persons belonging to national minorities.[165] In pursuing this objective, SAARC would have much to gain from OSCE feasibility studies on sharing norms, principles, commitments and values with other regions, in particular neighbouring areas.[166] Afghan interest in the OSCE Border Security and Management Concept should also be considered positively in view of the country's possible future proximity to OSCE norms and standards.[167] In this view, the current climate of

---

161 See Boris Wilke, "Regional Security Strategies for Afghanistan and Its Neighbours—A Role for the OSCE?", in Institute for Peace Research and Security Policy at the University of Hamburg (ed.), *OSCE Yearbook 2005* (Nomos Publishers, Baden Baden, 2005), 351-352.

162 The other Asian Partners for cooperation are Japan, Korea, Mongolia and Thailand.

163 See OSCE Ministerial Council in Madrid, second day of the 15th meeting, MC(15), Journal No. 2, Agenda Item 8, Decision No. 4/07 OSCE Engagement with Afghanistan, Doc. MC15ED04, 30 November 2007, 1. Cooperation should be enhanced through the early identification of areas of common interest and concern and possibilities for further coordinated action.

164 See *ibid.*, 3. With the 2003 strategy, the OSCE formally recognized that "threats to security and stability in the OSCE region are today more likely to arise as negative, destabilizing consequences of developments that cut across the politico–military, economic and environmental and human dimensions, than from any major armed conflict".

165 *Ibid.*, 4.

166 See OSCE 11th Meeting of the Ministerial Council, 1 and 2 December 2003, OSCE Strategy to Address Threats to Security and Stability in the Twenty-First Century, Art. 23.

167 See keynote address of H.E. Mr. Mohammad Kabir Farahi, Deputy Foreign Minister of Afghanistan, to the 2007 OSCE–Mongolia Conference on Strengthening the Cooperative Security between the OSCE and the Asian Partners for Cooperation, Ulaanbaatar, 12-13 June 2007, 15.

international commitment to peace and stability in Afghanistan should be complemented by a firm acknowledgement by SAARC members of the importance of a stable environment for regional cooperation in South Asia.[168] The association could also seize the opportunity to finally address the issue of policy cooperation with those regional bodies to which one or more of its member states belong—namely the Indian Ocean Rim Association for Regional Cooperation (IOC–ARC), Economic Cooperation Organization (ECO), Organization of Islamic Conference (OIC), and Bangladesh India Myanmar Sri Lanka Thailand Economic Cooperation (BIMSTEC).[169]

VI. Conclusion

The above analysis reveals several limitations in existing SAARC procedures and institutional development. The secretariat appears to be heavily constrained by difficulties in coping with an expanded range of activities. By contrast to the experience in Europe, developments at programme- and activity-level have not been complemented by adequate structural amendments, which has adversely impacted on the accountability of the association as a whole, and led to the lack of a clear long-term vision for its 'third decade of implementation'.

In addition, the absence of a dispute settlement mechanism within the association has negatively affected the development of a regional, South Asian, concept of peace and security. By failing to develop such a mechanism, SAARC has involuntarily bolstered the asymmetric configuration of the region in which a regional approach is the exception to a powerful Indian policy of bilateralism.

The above analysis has also indicated that the political dimension of SAARC is today the most problematic: deep-rooted tensions among member states and a strong predominance of bilateral issues have hampered the efforts of the association to achieve satisfactory regional results. The challenge is now to review the whole SAARC process and to agree on a roadmap for moving the association from a declaratory to an implementation phase. Within this context, amending the SAARC charter and its rules of procedures to permit consideration of both bilateral and contentious issues will be a crucial precondition for all future activities of the association, as will ensuring the full political commitment of its member states.

In any event, the development of a comprehensive security approach for South Asia will require an initial reassessment of the national security perspectives of SAARC member states. The current impossibility that members will agree on a common security perception is indeed the first obstacle to the development of a comprehensive regional framework for security. In this context, there is a pressing demand for a more balanced approach between traditional and non-traditional security issues, which will guide decision-makers in forging, through a multidimensional and comprehensive methodology, a collective regional mechanism capable both of resolving traditional interstate security issues and including non-traditional security challenges. Such a mechanism is a precondition for redirecting the attention of policy makers from the traditional to the non-traditional security paradigm.

---

168 See Wilke, *op.cit.* note 162, 348.

169 See CASAC, *op.cit.* note 159, 8-9.

More work should thus be dedicated to the advancement of the SAARC structure; increased attention should be paid to the concept of 'human and societal security', and a specific SAARC human dimension mechanism should be developed. An empowered SAARC could lead the regional cooperation process, thereby avoiding the regional imbalance of powers evident today, and influence collective efforts to forge a comprehensive security approach for South Asia. Proper harmonization of regional security concerns, coupled by a clear and firm political commitment on the part of its member states and a SAARC specific human rights mechanism, would certainly help South Asia, as a regional community under the aegis of SAARC, to move closer in practice to the standards of human and minority rights protection that have already agreed at the international level.

CHAPTER 10

Immigration to the UK from Commonwealth Countries and The Issue of "New Minorities" Defined by Religion: Between their Group Rights and Integration

Murtaza Hassan Shaikh*

I. Introduction

In the UK, persons belonging to minorities,[1] originating from Commonwealth countries, are inadequately protected on the basis of their religious identity. The UK interprets its obligations under the FCNM[2] as only having to protect its minorities against ethnic discrimination. This is born out in the Second State Report by the UK to the Advisory Committee on the Framework Convention on National Minorities (ACFC)[3] and its corresponding Opinion.[4] Nonetheless the UK denies Commonwealth minorities recourse to the FCNM on the basis of religion and evades responding to their legitimate claims to national minority. Such an interpretation works against the UK's own policy of integrating Commonwealth minorities as most also adhere to minority religions. Additionally the narrowness of the UK's interpretation risks incompatibility with the object and purpose of the FCNM. The ACFC, whilst playing an essential role in gradual and incremental realisation of group rights[5] for new minorities,[6] may nonetheless be able to increase compliance through greater reliance on its normative character and achieve genuine integration.

---

* The author is a Project Officer for the Initiative on Quiet Diplomacy and a PhD candidate at the School of Oriental and African Studies. He also sits on the International Human Rights Committee of the Law Society of England and Wales. All views expressed in the article are the authors alone.

1 Hereinafter the term "minorities" will be used to denote "persons belonging to minorities".

2 See Framework Convention for the Protection of National Minorities, adopted on 1 February 1995, entered into force on 1 February 1998, ETS No. 157.

3 See Second State Report submitted by the United Kingdom under FCNM Article 25, received on 22 February 2007 (Hereafter: 2nd State Report).

4 See ACFC Opinion on 2nd State Report (Hereafter: ACFC Opinion).

5 Hereinafter the term "group rights" will be used interchangeably with "minority rights" to refer to those rights accorded to persons belonging to minorities beyond non-discrimination i.e. linguistic, religious and cultural often requiring the attribution of positive duties to the State. Neither should be taken to mean "collective rights".

6 Hereinafter the term "new minorities" will be used to refer to persons belonging to minorities who have resulted in the territory of the State due to post-1945 immigration. While they may be ethnically, linguistically and religiously distinct they are denied the associated group rights.

II. A SHORT HISTORY: COMMONWEALTH IMMIGRATION TO THE UK

A. *The British Empire and the Commonwealth*

The British Empire, spanning over almost 500 years, at one time presided over half a billion subjects and enveloped a third of the world's territory. Its history can be divided into two distinct periods. The early Empire began with the colonisation of Newfoundland in 1497 and ended when the American Revolution resulting in the formal independence of the "Thirteen Colonies" in 1783. The second period, most commonly associated with the British Empire, had British India[7] as its jewel.

Britain was not the only European power to be engaged in Empire building. Aggressive policies of expansion and resultant intra-European tensions eventually sparked the First World War.[8] In its wake, the defeated German and Ottoman Empires were dismantled and distributed between the British and French as mandates. The British Empire's burgeoning size combined with the ruin wrought by the Great War set in motion its economic downturn. Consolidating political control over its colonies became increasingly difficult in the face of invigorated independence movements.[9] The Second World War catalysed these processes rendering the British Empire economically and politically unviable. The end of the second period began with the abdication of British India and its simultaneous partition into India and Pakistan in 1947. Decolonisation of the remaining Empire soon followed: first Arab and then African territories. Caribbean and Pacific colonies were the last to break away, while Hong Kong became the last major colony to be ceded in 1997.

The term, British Commonwealth of Nations, was first coined in 1884 by Lord Rosebury to describe the British Empire when settler colonies[10] started to become self-governing Dominions.[11] By 1926, all Dominions[12] were accorded status as autonomous communities, equal in status to each other and the Crown, but still retained within the British Empire.

In 1949, two years after the partition of British India into Pakistan and India, the latter declared itself a republic, dislodging the Queen as its head of State. Thus the modern Commonwealth was born vis-à-vis the London Declaration, which stated: "Governments of the United Kingdom, Canada, Australia, New Zealand, South Africa, India, Pakistan and Ceylon whose countries are united as Members of the British Commonwealth of Nations and owe a common allegiance to the Crown".[13] India, Pakistan and Ceylon (present day Sri Lanka) became the first non-settler former colonies to form part of the Commonwealth and those that later joined came to be known as the New Commonwealth. Today there are fifty three member States of the Commonwealth. All, with the exception of a few, are former colonies and the Queen remains the head of sixteen.

---

7 The term refers to the colony which is today divided into the independent States of Pakistan, India, Bangladesh, Sri Lanka and Burma.
8 See Roland J. Wenzlhuemer, "Colonialism: History", in Thomas M. Leonard (eds.), *Encycolpedia of the Developing World, Volume 1 A-E Index*, (Routledge, New York, 2006), 361.
9 *Ibid.*
10 Australia, Canada, Irish Free State, Newfoundland, New Zealand and South Africa.
11 A British politician in "at: http://www.thecommonwealth.org/Internal/191086/34493/history/.
12 See the Sixth Imperial Conference of Prime Ministers of the Dominions of the British Empire, London, 19 October to 22 November 1926.
13 See the London Declaration, 26 April 1949.

B. *Immigration from the New Commonwealth*

There were a number of factors which led to policies that facilitated immigration from non-settler colonies and New Commonwealth countries. Industry had suffered greatly as a result of two consecutive World Wars. Vast revenue streams had been severed with the dissipation of the Empire. Colonies like India had provided large quantities of raw materials such as cotton, silk and spices as well as a huge consumer market for British manufactured goods.[14] The British economy was in desperate need of reconstruction and there was a dire shortage of labour in the immediate aftermath of the Second World War. Consequently, in 1948, a "working party" was established to consider employment of colonial labour.[15] Through legislation and policy, they sought to facilitate immigration from Commonwealth countries to remedy the labour shortage. The ensuing scale of mass-immigration could not have been anticipated.[16]

The British Nationality Act 1948[17] allowed those belonging to territories of the Commonwealth absolute freedom of movement and full rights of citizenship. Initial immigration policies aimed towards Europeans[18] proved inadequate to meet the acute demand necessary to reinvigorate the war-ravaged industries and the UK turned to the New Commonwealth. The first wave of immigration came from the Caribbean and began with the arrival of the SS Empire Windrush on 22 June 1948 from the West Indies. Most immigration from India and Pakistan took place during the 1960s, of ethnic Indian from East Africa in the 1970s and from Hong Kong and Bangladesh in the 1980s. Most Black Africans came during the 1980s and 1990s.[19]

C. *Mollifying the Majority*

While such immigration policies filled gaps in industry, the government did not anticipate the sudden influx of New Commonwealth immigrants nor the widespread public resentment from the majority population. Commonwealth immigration had risen from 3000 per annum in 1953 to almost 50,000 in 1956 and rocketed to over 130,000 in 1961. It is estimated that in this period 250,000 "coloured" immigrants arrived in the UK from the New Commonwealth.[20]

The 1960s saw many arrive from Pakistan and India to work in the steel and textile industries of Yorkshire, Lancashire and West Midlands. This coincided with the completion of the Mangla Dam in the city of Mirpur, Azad Jammu and Kashmir,

---

14 See Dennison Berwick, *A Walk Along the Ganges* (Century Hutchinson, London, 1986), 42: "Exports of handloom textiles stopped and miles of cheap, machine-made cotton cloth from Lancashire mill began arriving at the ports of Calcutta and Bombay. [...] The cheap machine-made cloth destroyed the livelihood of handloom weavers in every village[...]. It was no wonder that Gandhi selected the burning of imported cloth for a mass protest against British rule".

15 See "Origins of Commonwealth immigration", in *The National Archives* (The Cabinet Papers 1915-1979), available at:
http://www.nationalarchives.gov.uk/cabinetpapers/themes/origins-commonwealth-immigration.htm.

16 *Ibid.*

17 See British Nationality Act, 1948, Chapter 56.

18 130,000 Poles arrived in the years after WWII, see "Immigration from Europe" in *The National Archives* (Post War Immigration) available at:
http://www.nationalarchives.gov.uk/pathways/citizenship/brave_new_world/immigration.htm.

19 See Office for National Statistics (UK), "Age distribution: by ethnic group", Annual Local Area Survey 2001/02, available at: http://www.statistics.gov.uk/cci/nugget.asp?id=272.

20 See Andrew Geddes, *The Politics of Migration and Immigration in Europe* (Sage Publications, London, 2005), 34.

causing 100,000 to be displaced[21] further catalysing the emigration of Pakistani Kashmiris. Today close to 70 percent of ethnic Pakistanis in the UK originate from Kashmir.[22] As mass immigration continued, so did racial prejudice and inter-communal friction.[23] In response, immigration controls were gradually tightened and primary immigration from the New Commonwealth was completely stopped.

The Commonwealth Immigration Act 1962[24] required Commonwealth passport holders to have secured employment before arrival or to apply for vouchers which graded their employment prospects.[25] Notwithstanding these measures, in 1967, ethnic Indians from Uganda and Kenya, fearing discrimination by their national governments, began arriving in the UK. The resentment against them was a direct legacy of imperial rule, which had enabled their free movement to East Africa and subsequent economic prosperity. Their retention of British passports rendered them immune from the 1962 Act. The impotency of the legislation to prevent "coloured" immigration, as was intended, further aggravated anti-immigration feeling. Enoch Powell, a Conservative Party politician, sensing the latent resentment of the masses, called for even tougher immigration controls in his notorious "Rivers of Blood" speech.[26] The incumbent Labour government responded with the Commonwealth Immigration Act 1968, which conditioned immigration on "substantial connection with the United Kingdom".[27] In practice, immigration was limited to those who could show the birth of a parent or grandparent in the UK and was the first step in reconceptualising British citizenship along ethnic lines.

By 1970 the anti-immigration mood in the UK had reached unprecedented levels with the Commonwealth minority population ballooning to 1.4 million from just a few thousand in the immediate aftermath of the Second World War.[28] The passing of the Immigration Act 1971[29] only allowed temporary residence and even introduced voluntary repatriation schemes. Patrials[30] were exempted and provided with a "right to abode" meaning, in essence, that "white" Commonwealth immigration could continue from settler colonies. Despite this, in 1972, the UK accepted 27,000 expelled ethnic Indians from Uganda in just two months, following Idi Amin's successful

---

21 See Ataullah Siddiqui, *"Muslims in Britain"*, in Sociological and Legal Data on Religion in Europe (EUREL) available at: www.eurel.info/telechargement/UK_muslims.pdf.

22 See Department for Communities and Local Government, *"The Pakistani Muslim Community in England: Understanding Muslim Ethnic Communities"*, March 2009 at: http://www.communities.gov.uk/documents/communities/pdf/1170952.pdf.

23 See Riots in Notting Hill 1958, Brixton 1981, Bradford 1995, in "Britain's worst race riots", *The Independent UK* of 28 May 2001 available at: http://www.independent.co.uk/news/uk/this-britain/britains-worst-race-riots-754137.html.

24 See Commonwealth Immigrants Act, 1962, Chapter 21.

25 See "Commonwealth Immigration Control Legislation" in *The National Archives* (The Cabinet Papers 1915-1979) available at: http://www.nationalarchives.gov.uk/cabinetpapers/themes/commonwealth-immigration-control-legislation.htm.

26 See transcript of 1968 speech available at: http://www.martinfrost.ws/htmlfiles/rivers_blood2.html#Enoch_was_right.

27 See Commonwealth Immigrants Act 1968, Chapter 9.

28 See Geddes, *op.cit.* note 20.

29 See Immigration Act 1971, Chapter 77.

30 *Ibid.*, Section 2 (6) meaning only those with parent or grandparents born in the UK.

coup. Legislation capable of refusing them entry was circumvented through a specially constituted Uganda Resettlement Board.[31]
Legislation was further tightened in the 1980s.[32] However immigration from Commonwealth countries continues for highly skilled workers and professionals.[33] Most notably the shortage of doctors in the newly formed National Health Service was filled by South Asian and Caribbean skilled migrants.[34] Despite decreased immigration, the minority population originating from New Commonwealth countries is rising, due to a young age structure, reflecting past immigration and fertility patterns. Conversely the "white" population is on the decline due to lower birth rates and an aging population.[35]
According to the 2001 UK Census, ethnic minorities constituted 7.9 percent of the population: 1.8 percent Indian, 1.3 percent Pakistani, 0.5 percent Bangladeshi, 1 percent Black Caribbean, 0.8 percent Black African, 0.4 percent Chinese and 1.2 percent mixed. The total percentage translated to 4.6 million having increased from 3 million in 1991.[36] The overwhelming majority originate from Commonwealth countries. Around half are from the Indian sub-continent and account for most of the religious minority population.

III. Commonwealth Minorities: New or National?

A. *What Makes Minorities National?*

There is no internationally agreed definition for which groups constitute minorities under international law.[37] However the United Nations Human Rights Committee (HRC) interprets CCPR Article 27[38] purely on a jurisdictional as opposed to a temporal basis allowing for its applicability to non-citizens.[39] Perhaps to counter such a wide interpretation, discussions pertaining to the drafting of a binding instrument at the Council of Europe had always centred on the rights of "national minorities" as

---

31 See "Commonwealth Immigration Control Legislation", *op.cit.* note 25.
32 See British Nationality Act 1981, Chapter 66.
33 See official website at:
http://www.ukba.homeoffice.gov.uk/workingintheuk/tier1/general/#header2.
34 See Geddes, *op.cit.* note 20, 32.
35 See "Age distribution: by ethnic group", *op.cit.* note 17: "The Bangladeshi group also had a young age structure, with 38 per cent aged under 16. This was double the proportion of the White group where only 19 per cent were under the age of 16. In contrast, the White group had the highest proportion of people aged 65 and over at 16 per cent."
36 See "Population: by ethnic group", UK Census, April 2001, Office for National Statistics at: http://www.statistics.gov.uk/cci/nugget.asp?id=273.
37 See Francesco Capotorti, Special Rapporteur of the Sub-commission on Prevention of Discriminating and Protection of Minorities, *Study on the Rights of Persons Belonging to Ethnic, Religious and Linguistic Minorities* (Centre of Human Rights, Geneva, United Nations, New York, 1991). See also Hannum, H. 'The Concept and Definition of Minorities', in Marc Weller (eds.), *Universal Minority Rights, A Commentary on the Jurisprudence of the International Courts and Treaty Bodies* (Oxford University Press 2007) and Packer, J. 'Problems in Defining Minorities', in D. Fottrell and B. Bowring (eds.), *Minority and Group Rights in the New Millennium* (Martinus Nijhoff Publishers, The Hague, Boston, London, 1999).
38 See International Covenant on Civil and Political Rights, G.A. res. 2200A (XXI), 21 U.N. GAOR Supp. (No. 16) at 52, U.N. Doc. A/6316 (1966), 999 U.N.T.S. 171, *entered into force* Mar. 23, 1976.
39 See Human Right Committee (HRC), General Comment 23 on Article 27, HRI/GEN/1/Rev.1 at 38 (1994), paras. 5.1-2.

opposed to "minorities". However "national" was interpreted by many States to imply a notion more extensive than legal citizenship. Council of Europe, Parliamentary Assembly (PACE) Recommendation 1134 defined "national" as requiring groups to be "established on the territory of a state"[40] while PACE Recommendation 1201 expressed it as "longstanding, firm and lasting ties with that state."[41] Furthermore Kymlicka has referred to this additional quality as "historical settlement".[42]

In contrast, the final text of the FCNM desists from defining "national minority" and lacks any such condition, let alone the explicit requirement of citizenship. Despite the exceptionally broad scope available, member States' interpretation of the FCNM has been closer to the restrictive definitions offered in PACE Recommendations 1134 and 1201. Most States have entered interpretative declarations on ratifying the FCNM requiring not only citizenship but also the fulfilment of the more abstract notion of "historical settlement" as a precondition to recognition as national minorities. This has led to the exclusion of new minorities resulting from immigration, from the FCNM's scope.[43] The length of time persons belonging to immigrant groups must exist in the territory of a State to be considered old or national is difficult to pinpoint. Nonetheless Tanase has observed that States have normally excluded new minorities resulting from post-1945 immigration.[44] Kymlicka has added that such settlement would reach the threshold of "national", if it dated back to a period prior to the formation of modern nation-States.[45]

B. Are Commonwealth Minorities National?

There are certain historical facts that can be seen as speaking in favour of national minority status for Commonwealth groups. The Commonwealth countries share a two century long history with the UK owing to the colonial legacy. In addition, the British had, prior to 1945, exercised direct political control over their colonies and thus the Commonwealth minorities can show their existence in territory controlled by the UK for that period. In fact it was on the basis of these longstanding and firm ties that the UK allowed for an expanded notion of British nationality to persist despite the independence of many of its colonies, thus allowing for unrestricted immigration for Commonwealth citizens:

From an expansive, imperial notion of citizenship that gave all subjects of the crown the right to enter Britain – formalised by the 1948 British Nationality Act – there was a swift movement towards restriction. This was elaborated in three main pieces of

---

40 See Parliamentary Assembly of the Council of Europe (PACE), Recommendation 1134 (1990) on the rights of minorities, dated 1 October 1990, paras.10-11.

41 See Parliamentary Assembly of the Council of Europe (PACE), Recommendation 1201 (1993) on an Additional Protocol on the Rights of National Minorities to the European Convention on Human Rights, dated 1 February 1993, para. 1(b).

42 See Will Kymlicka, "The Internationalisation of Minority Rights", 6 International Journal of Constitutional Law (2008), 1-22, at 5.

43 See Rainer Hofmann, "Review of the Monitoring Process of the Council of Europe Framework Convention for the Protection of National Minorities", 1 European Yearbook of Minority Issues (EYMI 2001/2), 435-60, at 447: Given the absence of an internationally agreed definition, many States sought to exclude application to "new minorities".

44 See Ioana Tanase, *"Defining National Minorities: Old Criteria and New Minorities"*, St Antony's College, University of Oxford, Seminar Series "Citizenship and National Minorities in Europe", January 2003, at http://www.sant.ox.ac.uk/esc/esc-lectures/Tanase.htm.

45 See Kymlicka, *op.cit.* note 41, 6.

legislation between 1962 and 1971 with the idea of citizenship downsized from the imperial understanding of the 1948 British Nationality Act to a more restricted ethnic understanding by the 1981 British Nationality Act.[46]

The fulfilment of the "national" quality by immigrant groups from the Commonwealth is further strengthened by their extensive participation in the World Wars. British India alone provided almost one and half and a staggering two and half million men in the First[47] and Second World Wars, respectively.[48] Imperial policies espoused in London gave little or no importance to the interests of the local populations. Imperial rule subjugated its non-settler, while nurturing its settler colonies. The New Commonwealth countries used to be colonies of domination without a significant percentage of permanent settlers where the greatest part of the financial profit was not reinvested but transferred to the mother country.[49] Even the establishment of English schools was motivated by the need for the local elite to become imperial proxies and act as translators between the British and the, mostly rural, masses.[50]

The unorganised and rushed process of decolonisation, owing to economic necessity and the emergence of nationalist movements,[51] lies at the root of many of today's unresolved territorial conflicts in Africa, the Middle East and in South Asia.[52] The most glaring example is the partition of the Indian sub-continent, which led to "mass exodus on both sides and the death of more than 1 million people in the resulting atrocities".[53] In reality, three particular ethno-linguistic peoples and their territories were subjected to partition between Pakistan and India. These were Punjab, Kashmir and Bangladesh.[54] Today, these groups account for the majority of the ethnic Indian, Pakistani, Bangladeshi populations in the UK, who cumulatively form half its ethnic minority population. Similarly the decolonisation of East Africa gave little consideration to models of coexistence between the immigrant ethnic Indian minority and the indigenous Black majority.

C. The UK Treats Commonwealth Immigrants as New Minorities

The above arguments are not intended to conclusively prove the eligibility of Commonwealth minorities to national minority status. The legal and moral issues raised are intended to highlight the implications of simply assuming that they, as minorities, must be "new" because they resulted from post-1945 immigration. The

---

46 See Geddes, *op.cit.* note 20.
47 See "India and World War One" available at:
http://www.historylearningsite.co.uk/india_and_world_war_one.htm.
48 See Wenzlhuemer, *op.cit.* note 8.
49 *Ibid.,* 362.
50 See Berwick, *op.cit.* note 14: In 1813 "Governor-General Bentinck followed the new spirit of the age and encouraged and instituted many reforms and improvements [...]. His most important reform was to make English the medium of education and administration, replacing Persian which had been the language of the Moghul Court. 'We must at present do our best to form a class who may be interpreters between us and the millions whom we govern; a class of persons, Indian in blood and colour, but English in taste, in opinions, in morals, and in intellect,' advised the Governor-General's Law Member, Lord Macaulay."
51 See Wenzlhuemer, *op.cit.* note 8.
52 *Ibid.*, 362.
53 *Ibid.*, 361.
54 See Siddiqui, *op.cit.* note 21.

UK evades responding to such claims by limiting its obligations to solely being "committed to the elimination of all forms of racism and to the development of policies which address racial discrimination, intolerance and violence",[55] thus rejecting the notion of group rights, outright. The UK further fails to accord its religious minorities even the minimum accepted standards for new minorities by excluding them from the scope of the FCNM by interpreting it "on the understanding that it would be applied with reference to 'racial groups' within the meaning of Section 3(1) of the Race Relations Act 1976 (RRA), which is to say any groups defined by 'colour, race, nationality or national or ethnic origins'."[56] While this allows for Commonwealth minorities to fall within the scope of the FCNM, they so do only on the basis of their ethnicity defined by national origin and not their religious identity.

IV. Flawed Integration

A. *Ethnicity Privileged over Religious Identity*

The UK interprets the FCNM so as to only accept the necessity of racial non-discrimination rights for its Commonwealth minorities under a purported policy of equality and integration.[57] It is aimed at creating cohesive communities[58] and offers extensive protection from discrimination, intolerance and violence to its Commonwealth minorities as ethnic but not as religious groups.

Religious minorities were recorded for the first time in the 2001 Census on a voluntary basis. These groups were as follows: 2.7 percent Muslim, 1 percent Hindu, 0.6 percent Sikh, 0.5 percent Jewish and 0.3 percent Buddhist. With the exception of the Jewish population, the remainder (4.6 percent) of the declared religious minority population is attributable to those who also constitute an ethnic minority originating from Commonwealth countries. Furthermore 80 percent (4.3 percent) of the religious minority population is attributable to those who originate from the countries of the Indian sub-continent.[59]

The RRA[60] applies to the fields of employment, planning, housing, public authorities as well as provision of goods, facilities and services and education. The ACFC applauded its recent strengthening by the Race Relations (Amendment) Act 2000[61] as an "innovative system of positive duties which requires public authorities to actively promote racial equality and good race relations."[62] While Commonwealth minorities are referred to as "racial groups" for the purposes of the FCNM in relation to their national origin, discrimination on the basis of their religious identity is denied the same level of protection. Privileging protection on the basis of ethnicity over religion

---

55 See 2nd State Report, para. 2.
56 *Ibid.*, para. 17.
57 *Ibid.*, para. 1.
58 *Ibid.*, para. 2.
59 See *"Focus on Ethnicity and Religion"* by Office of National Statistics (Palgrave Macmillan, 2006), 22.
60 See Race Relations Act 1976, Chapter 74.
61 See Race Relations (Amendment) Act 2000, Chapter 34 prompted in large part to accusations of institutional racism within the Police in the wake of the Stephen Lawrence Inquiry.
62 See ACFC Opinion, para. 11.

runs against the UK's underlying policy of promoting equality and integration and creating cohesive communities.

Based on this determination by the ACFC as well as EU legislation, the UK has, in recent years, strengthened its legislative framework to improve protection against religious discrimination. The implementation of the EU Race[63] and Employment Directives[64] have allowed for the development of domestic law relating to religion or belief. The Equality Act[65] prohibits discrimination on grounds of religion or belief in the provision of goods, facilities and services and public functions in Great Britain adding to previously existing protections in the areas of employment and vocational training.[66] Other improvements in the criminal law have meant that religiously motivated attacks can now attract the same maximum sentences as those available for racially aggravated offences.[67]

However significant gaps persist in the criminal law between racist and religious offences. The introduction of an offence for the incitement of religious hatred[68] criminalises "threatening" but not "abusive or insulting" expressions. While the maximum sentence for this new offence is equivalent to that of inciting racial hatred,[69] the threshold for securing a conviction is much higher. Similarly racist chanting at football matches is a criminal offence[70] while there is no equivalent offence for abusive chanting of a religious nature. We are led to believe that the rationale behind racial equality is to integrate ethnic minority communities originating from Commonwealth countries through the elimination of discrimination, intolerance and violence. Nonetheless this cannot be achieved when the door to racial discrimination is slammed shut while the door to religious discrimination towards those same minorities is left ajar.

It is incoherent policy for a State committed to integrating its minorities on a firm footing of non-discrimination and equality to criminalising *any* racist speech, while only criminalising expressions of religious hatred if they are deemed to be inciting violence. In fact, only when a violent attack has been carried out and religious aggravation proven does the offence become indistinguishable, in ease of prosecution and maximum sentence, from one that is racially aggravated. This means that a person belonging to a minority may be subjected to religious insults,[71] without recourse to the law. The framework for protection against religious discrimination, according to the ACFC, remains inadequate in that none of the new religious discrimination laws "create positive duties on public institutions to promote religious equality."[72]

---

63 See Council Directive 2000/43/EC of 29 June 2000 Implementing the Principle of Equal Treatment Between Persons Irrespective of Racial or Ethnic Origin.

64 See Council Directive 2000/78/EC of 27 November 2000 Establishing a General Framework for Equal Treatment and Occupation.

65 See Equality Act 2006, Chapter 3.

66 *Ibid.*

67 See Crime and Disorder Act 1998 as amended by Part 5 of the Anti-Terrorism, Crime and Security Act 2001.

68 See Racial and Religious Hatred Act 2006, Chapter 1. Part III Public Order Act 1986, Incitement to Racial Hatred did not cover religion.

69 See Part III Public Order Act 1986.

70 See Racialist chanting at football matches - Section 3 Football Offences Act 1991 (as amended).

71 See homepage of English Defence League *"Peacefully Protesting Against Militant Islam"* at http://www.englishdefenceleague.org/.

72 See ACFC Opinion, para. 60.

B. *Some more equal than others*

The disparity in the protections afforded under these two heads of discrimination has led Commonwealth minorities with compound ethnic *and* religious identities to attempt to widen the scope of "racial group" under the RRA so as to have their religious identity accorded equal rights of non-discrimination. The Sikh[73] and Jewish[74] religious minorities have, through litigation, succeeded in this. Both religious groups are now considered "ethnic" and thus within the scope of "racial groups" for the purposes of the RRA. Their contention was that, as religious communities, they were ethnically homogenous and distinct. Therefore blurring the line between their religious and ethnic identities proved an effective litigation strategy in persuading the House of Lords that such ethno-religious minorities should be protected from discrimination on the basis of their ethnic identity, which included but was not limited to their religion.[75] Only their specific situations warranted their protection as racial groups.[76] Consequently Sikhs and Jews are not only protected on account of their national origin but also their religious identities under the RRA.

Whereas the Sikh and Jewish identities are accepted to be "ethnic", neither the scope of "ethnic" nor "racial group" is extendable to Muslims, Hindus or Buddhists, as they cannot lay claim to ethnic homogeneity.[77] The ACFC points out that "the 'racial group' criterion may result in exclusions from the Framework Convention's scope of application of groups that have legitimate claims to be covered."[78] While Sikhs and Jews are protected separately on the basis of their national origin and their religious identity, the Muslim, Hindu and Buddhist minorities can only avail the comprehensive protections of the RRA and thus the FCNM, on the basis of their national origins. While Sikhs and Jews may invoke discrimination on the basis of their faith across all

---

73 See *Mandla v Dowell-Lee* [1983] 2 AC 548 (House of Lords).

74 See *Seide v Gillette Industries Ltd* [1980] IRLR 427, a decision of the Employment Appeal Tribunal and *R. (on the application of E) v JFS Governing Body Court of Appeal* (Civil Division), 25 June 2009.

75 See Lord Fraser of Tullybelton's leading opinion stated that an "ethnic group" must "regard itself, and be regarded by others, as a distinct community by virtue of certain characteristics. Some of these characteristics are essential others are not essential but one or more of them will commonly be found and will help to distinguish the group from the surrounding community. The conditions which appear to me to be essential are these:

1. a long shared history, of which the group is conscious as distinguishing it from other groups, and the memory of which it keeps alive.
2. a cultural tradition of its own, including family and social customs and manners, often but not necessarily associated with religious observance. In addition to those two essential characteristics the following characteristics are in my opinion, relevant;
3. either a common geographical origin, or descent from a small number of common ancestors
4. a common language, not necessarily peculiar to the group
5. a common literature peculiar to the group
6. a common religion different from that of neighbouring groups or from the general community surrounding it
7. being a minority or being oppressed or a dominant group within a larger community, for example a conquered people."

76 Gypsies and travellers also treated as "racial groups" see *Commission for Racial Equality v. Dutton* [1989] 2 WLR 17 (Court of Appeal) cited in Jenny Turner, "Minority Rights Protection in the United Kingdom", 1 EYMI (2001/2), 395-419, at 396.

77 See *Ibid.*, 402 on how a Bill which would have brought "religion" within the scope of RRA was rejected.

78 See ACFC Opinion, para. 12.

sectors and even claim the non-performance of positive duties,[79] the other religious minorities can only resort to the weaker framework for religious discrimination and are excluded from the scope of the FCNM.

Furthermore those who do not belong to any of the ethnic minority groups but nonetheless adhere to a minority religion have no resort to the RRA, let alone rights stipulated in the FCNM: "a percentage of Muslims are British converts to Islam, who are not covered by the Framework Convention." Furthermore many Muslims already protected on the basis of their Commonwealth national origin "consider that their religious identity, rather than their ethnic identity, should be the basis for their inclusion."[80] Since "September 11" and "7 July", the Muslim ethnic minority population has been more vulnerable to discrimination, intolerance and violence on the basis of their religion as opposed to their national origin. While the media has exasperated the situation with sensationalist reporting[81] the Government has sanctioned religious profiling in the form of anti-terror laws, which inadvertently target Muslims.[82] These factors combine to alienate the Muslim minority thus making their integration the most difficult.

V. Flawed Interpretation: Minimising Scope and Maximising Discretion

A. *Discretion Limited by "Object and Purpose"*

The Explanatory Report to the FCNM (Exp. Rep. FCNM) states that "a choice was made for a framework Convention which contains mostly programme-type provisions [...] which [...] leave the States concerned a measure of discretion in the implementation of the objectives which they have undertaken to achieve."[83] Notwithstanding its programmatic nature and in-built State discretion, the FCNM remains "the first *legally binding* [italics added] multilateral instrument devoted to the protection of national minorities".[84] Thus the UK, in excluding from the FCNM's scope religious minorities raises serious questions as to the legality of such an interpretation.

The Vienna Convention on the Law of Treaties (VCLT)[85] states that parties are bound by the treaties they enter and obliges their performance in good faith.[86] An interpretative declaration[87] cannot alter or modify obligations under a treaty to the extent that they become incompatible with the object and purpose of the treaty.[88] The UK, in limiting the scope of the FCNM to just protecting against racial discrimination

---

79 See Race Relations (Amendment) Act 2000, *op.cit.* note 62.
80 See ACFC Opinion, para. 34.
81 *Ibid.*, para. 18.
82 For example, Section 41 and Schedule 7 of Terrorism Act 2000, Chapter 11.
83 See Exp. Rep. FCNM, para. 11.
84 *Ibid.*, para. 10
85 See the Vienna Convention on the Law of Treaties (VCLT), concluded on 23 May 1969, entered into force on 27 January 1988, 1155 UNTS 331.
86 *Ibid.*, Article 26.
87 *Ibid.*, Article 19.
88 *Ibid.*, Article 2(d) and International Law Commission, *Text of the draft guidelines on reservations to treaties, Guide to practice,* Directive 1.2. "Definition of reservations", provisionally approved by the Commission. Report of the International Law Commission 60th session, supplement No. 10 (A/63/10).

resulting in the exclusion of religious and linguistic identities explicitly protected under the treaty, constitutes a substantial modification of its obligations. Therefore we must determine whether these modifications compromise the object and purpose of the FCNM.

Not only is the FCNM programmatic in nature but it desists from defining national minority. The resultant discretion available to States, to interpret the FCNM to fit their specific contexts, though extensive is by no means absolute. While the term is elastic and has been interpreted by many States to exclude new minorities, such a narrowing of scope must not encroach on the FCNM's object and purpose. Hence, the available discretion cannot extend beyond the point where a State's interpretation is incompatible with the object and purpose of a treaty. Therefore the discretion available under the FCNM is limited by its object and purpose especially as the aim of such discretion is to allow for the "implementation of the objectives".[89]

B. Object and Purpose of the FCNM

The essence of all normative minority rights development has been premised on the fundamental principle of preservation of group identity and the enjoyment of their culture.[90] The FCNM sets out this essential purpose in its Preamble: "a pluralist and genuinely democratic society should not only respect the ethnic, cultural, linguistic and religious identity of each person belonging to a national minority, but also create appropriate conditions enabling them to express, preserve and develop this identity."[91] Elaboration of this preambular aspiration is to be found in Section I[92] of the operative part, which "contains provisions which, in a general fashion, stipulate certain fundamental principles which may serve to elucidate the other substantive provisions of the framework Convention."[93] Therefore while the specific principles enumerated in Section II[94] may be subject to a measure of discretion, violating any of the fundamental principles of Section I would be incompatible with the object and purpose of the FCNM. Article 3 lays out two separate but symbiotic fundamental principles that constitute the core of the FCNM and all minority rights.

Article 3 (1) states: "Every person belonging to a national minority shall have the right freely to choose to be treated or not to be treated as such and no disadvantage shall result from this choice or from the exercise of the rights which are connected to that choice."

"This provision leaves it to every such person to decide whether or not he or she wishes to come under the protection flowing from the principles of the framework Convention."[95] This right to self-identification is rendered meaningless if the minority group is not able to ascribe to whichever identity they so choose. Identity by its very nature must emanate from the self and defies imposition. However this "does not imply a right for an individual to choose arbitrarily to belong to any national minority.

---

89 See Exp. Rep. FCNM, para, 11.

90 See "Commentary of the Working Group on Minorities to the United Nations Declaration on the Rights of Persons Belonging to National or Ethnic, Religious and Linguistic Minorities", by Asbjørn Eide, 4 April 2005, E/CN.4/Sub.2/AC.5/2005/2 (Com.UN Decl. Min), para. 4.

91 See FCNM Preamble.

92 See FCNM Arts. 1-3.

93 See Exp. Rep. FCNM, para. 15.

94 See FCNM Arts. 4-19.

95 See Exp. Rep. FCNM, para. 34.

The individual's subjective choice is inseparably linked to objective criteria relevant to the person's identity."[96] Consequently the freedom to choose ones group identity is not absolute but must be within the categories envisaged by the FCNM. While there is no definitive definition for national minority under the FCNM, we observe that it protects and preserves ethnic, cultural, linguistic or religious identity.[97] Hence religious minorities are explicitly included within the objective scope of national minority and there are provisions that lay out specific principles of religious group rights.[98]

Therefore the principle of self-identification is deferential to the self-perception of the minority group as long as it is within the objectively discernable bounds envisaged by the FCNM. While the UK may prevent religious minorities from recognition as ethnic minorities, as is the case with Muslims[99], based on objective grounds,[100] it cannot not exclude them on the basis of a blanket non-recognition of all religious groups. When a non-discrimination framework itself discriminates on the basis of religion, religious groups are coerced into self-identifying as ethnic minorities. This constitutes an indirect erosion of the principle of self-identification, which becomes somewhat illusory and lacks legitimacy when groups are offered a choice between their true identity and the best scheme of protection from discrimination. Thus restricting the choice of identity to ethnicity is irreconcilable with the principle of self-identification. Religious minorities are compelled to identify as ethnic groups restricted to rights of non-discrimination when their true identity and group needs are religious in nature. The UK's interpretation in reducing the FCNM's scope to only ethnic groups could therefore be incompatible with the right freely to choose.

Article 3 (2) states: "Persons belonging to national minorities may exercise the rights and enjoy the freedoms flowing from the principles enshrined in the present framework Convention individually as well as in community with others."

By solely being "committed to the elimination of all forms of racism and to the development of policies which address racial discrimination, intolerance and violence",[101] The UK absolves itself from providing any group rights under the FCNM by refusing to recognise *any* groups as "national minorities":

"[T]here is no mechanism under any of the UK's legal jurisdictions to grant "national minority status" to any particular group nor is it proposed to introduce such a mechanism. The UK's discrimination laws protect all individuals from being treated less favourably on racial grounds, whether they belong to a "minority" group or a "majority" group. There is no comprehensive list of "recognised" groups."[102]

Based on these statements, the UK refuses to *formally* recognise *any* national minorities within its territory. This appears to amounts to a rejection of the group rights approach on which the FCNM is premised. It even states that the law does not distinguish between minority and majority groups. However both special measures in relation in non-discrimination and group rights rely on a legitimate difference in

96 See Exp. Rep. FCNM, para. 35.
97 See Arts. 5, 6 & 7 FCNM.
98 See FCNM Arts. 7, 8 & 12.
99 In *Nyazi v. Rymans Ltd* (1988), ethnic status was denied to Muslims on the basis that they include people of many nations and colours, who speak many languages and whose only common denominator is religion and religious culture.
100 As established in *Mandla, op.cit.* note 73.
101 See 2nd State Report, para. 2.
102 See 2nd State Report, para. 16.

treatment based on relative vulnerability. Other State parties also made interpretative declarations on ratification, but those sought to exclude new minorities from the FCNM's scope. The UK has instead rejected the notion of national minority and thus group rights, outright restricting the FCNM only to its new ethnic minorities and only as far as their rights of racial non-discrimination are concerned. As such, it *formally* desists from even recognising established minorities as national minorities. In fact it does not once use the term "national minority" throughout its 2nd State Report except to limit the scope of the FCNM.
Therefore to restrict minority rights to just non-discrimination of ethnic groups raises serious questions as to compliance with the fundamental principles set out in Article 3 and thus compatibility with the object and purpose of the FCNM.

VI. THE ROLE OF THE ADVISORY COMMITTEE: TOWARDS MAXIMISING SCOPE AND MINIMISING DISCRETION

A. *Explaining the ACFC's Lack of Criticism*

The UK's interpretative declarations seem to be tantamount to a rejection of the minority rights approach and offer no more than the protections already afforded under the CERD,[103] not to mention the UK limits its international obligations on the basis of national laws.[104] The ACFC's mild critique thus seems to be disproportionate to the gravity and potential unlawfulness of the UKs restrictive interpretation.
However this may be explained by the wide gap between the UK's *de jure* interpretation and its *de facto* application of the FCNM. Groups such as the Scots, Welsh and Irish are in fact accorded ad-hoc devolved structures of government based on territoriality which allow for enjoyment of cultural rights, especially those of language. In addition despite refusing to treat differently majority and minority groups, the Race Relations (Amendment) Act 2000 clearly imposes positive duties on public bodies specifically in relation to ethnic minorities. While the UK is not willing to *formally* recognise even these old minorities as national minorities, the ACFC infers as much.[105] The UK also remains one of the few member-States of the FCNM that extends its application to individuals belonging to groups despite of their citizenship or long lasting ties with the territory concerned. In addition the article-by-article approach[106] highly encouraged by the ACFC has allowed for, in part, the inclusion of Commonwealth religious minorities within the scope of the FCNM. Therefore it appears the ACFC's Opinion is based on the UK's treatment of its minorities as opposed to its stated interpretation of the FCNM, which is extremely narrow.

B. *Drawing on the ACFC's Judicial Capacity*

The ACFC, as the supervisory and monitoring body for the first binding minority rights instrument, must be commended on its efforts to encourage member States to

---

103 International Convention on the Elimination of All Forms of Racial Discrimination, concluded on 7 March 1966, entered into force on 4 January 1969, 660 UNTS 195.
104 Impermissible under VCLT Article 27.
105 See ACFC Opinion, para. 85.
106 See 2nd State Report, para. 18.

extend the scope of application of the FCNM on an article-by-article basis in order to include new minority groups originating from immigration. The ACFC seems to perceive such a diplomatic approach to be paying dividends. Subsequently not criticizing on a tougher normative basis is perhaps seen as a worthwhile trade-off for the practical improvement in the situation of minorities, whether new or old.

However the ACFC underutilises its competence as a judicial organ. As such, the UK escapes having to interpret the FCNM in a manner compatible with its object and purpose and thus justify recognition of some groups as national minorities to the exclusion of others. The ACFC should consider modifying its approach. The main reason is that at present, the UK avoids having to respond to claims to national minority status by Commonwealth religious minorities. In this context the article-by-article approach allows the UK to broaden the application and scope of certain provisions of the FCNM at its discretion. Neither the discharge of positive duties nor the granting of group rights is intended to constitute an antecedent or precedent to which the UK can be held to in the future.[107] In minimising the scope of the FCNM, the UK maximises the measure of discretion available to it. The ACFC sidesteps having to comment on the legality of the UK's interpretation and its compatibility with the FCNM's object and purpose. It merely states, I this regard, that the "Government should *consider* [italics added] supplementing its current criterion based on recognition as a 'racial group' in case law with other criteria."[108]

C. *The Scope for the Inclusion of New Minorities*

In order for this shift in approach to be realistic, we must first establish whether the text of the FCNM itself allows for the inclusion of new minorities. Firstly the FCNM desists from defining national minority unlike PACE Recommendations 1144 and 1201. The omission allows for a scope wide enough for even non-citizen immigrant groups to be potentially included. Based on the text alone, it becomes difficult to isolate the normative basis for the category of minority rights reserved for migrant groups referred to as new minorities.

Professor John Packer[109] has advanced such an argument articulating powerfully that in textually interpreting the FCNM, the only support to be found for the term new minority is the word "traditional". This condition is however only one route by which groups can claim national minority status. The wording of the FCNM actually reads "traditional *or* [italics added] substantial number,"[110] meaning that the "traditional" criterion need not be satisfied if the minority group constitute a substantial number. Additionally the term "inhabited [...] traditionally" only attaches to three provisions and is somewhat weaker than the condition of being "established" or having "longstanding, firm and lasting ties".[111] The Exp. Rep. FCNM further states that *traditional* inhabitation "does not refer to historical minorities, but only to those still living in the same geographical area".[112] The possibility for including new minorities

107 See ACFC Opinion, para. 30.
108 *Ibid.*, para. 13.
109 See John Packer commenting on Stefan Oeter's presentation, "*Minority Protection and the European Union: The Way Forward*", Conference, 30-31 January 2004, European Academy, Bolzano available at: http://www.eurac.edu/Org/Minorities/eld/projects/PECEDE/The_conference.htm.
110 See FCNM Arts. 10, 11 & 14.
111 See PACE Recommendations 1134 and 1201.
112 See 2nd State Comments, Para. 66.

within the wide and indeterminate scope of national minority is evidenced by the fact that the ACFC welcomes developments where new minorities are granted group rights on a discretionary basis.

Despite the available flexibility in interpretation, the ACFC never of its own accord criticises the non-attribution of group rights to Commonwealth minorities. This is evident in the absence of any such issues raised in its second Opinion, particularly those pertaining to religious rights.[113] Such a practice of denying new minorities' group rights and the lack of criticism from the ACFC is common among other member States.[114] Consistent State practice of parties to the FCNM shows that the exclusion of new minorities from its ambit is an accepted practice under the FCNM and more in line with the definition of national minority in Recommendations 1134 and 1201.

D. Deferring to Higher Standards of Minority Protection

Given the ACFC's quasi-judicial nature, it has the ability to maximise the scope of the FCNM and to minimise State discretion. Therefore it must interpret the FCNM in light of the international law on minority rights as stipulated in FCNM Section III. These provisions allow for the application of international standards that may be relied on to challenge the normative soundness of the UK's interpretation, hence providing the ACFC with the interpretative means necessary for the attribution of group rights to new minorities under the FCNM. FCNM Article 22 is aimed at ensuring "that persons belonging to 'national minorities' benefit from whichever of the relevant national or international human rights legislation is most favourable to them."[115] The scope of CCPR Article 27 is wider than the FCNM as the HRC explicitly includes immigrant minority groups within its scope.[116]

The UN Decl. Min.[117] builds on the HRC's interpretative work:

"Those who live compactly together in a part of the State territory may be entitled to rights regarding the use of language, and street and place names which are different from those who are dispersed, and may in some circumstances be entitled to some kind of autonomy. Those who have been established for a long time on the territory may have stronger rights than those who have recently arrived."[118]

This reveals that the UN Decl. Min. in differentiating between the strength of the rights of the two groups does not exempt new minorities from claiming group rights confining this relative disadvantage to those rights attached to territory. Therefore when it comes to non-territorial group rights, particularly religious, "being established for a long time" is immaterial and all that needs to be established to claim and access such rights is substantial numbers of persons belonging to that minority.

If the ACFC was to apply Article 22 in its fullest sense, it would undoubtedly be more inclined to raise the issue of group rights for Commonwealth minorities:

"[E]ven if a group is held not to constitute a national minority, it can still be an ethnic, religious or linguistic minority and therefore be covered by the Declaration. This can

---

113 See FCNM Arts. 7, 8 & 12.

114 See Hoffman, *op.cit.* note 43.

115 See Exp. Rep. FCNM, para. 91.

116 See HRC, *op.cit.* note 39.

117 Declaration of the Rights of Persons Belonging to National or Ethnic, Religious and Linguistic Minorities, adopted by the UN GA on 18 December 1992, GA Res. 47/135.

118 See Com.UN Decl. Min, para. 10.

be important in several respects. In relation to the European regional instruments, some States argue that 'national minorities' only comprise groups composed of citizens of the State. Even if that is accepted (at present it is a matter of some controversy), it would not apply to the United Nations Declaration on Minorities because it has a much wider scope than "national minorities."[119]
The ACFC has recourse to the HRC's interpretation of CCPR Article 27 as well as UN Decl. Min. to develop and embolden its arguments for allowing for group rights for Commonwealth minorities and thus new minorities generally. The UN Decl. Min. is not legally binding and more crucially has no monitoring or implementation mechanisms. Nonetheless its normative effect can be made to bear by bodies such as the ACFC which have specific interpretative tools codified as operative provisions. Similarly the European Convention on Human Rights restricts the lowering of standards already protected under other treaty obligations[120] and the African Charter on Human Peoples' Rights allows for UN Declarations as well as comparative regional jurisprudence to be relied on as authorities.[121] FCNM Article 22 is the equivalent of these provisions and reiterates established customary international law that deals with conflicting or varying standards of international and regional law by deferring to the higher standard of protection.[122]

VII. CONCLUSION

It has been the consistent practice of State parties to the FCNM to deny their ethnic, religious and linguistic minorities resulting from post-1945 immigration recognition as national minorities. At the most these new minorities are availed rights of non-discrimination justified by a policy of integration. Such practice has found legitimacy in the work of the ACFC tasked with monitoring compliance with the FCNM. However the old/new or immigrant/national dichotomy becomes blurred in the UK. In the period following World War II, the British Empire shrunk rapidly prompting immigration from its former settled colonies driven by economic and political factors. The historical links resulted in a notion of nationality far more expansive than along ethnic lines, prevalent today.
The UK treats some minorities in its territory as national while others as new. It accords rights in line with these characterisations: group and territorial rights for the former and the rights to racial non-discrimination for the latter. However in its interpretation of the FCNM, the UK rejects the concept of national minority outright and precludes the possibility of any group rights from the scope of the FCNM except those of racial non-discrimination. In doing so, it excludes even old minorities *de jure* from the scope of national minority accepting only its obligation to implement non-

---

119 See Com. UN Decl. Min, paras. 8-9.
120 See European Convention on Human Rights and Fundamental Freedoms, dated 4 November 1950, ETS No. 5, Article 60.
121 African Charter on Human and Peoples' Rights, concluded on 26 June 1981, entered into force on 21 October 1986, O.A.U. Doc. CAB/LEG/67/3 Rev. 5, Article 60.
122 The UK Government has sought to argue the opposite in a pending case at the ECtHR in that the general international law obligation to respect Iraq's sovereignty trumps their obligation under Protocol 13 not to subject any individual within their jurisdiction to the Death Penalty or a real risk of it. ECtHR. Appl. No. 61498/08, *Al-Saadoon and Mufdhi v. United Kingdom*, decision of 30 June 2009, para. 106. See also ECtHR. Appl. No. 37201/06, *Saadi v.Italy,* judgement of 28 February 2008, para. 127.

discrimination measures aimed at integrating its minorities on the basis of ethnic identity. Almost the entirety of this ethnic minority population originates from Commonwealth immigration and they are recognised as ethnic minorities based on their national origins and so are protected from racial discrimination.

Minority rights theory seeks to protect against discrimination on the basis of identity followed by attribution of group rights so as to enable the preservation of culture. The latter constitutes a legitimate difference in treatment. It is a means by which to accommodate difference and address entrenched systematic inequality. The UK denies religious minorities equivalent non-discrimination protections as well as group rights by excluding them from the scope of the FCNM.

The proposed arguments for changing such a practice were manifold. The first aimed at UK Government proposed that pursuing a policy of purely racial non-discrimination undermines their own aim of integrating Commonwealth minorities in particular originating from the countries of the Indian sub-continent who account for 80 percent of the religious minority population as well as contravening their international obligations to treat different groups within an equitable framework. Secondly the legality of the UK's interpretation is questionable due to its potential incompatibility with the object and purpose of the entire treaty notwithstanding the *de facto* ad-hoc attribution of group rights. Thirdly the ACFC has the space in which to increase the scope of the FCNM and reduce the discretion available to the UK to allow for the attribution of group rights to new minorities. The interpretative tools necessary for reading FCNM provisions in light of international law are codified within its operative part. As such it has the faculty and authority to push for the normative development in a direction more beneficial to new minorities. Immigrant communities from Commonwealth countries in the UK, after centuries of economic and political subjugation, are denied the most basic of rights of identity and the enjoyment of their culture.

The national/new distinction when read in light of other international instruments, seems to be misapplied and abused by FCNM member States. Connection to territory can only logically result in rights linked to territory such as land or devolved political structures, as opposed to cultural ones which attach to individuals and not territory. Therefore they do not diminish or strengthen over time except by the volition of individuals themselves.

Furthermore the UK's integration policies are flawed with regards to religious identity. It is almost impossible to integrate religious minorities without offering protection against discrimination on a par with ethnic groups. Religion by its very nature and its claim to absolute truth can only ever exist as a singularity. Thus integration cannot aim at sameness as this will give religious minorities an either/or choice which will alienate them further. Language, on the other hand, must be learnt for practical reasons, but learning English does not result in the forfeiture of one's linguistic identity. Therefore the State must redefine its understanding of integration when it comes to religious minorities as one of coexistence, accommodation of difference and plurality.[123] In fact the more group rights granted, the closer the religious minority is bound to feel to the State, thus facilitating genuine integration premised on pluralism.

---

123 See Com. UN Decl. Min, paras. 21-22.

www.ingramcontent.com/pod-product-compliance
Ingram Content Group UK Ltd.
Pitfield, Milton Keynes, MK11 3LW, UK
UKHW021832100926
8556IPUK00004B/294

9 783631 609163